Fourth Workshop on Fact Extraction and VERification (FEVER 2021)

Punta Cana, Dominican Republic
10 November 2021

ISBN: 978-1-7138-9171-0

Printed from e-media with permission by:

Curran Associates, Inc.
57 Morehouse Lane
Red Hook, NY 12571

Some format issues inherent in the e-media version may also appear in this print version.

Printed with permission by Curran Associates, Inc. (2024)

Association for Computational Linguistics
209 N. Eighth Street
Stroudsburg, Pennsylvania 18360

Phone: 1-570-476-8006
Fax: 1-570-476-0860

acl@aclweb.org

Additional copies of this publication are available from:

Curran Associates, Inc.
57 Morehouse Lane
Red Hook, NY 12571 USA
Phone: 845-758-0400
Fax: 845-758-2633
Email: curran@proceedings.com
Web: www.proceedings.com

EMNLP 2021

FEVER

Fact Extraction and VERification

Proceedings of the Fourth Workshop

November 10, 2021

We thank our sponsor Amazon for their generous support.

Introduction

With billions of individual pages on the web providing information on almost every conceivable topic, we should have the ability to collect facts that answer almost every conceivable question. However, only a small fraction of this information is contained in structured sources (Wikidata, Freebase, etc.) – we are therefore limited by our ability to transform free-form text to structured knowledge. There is, however, another problem that has become the focus of a lot of recent research and media coverage: false information coming from unreliable sources.

To ensure accuracy, this content must be verified. However, the volume of information precludes human moderators from doing so. It is paramount to research automated means to verify accuracy and consistency of information published online and the downstream systems (such as Question Answering, Search and Digital Personal Assistants) which rely on it. The FEVER series of workshops has been a venue for ongoing research in this area.

Organizers:

Ramy Aly (University of Cambridge)
Christos Christodoulopoulos (Amazon)
Oana Cocarascu (King's College London)
Zhijiang Guo (University of Cambridge)
Arpit Mittal (Facebook)
Michael Schlichtkrull (University of Cambridge)
James Thorne (University of Cambridge)
Andreas Vlachos (University of Cambridge)

Invited Speakers:

Mohit Bansal (UNC Chapel Hill)
Mirella Lapata (University of Edinburgh)
Maria Liakata (Queen Mary University London)
Pasquale Minervini (University College London)
Preslav Nakov (Qatar Computing Research Institute)
Steven Novella (Yale University School of Medicine)
Brendan Nyhan (Dartmouth College)

Program Committee:

Pepa Atanasova (University of Copenhagen) Esma Balkir (University of Edinburgh) Nicola De Cao (University of Amsterdam, The University of Edinburgh) Martin Funkquist (Independent) Ivan Habernal (Technische Universität Darmstadt) Andreas Hanselowski (Cerence Inc) Neema Kotonya (Imperial College London) Christopher Malon (NEC Laboratories America) Laura Mascarell (ETH Zurich) Joonsuk Park (University of Richmond) Hugo Perrin (Buster.ai) Tamara Polajnar (University of Cambridge) Mohammed Saeed (Eurecom) Dominik Stammbach (ETH Zürich) Motoki Taniguchi (Fujifilm, Tokyo Metropolitan University) Orkun Temiz (Middle East Technical University) Richard Tzong-Han Tsai (Academia Sinica) Takehito Utsuro (University of Tsukuba) Menglin Xia (Amazon)

Table of Contents

The Fact Extraction and VERification Over Unstructured and Structured information (FEVEROUS) Shared Task
Rami Aly, Zhijiang Guo, Michael Sejr Schlichtkrull, James Thorne, Andreas Vlachos, Christos Christodoulopoulos, Oana Cocarascu and Arpit Mittal 1

Evidence Selection as a Token-Level Prediction Task
Dominik Stammbach 14

Graph Reasoning with Context-Aware Linearization for Interpretable Fact Extraction and Verification
Neema Kotonya, Thomas Spooner, Daniele Magazzeni and Francesca Toni 21

FaBULOUS: Fact-checking Based on Understanding of Language Over Unstructured and Structured information
Mostafa BOUZIANE, Hugo Perrin, Amine Sadeq, Thanh Nguyen, Aurélien Cluzeau and Julien Mardas 31

Team Papelo at FEVEROUS: Multi-hop Evidence Pursuit
Christopher Malon 40

Modeling Entity Knowledge for Fact Verification
Yang Liu, Chenguang Zhu and Michael Zeng 50

Verdict Inference with Claim and Retrieved Elements Using RoBERTa
In-Zu Gi, Ting-Yu Fang and Richard Tzong-Han Tsai 60

Stance Detection in German News Articles
Laura Mascarell, Tatyana Ruzsics, Christian Schneebeli, Philippe Schlattner, Luca Campanella, Severin Klingler and Cristina Kadar 66

FANG-COVID: A New Large-Scale Benchmark Dataset for Fake News Detection in German
Justus Mattern, Yu Qiao, Elma Kerz, Daniel Wiechmann and Markus Strohmaier 78

Combining sentence and table evidence to predict veracity of factual claims using TaPaS and RoBERTa
Martin Funkquist 92

Automatic Fact-Checking with Document-level Annotations using BERT and Multiple Instance Learning
Aalok Sathe and Joonsuk Park 101

Neural Re-rankers for Evidence Retrieval in the FEVEROUS Task
Mohammed Saeed, Giulio Alfarano, Khai nguyen, Duc Pham, Raphael Troncy and Paolo Papotti 108

A Fact Checking and Verification System for FEVEROUS Using a Zero-Shot Learning Approach
Orkun Temiz, Özgün Ozan Kılıç, Arif Ozan Kızıldağ and Tuğba Taşkaya Temizel 113

Conference Program

10th November

09:00–09:05 Opening

09:05–10:20 Keynote Talks

09:05–09:35 *Keynote Talk*
Preslav Nakov

09:35–10:05 *Keynote Talk*
Maria Liakata

10:05–10:20 *Q & A*

10:20–11:00 Research Talks

10:20–10:35 *Evidence Selection as a Token-Level Prediction Task*
Dominik Stammbach

10:35–10:50 *Graph Reasoning with Context-Aware Linearization for Interpretable Fact Extraction and Verification*
Neema Kotonya, Thomas Spooner, Daniele Magazzeni and Francesca Toni

10:50–11:00 *Q & A*

11:00–11:15 *Break*

10th November (continued)

11:15–12:30 Keynote Talks

11:15–11:45 *Keynote Talk*
Mirella Lapata

11:45–12:15 *Keynote Talk*
Pasquale Minervini

12:15–12:30 *Q & A*

12:30–13:30 *Lunch*

13:30–14:45 Keynote and Shared Task

13:30–14:00 *Keynote Talk*
Mohit Bansal

14:00–14:10 *The Fact Extraction and VERification Over Unstructured and Structured information (FEVEROUS) Shared Task*
Rami Aly, Zhijiang Guo, Michael Sejr Schlichtkrull, James Thorne, Andreas Vlachos, Christos Christodoulopoulos, Oana Cocarascu and Arpit Mittal

14:10–14:20 *FaBULOUS: Fact-checking Based on Understanding of Language Over Unstructured and Structured information*
Mostafa BOUZIANE, Hugo Perrin, Amine Sadeq, Thanh Nguyen, Aurélien Cluzeau and Julien Mardas

14:20–14:30 *Team Papelo at FEVEROUS: Multi-hop Evidence Pursuit*
Christopher Malon

14:30–14:45 *Q & A*

10th November (continued)

14:45–16:15 Virtual Poster Session

Modeling Entity Knowledge for Fact Verification
Yang Liu, Chenguang Zhu and Michael Zeng

Verdict Inference with Claim and Retrieved Elements Using RoBERTa
In-Zu Gi, Ting-Yu Fang and Richard Tzong-Han Tsai

Stance Detection in German News Articles
Laura Mascarell, Tatyana Ruzsics, Christian Schneebeli, Philippe Schlattner, Luca Campanella, Severin Klingler and Cristina Kadar

FANG-COVID: A New Large-Scale Benchmark Dataset for Fake News Detection in German
Justus Mattern, Yu Qiao, Elma Kerz, Daniel Wiechmann and Markus Strohmaier

Combining sentence and table evidence to predict veracity of factual claims using TaPaS and RoBERTa
Martin Funkquist

Automatic Fact-Checking with Document-level Annotations using BERT and Multiple Instance Learning
Aalok Sathe and Joonsuk Park

Neural Re-rankers for Evidence Retrieval in the FEVEROUS Task
Mohammed Saeed, Giulio Alfarano, Khai nguyen, Duc Pham, Raphael Troncy and Paolo Papotti

A Fact Checking and Verification System for FEVEROUS Using a Zero-Shot Learning Approach
Orkun Temiz, Özgün Ozan Kılıç, Arif Ozan Kızıldağ and Tuğba Taşkaya Temizel

10th November (continued)

16:15–17:30 Keynote Talks

16:15–16:45 *Keynote Talk*
Steven Novella

16:45–17:15 *Keynote Talk*
Brendan Nyhan

17:15–17:30 *Q & A*

17:30–17:45 Closing Remarks

The Fact Extraction and VERification Over Unstructured and Structured information (FEVEROUS) Shared Task

Rami Aly, Zhijiang Guo, Michael Schlichtkrull, James Thorne, Andreas Vlachos
Department of Computer Science and Technology
University of Cambridge
{rmya2,zg283,mss84,jt719,av308}@cam.ac.uk

Christos Christodoulopoulos
Amazon Alexa
chrchrs@amazon.co.uk

Oana Cocarascu
Department of Informatics
King's College London
oana.cocarascu@kcl.ac.uk

Arpit Mittal
Facebook
arpitmittal@fb.com

Abstract

The Fact Extraction and VERification Over Unstructured and Structured information (FEVEROUS) shared task, asks participating systems to determine whether human-authored claims are SUPPORTED or REFUTED based on evidence retrieved from Wikipedia (or NOTENOUGHINFO if the claim cannot be verified). Compared to the FEVER 2018 shared task, the main challenge is the addition of structured data (tables and lists) as a source of evidence. The claims in the FEVEROUS dataset can be verified using only structured evidence, only unstructured evidence, or a mixture of both. Submissions are evaluated using the FEVEROUS score that combines label accuracy and evidence retrieval. Unlike FEVER 2018 (Thorne et al., 2018a), FEVEROUS requires partial evidence to be returned for NOTENOUGHINFO claims, and the claims are longer and thus more complex. The shared task received 13 entries, six of which were able to beat the baseline system. The winning team was "Bust a move!", achieving a FEVEROUS score of 27% (+9% compared to the baseline). In this paper we describe the shared task, present the full results and highlight commonalities and innovations among the participating systems.

1 Introduction

Automated fact verification has become an important field of research, as fact-checkers and journalists are facing an even-increasing volume of claims to verify (Thorne and Vlachos, 2018). This task has been explored by the NLP community through forums and shared tasks such as CLEF CheckThat! (Nakov et al., 2021), SemEval (Wang et al., 2021) and FEVER (Thorne et al., 2018b), as well as a number of datasets aimed at modelling parts of the task (Karadzhov et al., 2017; Wang, 2017; Augenstein et al., 2019; Chen et al., 2020; Gupta et al., 2020).

While these previous works focus on claims that are verified against a single type of evidence, such as text *or* structured information, the new FEVEROUS dataset (Aly et al., 2021) we study in this shared task requires the models to reason about *both* types of evidence. This helps better approximate real-world fact checking, where both the claims and the sources of evidence are more complex in nature.

FEVEROUS models the task of Fact Extraction and VERification Over Unstructured and Structured information, overcoming some limitations of the previous FEVER dataset (Thorne et al., 2018a), which only considers text as evidence, and improving the quality of the annotations as well as removing known biases from the dataset. FEVEROUS contains 87,026 new claims which are more complex (25.3 word/claim on average compared to 9.4 for FEVER), and a larger pool of evidence (tables, lists, and sentences from the entirety of Wikipedia), bringing us closer to real-world scenarios, while maintaining the experimental control of an artificially designed dataset.

This paper presents a short description of the task and dataset, the final test phase leaderboard, and a summary of the submissions with a comparison to previous FEVER shared tasks, an analysis of current challenges and a discussion around interesting research directions for this task. The shared task received 13 entries in total, with the winning team, *"Bust a move!"*, achieving a score of 27%, 9 percentage points higher than the baseline system we released. While considerable progress was made by the participants of the task, there are still plenty of opportunities for systems to improve. We will leave the scoring system open to allow future work to build upon the advances made in this shared task.

Proceedings of the Fourth Workshop on Fact Extraction and VERification (FEVER) at EMNLP 2021, pages 1–13
November 10, 2021.

Claim: In the 2018 Naples general election, Roberto Fico, an Italian politician and member of the Five Star Movement, received 57,119 votes with 57.6 percent of the total votes.

Evidence:

Page: `wiki/Roberto_Fico`
$\mathbf{e}_1$(Electoral history):

2018 general election: Naples -Fuorigrotta		
Candidate	Party	Votes
Roberto Fico	Five Star	61,819
Marta Schifone	Centre-right	21,651
Daniela Iaconis	Centre-left	15,779

Verdict: Refuted

Claim: Red Sundown screenplay was written by Martin Berkeley; based on a story by Lewis B. Patten, who often published under the names Lewis Ford, Lee Leighton and Joseph Wayne.

Evidence:

Page: `wiki/Red_Sundown`
$\mathbf{e}_1$(Introduction):

Red Sundown	
Directed by	Jack Arnold
Produced by	Albert Zugsmith
Screenplay by	Martin Berkeley
Based on	Lewis B. Patten
...	

Page: `wiki/Lewis_B._Patten`
$\mathbf{e}_2$(Introduction): He often published under the names Lewis Ford, Lee Leighton and Joseph Wayne.

Verdict: Supported

Figure 1: FEVEROUS sample instances. Evidence in tables is highlighted in red. Each piece of evidence e_i has associated context, i.e. page, section title(s) and the closest row/column headers (highlighted in dark gray). Left: evidence consists of two table cells refuting the claim. Right: Evidence consists of two table cells and one sentence from two different pages, supporting the claim.

2 Task Description

Given a human-authored claim, systems had to first retrieve evidence from Wikipedia in the form of sentences and table cells, each accompanied by the page/section titles and column headers they were found under respectively. They then had to classify whether the claim is SUPPORTED or REFUTED based on the evidence, or NOTENOUGHINFO if the claim cannot be verified. System responses would be scored both on the evidence retrieval and the label classification. Note that unlike in the original FEVER shared task, (partial) evidence needs to be provided for the NOTENOUGHINFO claims. Each claim in the FEVEROUS dataset could have multiple ways of being verified, which is represented in the different *evidence sets* - each with potentially multiple pieces of evidence. The participating systems only had to provide one complete evidence set for their response to be considered correct.

2.1 Dataset

We provided the training and development datasets through the FEVER website[1] and as an open source dataset[2]. A reserved portion of the dataset was released as a blind test set without the gold annotations (labels + evidence) to be used in the final phase of the challenge. The training data and the blind test set are described in (Aly et al., 2021), with each split's label distribution being thus known in advance. The label distribution of the dataset is only roughly balanced for the blind test set. The number of evidence sets with only textual evidence is slightly higher than sets that contain only textual evidence or sets that require a combination of different evidence types (c.f. Table 1).

	Train	Dev	Test
Supported	41,835	3,908	3,372
Refuted	27,215	3,481	2,973
NEI	2,241	501	1,500
Total	71,291	7,890	7,845
$\mathrm{E}_{Sentences}$	31,607	3,745	3,589
E_{Cells}	25,020	2,738	2816
$\mathrm{E}_{Sentences+Cells}$	20,865	2,468	2062

Table 1: Quantitative characteristics in each split of FEVEROUS, with $E_{Sentences}$, E_{Cells}, and $E_{Sentences+Cells}$ being claims requiring only sentence evidence, cell evidence, or both, respectively.

[1] https://fever.ai/dataset/feverous.html

[2] https://doi.org/10.5281/zenodo.4911507

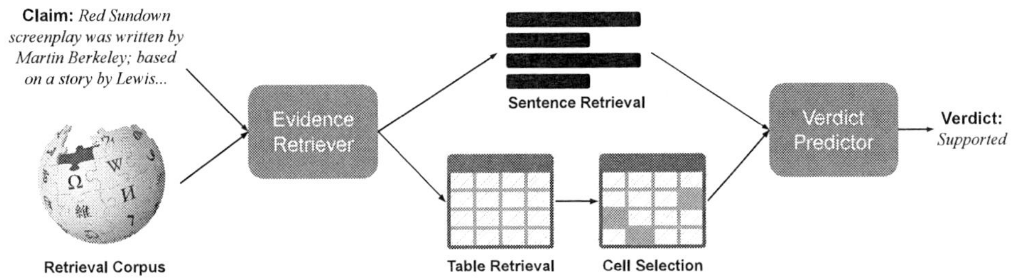

Figure 2: The pipeline of the FEVEROUS baseline, illustration taken from (Aly et al., 2021).

2.2 Submissions

The FEVEROUS shared task was hosted as a challenge on EvalAI[3] where participants were invited to submit predictions against the blind test set. Participants had about three days (24th July to 27th July 2021) starting from the release of the unlabeled blind test set to submit up to three submissions. Only a team's final submission was considered. The platform was open to submission on the development split one month prior, to allow participants to become familiar with the submission environment.

2.3 Baseline

The FEVEROUS baseline, shown schematically in Figure 2, employs a multi-stage retrieval pipeline, followed by a verdict prediction module. The most relevant documents are retrieved using a combination of entity matching and TF-IDF. The latter is then used to to extract the most relevant sentences and tables from the selected documents. To retrieve relevant cells from extracted tables, a cell extraction model linearizes them and treats the extraction as a sequence labelling task. A RoBERTa classifier (Liu et al., 2019) pre-trained on multiple NLI datasets, and fine-tuned on the FEVEROUS data[4], then predicts the veracity of the claim using the retrieved evidence and its context. Since the FEVEROUS dataset is imbalanced regarding NEI labels (5% of claims), the baseline additionally samples artificial NEI instances for training by partially removing evidence pieces from annotations. This baseline substantially outperforms the sentence-only and table-only baselines (Aly et al., 2021).

2.4 FEVEROUS score

Similar to the previous shared tasks of the FEVER Workshop (Thorne et al., 2018b), the scoring in FEVEROUS considers both the evidence retrieval and the claim labels. While we track the scores for each of these aspects individually (label accuracy, evidence P/R/F1), we use the FEVEROUS score defined in Aly et al. (2021) as the primary score for the challenge, defined as follows. For a given claim, a prediction is considered correct only if at least one complete gold evidence set E is a subset of the predicted evidence $\hat{E}$ and the predicted label is correct. We recognise that the evidence annotations are unlikely to be exhaustive, and measuring precision would penalise correct evidence missed by the annotators. Instead, we set a limit to the number of evidence pieces systems can return for each claim and allow only 5 predicted sentences items and 25 predicted table cells (the latter include table captions and list items). If additional evidence was returned it was discarded without penalty.

3 Results

The results for all submissions to the shared task are in Table 2. Further break downs are provided with results of each class (SUPPORTED, REFUTED NOTENOUGHINFO) in Table 2, and according to different types of evidence needed (textual-only, tabular-only, or both) in Table 4. The latter results are further analysed in Table 6 for each type of evidence. In Table 3, we further report results for claims that are particularly challenging, requiring numerical reasoning, multi-hop reasoning, entity disambiguation, or search terms beyond entities mentioned in the claim. Each of the 12 teams that submitted results for the blind test phase was invited to submit a paper to be reviewed in the FEVER workshop, as well as a 200-word descrip-

[3] https://eval.ai/web/challenges/challenge-page/1091

[4] For early reported scores of the baseline the classifier was not trained on the entire FEVEROUS data. These preliminary scores were almost identical to the final ones, with accuracy, evidence precision, and F_1 being around 0.01 points higher than here, but FEVEROUS score being marginally lower.

Rank	Team Name	Label Accuracy	Evidence Precision	Evidence Recall	Evidence F1	FEVEROUS Score
1	Bust a move!	0.56	0.08	**0.43**	0.13	**0.27**
2	Papelo	**0.58**	0.07	0.35	0.12	0.26
3	NCU	0.52	0.1	0.39	0.16	0.25
4	Z team	0.49	0.08	**0.43**	0.13	0.23
5	EURECOM_Fever	0.48	**0.14**	0.34	**0.2**	0.2
6	*Baseline*	0.46	0.10	0.29	0.15	0.18
7	Saturday Night Fever	0.48	0.11	0.29	0.16	0.18
8	Martin Funkquist	0.43	0.06	0.28	0.1	0.13
9	Albatross	0.41	0.06	0.19	0.1	0.12
10	METUIS	0.39	0.05	0.1	0.06	0.06
11	ChaCha	0.42	0.03	0.1	0.04	0.04
12	seda kaist	0.43	0.07	0.12	0.09	0.05
13	qmul uou iiith	0.4	0.02	0.03	0.03	0.02

Table 2: Final results of the blind test phase of the FEVEROUS challenge.

tion of their approach. 7 teams sent us system descriptions, six of which also submitted a paper. The descriptions appear in Appendix A (as sent by the authors except from minor typographic corrections), with the accompanying paper citation if one was submitted. In the remainder of this section we present our observations on the techniques used by the participants. The architecture followed by participating teams consisted of evidence retrieval followed by verdict prediction. Evidence retrieval was decomposed into page retrieval, followed by selecting textual (i.e. sentences) and tabular evidence (i.e. table cells) from the retrieved pages. Verdict prediction combined the retrieved evidence to return a label for the claim.

Page retrieval Page retrieval was mostly kept simple relying on term-matching for efficiency *Bust a move!*, *NCU* and *METUIS* used BM25 (the latter two using the implementation of Anserini (Yang et al., 2017)), while *Martin Funkquist* used vanilla TF-IDF matching. *Papelo* and *Albatross*, following the baseline, combined TF-IDF matching with entity matching, and *EURECOM_Fever* reranked its results with a BERT model pre-trained on MS-MARCO (Nguyen et al., 2016). Overall, focusing on the entities in the claim for page retrieval was found to be beneficial by the participants.

Sentence selection In order to select sentences to used as evidence, many teams used continuous representations in order to capture semantic affinity with the claim. *Bust a move!* applied a three stage-process to the task consisting of multi-hop dense passage-retrieval (Xiong et al., 2021) trained on FEVEROUS data, followed by BM25 filtering to ensure that sentences containing named entities mentioned in the claim are not ranked below those sentences semantically related to the claim but for different entities, and a final re-ranking step using a fine-tuned RoBERTa model. The latter is trained iteratively using a scheme to identify hard negative examples using previous versions of the model. Their method performs better than other systems on claims where the disambiguation of a claim's entity was a major challenge or when an article's name is not mentioned in the claim itself (c.f. Table 3), suggesting that their negative sampling method is effective. Papelo used a fine-tuned RoBERTa model for sentence selection combined with a next hop predictor based on T5 (Raffel et al., 2020) that aims to retrieve evidence complementing the pieces already retrieved. *NCU* used a BERT evidence classifier fine-tuned on FEVEROUS data, while *METUIS* developed a BERT-based QA model using the data provided. *Martin Funkquist* and *EURECOM_Fever* used TF-IDF matching following the baseline.

Table/cell selection Table selection was often done term-based using the same approaches as for page selection, i.e. TF-IDF as in the baseline (*Papelo, EURECOM_Fever*) and BM25 (*Bust a move!*), while *Martin Funkquist* used the dense table retriever of Herzig et al. (2021). *NCU* considers all tables in retrieved documents for cell extrac-

Team Name	Numerical Reasoning	Multi-hop Reasoning	Entity Disambiguation	Search terms not in Claim
Bust a move!	0.11	**0.14**	**0.20**	**0.15**
Papelo	**0.21**	0.10	0.10	0.02
NCU	0.10	**0.14**	**0.20**	0.12
Z team	0.10	0.13	0.18	0.11
EURECOM_Fever	0.07	0.12	0.17	0.10
Baseline	0.07	0.11	0.12	0.12
Saturday_Night_Fever	0.07	0.12	0.12	0.11
Martin Funkquist	0.01	**0.14**	0.12	0.09
Albatross	0.02	0.09	0.10	0.12
METUIS	0.04	0.00	0.04	0.01
ChaCha	0.03	0.01	0.01	0.00
seda_kaist	0.02	0.01	0.01	0.00
qmul_uou_iiith	0.02	0.01	0.01	0.01

Table 3: FEVEROUS scores on the blind test phase, requiring numerical reasoning (740 samples), multi-hop reasoning (1,195 samples), entity disambiguation (200 samples) and search terms beyond entities mentioned in claim (193 samples).

tion. The cells from the tables were often chosen using the same approach used by teams to select sentences from documents but trained on tabular data from the task (*Bust a move!, Papelo, NCU, EURECOM_Fever*). Cells are treated as text by linearzing them through concatenating their content and context with special markup. The teams considered as context a table's caption, table headers, and the page name, with the latter improving scores substantially for *NCU*. While *Bust a move!* and *Papelo* train a separate model for sentence and cell retrieval, *NCU* trains a single model on the joint tabular and textual data. *Martin Funkquist* and *METUIS* used the TAPAS QA model (Herzig et al., 2020) for retrieving cells. Using continuous representations to retrieve sentences and cells from retrieved documents have generally been successful, however, using specialised methods (i.e. TAPAS) explored by participants for table retrieval and cell selection seems to be have been less successful. Instead, term-based table retrieval, and treating tables as sequences of cells was overall more successful.

Evidence retrieval from different locations Claims requiring information from two or more different sections or articles (termed multi-hop reasoning in FEVEROUS), was a challenge to all systems, with neither of the two systems employing multihop evidence retrieval (*Bust a move!*, *Papelo*) scoring better (c.f. Table 3). However, we note that both teams' multihop evidence retrieval focus on the iterative retrieval of evidence, while for multi-hop claims labelled in FEVEROUS direct semantic matching with only the claim is sufficient in many cases.

Verdict prediction For verdict prediction, the top two teams developed models taking into account the fact that the evidence during testing will be noisy given that retrieval is imperfect. Thus they trained models using retrieved evidence (*Papelo*) or combining it with gold evidence from the data (*Bust a move!*). The latter considered all evidence to be of tabular form and used two instantiations of a TAPAS model, whose predictions were aggregated using an MLP. On the other hand, *Papelo* considered all evidence to be of sentence form using a simple markup to encode the table structure, and trained a T5 model on FEVEROUS data. In addition they facilitated the handling of mathematical reasoning at this stage by encoding numbers and relations between into "math hints" that were added as a prefix to the input. By using these hints, *Papelo* achieves by far the highest scores on claims that require numerical reasoning, as seen in Table 3. As this type of reasoning is typically also more relevant to claims requiring tabular evidence, it is possibly part of the reason *Papelo* performs substantially better in such claims (Table 4). Yet, all systems appear to struggle when a claim requires both textual and tabular evidence, as seen in Table 4. With exception to *Papelo*, the score tends to follow the tabular-only performance, which was more challenging for most systems. Following the baseline, *NCU*, *EURECOM_Fever* and *Albatross* treated all evidence as text and relied on some form of pre-trained NLI model fine-tuned to the data from the shared task. *Albatross* fine-tuned several existing NLI models and used majority voting to obtain the final verdict. METUIS used a pre-trained NLI model without further tuning which was applied to each piece of evidence retrieved, combining the predictions heuristically. Finally, *Martin Funkquist* handled textual evidence using RoBERTa and tabular evidence using TAPAS, aggregating their results using an MLP.

Team Name	Textual	Tabular	Combined
Bust a move!	**0.35**	0.23	0.22
Papelo	0.28	**0.33**	0.20
NCU	0.32	0.21	**0.23**
Z team	0.29	0.16	0.22
EURECOM_Fever	0.29	0.14	0.15
Baseline	0.27	0.12	0.12
Saturday_Night_Fever	0.26	0.11	0.14
Martin Funkquist	0.22	0.04	0.09
Albatross	0.26	0.03	0.01
METUIS	0.12	0.03	0.01
ChaCha	0.05	0.05	0.03
seda_kaist	0.05	0.05	0.03
qmul_uou_iiith	0.03	0.02	0.01

Table 4: FEVEROUS scores on the blind test phase, only considering samples that require exclusively textual evidence, tabular evidence, or both, respectively.

4 Analysis

Handling NOTENOUGHINFO (NEI) claims in FEVEROUS is substantially more challenging than in the FEVER shared task for two reasons: i) (partial) evidence must be retrieved for a prediction to be considered correct, ii) the dataset is very imbalanced, with relatively few NEI instances in the training set. As seen in Table 5, NEI performance was poor on the whole, with the top two systems opting not to predicting any NEI instances. In contrast to *Bust a move!*, *Papelo* by design does not predict any NEI instances, replacing instances in the training set labelled as NEI with Supported, turning the task into a binary classification task. While *Papelo* explored sampling artificial NEI instances, by labelling any instance with incomplete extracted evidence as NEI, their model performs much worse in this scenario, overpredicting NEI. A possible cause is that their prediction model is still trained on noisy evidence, creating the additional challenge of distinguishing a complete evidence set with possibly irrelevant evidence from an incomplete evidence set. This further presents an explanation for *Bust a move!*'s performance on NEI, as they also train their prediction model on both complete and incomplete evidence, which makes it more robust to imperfect retrieval for supported and refuted instances, yet making it impossible for the model to correctly distinguish these from instances with not enough information. Interestingly, worse overall systems did better on NEI predictions, with *Albatross* and *METUIS* receiving a relatively balanced F_1 score across all classes. This can possibly be attributed to their explicit treatment of the NEI class, with *METUIS* using a verdict heuristic to predict the NEI class if none of the extracted evidence pieces provides enough confidence in supporting or refuting a claim. They also report that their model overpredicts NEI instances on the development split, suggesting that it should be fine-tuned on the dataset.

Team Name	Supported	Refuted	NEI
Bust a move!	**0.66**	0.57	0.00
Papelo	0.65	**0.63**	0.00
NCU	0.61	0.54	0.26
Z team	0.62	0.38	0.01
EURECOM_Fever	0.58	0.46	0.19
Baseline	0.55	0.47	0.26
Saturday_Night_Fever	0.58	0.48	0.17
Martin Funkquist	0.60	0.01	0.00
Albatross	0.46	0.45	**0.29**
METUIS	0.35	0.49	**0.29**
ChaCha	0.53	0.35	0.11
seda_kaist	0.52	0.36	0.09
qmul_uou_iiith	0.32	0.51	0.17

Table 5: Label F_1 score per-class.

We measured how the metric of the FEVEROUS shared task correlates to its performance on both components of the task, namely evidence retrieval and veracity prediction and how the FEVEROUS scores compare to the scores obtained in FEVER (Thorne et al., 2018b). As seen in Figure 3, both FEVER and FEVEROUS scores for systems participating in the respective shared tasks strongly positively correlate with an increased label accuracy (Pearson correlation of $\rho = 0.92$ for both). However, concerning the retrieval component, it can be seen that the FEVEROUS scores correlate with the evidence F1 ($\rho = 0.83$) more strongly than the FEVER scores ($\rho = 0.41$), especially in terms of recall ($\rho = 0.97$ and $\rho = 0.53$, respectively). Again, this is a consequence of correct NEI predictions not requiring any evidence in FEVER.

The FEVEROUS baseline system is stronger than the one proposed for FEVER relatively to the respective submitted systems, achieving a higher

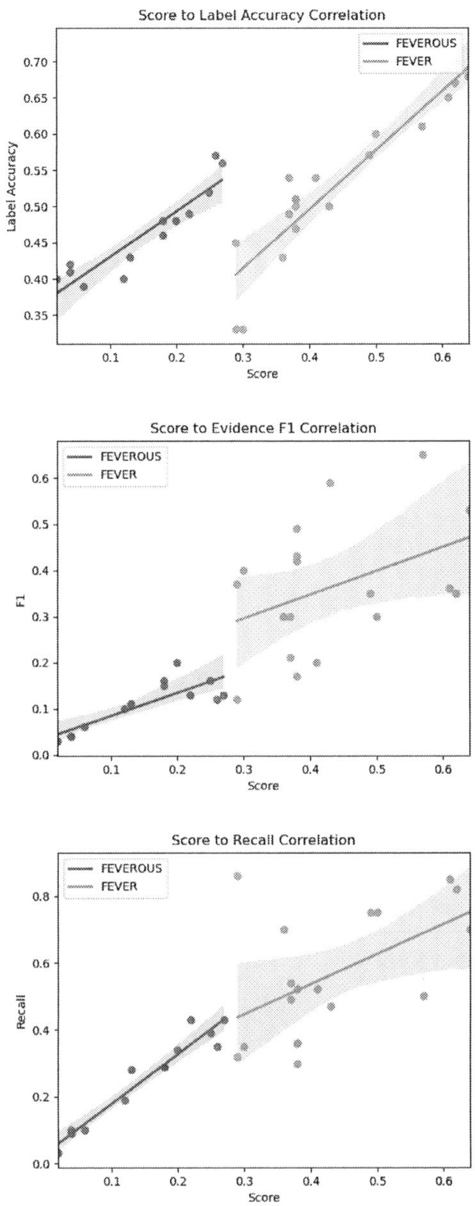

Figure 3: Correlation between FEVER/FEVEROUS score and Label Accuracy, F1, and Recall, respectively.

score than more than half of participating teams, while the FEVER baseline only performed better than around a fifth of all systems. Generally, FEVEROUS scores are generally much lower than FEVER scores, with retrieval scores being particularly low for FEVEROUS. While this is likely partly due to the NEIs being easier to predict and more numerous in FEVER (by only predicting NEI, a system would already get a score of 0.33), it might also be a result of artefacts in the original FEVER dataset, as a claim-only baseline was able to get an accuracy score of about 62% (Schuster et al., 2019), compared to a majority-class baseline of 33%. In contrast, the claim-only baseline on FEVEROUS achieves a score of 58% against a majority-class baseline of 56%. Yet, peculiarities of the FEVEROUS dataset observed by participants is a higher number of redundant evidence pieces than in FEVER (Malon, 2021) (likely a result of the higher complexity of evidence annotation), as well as a considerable number of claims that are refuted/NEI due to a single piece of information being incorrect/missing in an otherwise supported claim (Bouziane et al., 2021). Since claims are much longer in FEVEROUS than FEVER, such cases are much harder to identify. Similar to the FEVER 2.0 challenge (Thorne et al., 2019) where in a *build-it, break-it, fix-it* competition teams created adversarial attacks (*breakers*) against systems that were trained on the FEVER dataset (*builders*), to identify biases and weaknesses and address them (*fixers*), such a challenge might provide highly valuable insights to the FEVEROUS dataset to foster further research on this task.

Acknowledgements

We would like to thank Amazon for sponsoring the dataset generation and supporting the FEVER workshop and the FEVEROUS shared task. Rami Aly is supported by the Engineering and Physical Sciences Research Council Doctoral Training Partnership (EPSRC). James Thorne is supported by an Amazon Alexa Graduate Research Fellowship. Zhijiang Guo, Michael Schlichtkrull and Andreas Vlachos are supported by the ERC grant AVeriTeC (GA 865958).

References

Rami Aly, Zhijiang Guo, Michael Sejr Schlichtkrull, James Thorne, Andreas Vlachos, Christos Christodoulopoulos, Oana Cocarascu, and Arpit Mittal. 2021. FEVEROUS: Fact extraction and VERification over unstructured and structured information. In *Thirty-fifth Conference on Neural Information Processing Systems Datasets and Benchmarks Track*.

Isabelle Augenstein, Christina Lioma, Dongsheng Wang, Lucas Chaves Lima, Casper Hansen, Christian Hansen, and Jakob Grue Simonsen. 2019. MultiFC: A real-world multi-domain dataset for evidence-based fact checking of claims. In *Proceedings of the 2019 Conference on Empirical Methods in Natural Language Processing and the 9th International Joint Conference on Natural Language Processing (EMNLP-IJCNLP)*, pages 4685–4697, Hong Kong, China. Association for Computational Linguistics.

Mostafa Bouziane, Hugo Perrin, Amine Sadq, Thanh Nguyen, Aurélien Cluzeau, and Julien Mardas. 2021. FaBULOUS: Fact-checking based on understanding of language over unstructured and structured information. In *Proceedings of the Fourth Workshop on Fact Extraction and VERification (FEVER)*, pages 31 – 40. Association for Computational Linguistics.

Danqi Chen, Adam Fisch, Jason Weston, and Antoine Bordes. 2017. Reading wikipedia to answer open-domain questions. *arXiv preprint arXiv:1704.00051*.

Wenhu Chen, Hongmin Wang, Jianshu Chen, Yunkai Zhang, Hong Wang, Shiyang Li, Xiyou Zhou, and William Yang Wang. 2020. TabFact: A Large-scale Dataset for Table-based Fact Verification. In *ICLR*, pages 1–14.

Martin Funkquist. 2021. Combining sentence and table evidence to predict veracity of factual claims using TaPaS and RoBERTa. In *Proceedings of the Fourth Workshop on Fact Extraction and VERification (FEVER)*, pages 92 – 101. Association for Computational Linguistics.

In-Zu Gi, Ting-Yu Fang, and Richard Tzong-Han Tsai. 2021. Verdict inference with claim and retrieved elements using roberta. In *Proceedings of the Fourth Workshop on Fact Extraction and VERification (FEVER)*, pages 60 – 66. Association for Computational Linguistics.

Jiafeng Guo, Yixing Fan, Liang Pang, Liu Yang, Qingyao Ai, Hamed Zamani, Chen Wu, W Bruce Croft, and Xueqi Cheng. 2020. A deep look into neural ranking models for information retrieval. *Information Processing & Management*, 57(6):102067.

Vivek Gupta, Maitrey Mehta, Pegah Nokhiz, and Vivek Srikumar. 2020. INFOTABS: Inference on tables as semi-structured data. In *Proceedings of the 58th Annual Meeting of the Association for Computational Linguistics*, pages 2309–2324, Online. Association for Computational Linguistics.

Jonathan Herzig, Thomas Müller, Syrine Krichene, and Julian Eisenschlos. 2021. Open domain question answering over tables via dense retrieval. In *Proceedings of the 2021 Conference of the North American Chapter of the Association for Computational Linguistics: Human Language Technologies*, pages 512–519, Online. Association for Computational Linguistics.

Jonathan Herzig, Pawel Krzysztof Nowak, Thomas Müller, Francesco Piccinno, and Julian Eisenschlos. 2020. TaPas: Weakly supervised table parsing via pre-training. In *Proceedings of the 58th Annual Meeting of the Association for Computational Linguistics*, pages 4320–4333, Online. Association for Computational Linguistics.

Georgi Karadzhov, Preslav Nakov, Lluís Màrquez, Alberto Barrón-Cedeño, and Ivan Koychev. 2017. Fully automated fact checking using external sources. In *Proceedings of the International Conference Recent Advances in Natural Language Processing, RANLP 2017*, pages 344–353, Varna, Bulgaria. INCOMA Ltd.

Yinhan Liu, Myle Ott, Naman Goyal, Jingfei Du, Mandar Joshi, Danqi Chen, Omer Levy, Mike Lewis, Luke Zettlemoyer, and Veselin Stoyanov. 2019. Roberta: A robustly optimized bert pretraining approach. *arXiv preprint arXiv:1907.11692*.

Christopher Malon. 2021. Team Papelo at feverous: Multi-hop evidence pursuit. In *Proceedings of the Fourth Workshop on Fact Extraction and VERification (FEVER)*, pages 40–46. Association for Computational Linguistics.

Bhaskar Mitra, Fernando Diaz, and Nick Craswell. 2017. Learning to match using local and distributed representations of text for web search. In *Proceedings of the 26th International Conference on World Wide Web*, WWW '17, page 1291–1299, Republic and Canton of Geneva, CHE. International World Wide Web Conferences Steering Committee.

Preslav Nakov, Giovanni Da San Martino, Tamer Elsayed, Alberto Barrón-Cedeño, Rubén Míguez, Shaden Shaar, Firoj Alam, Fatima Haouari, Maram Hasanain, Nikolay Babulkov, Alex Nikolov, Gautam Kishore Shahi, Julia Maria Struß, and Thomas Mandl. 2021. The CLEF-2021 checkthat! lab on detecting check-worthy claims, previously fact-checked claims, and fake news. In *Advances in Information Retrieval - 43rd European Conference on IR Research, ECIR 2021, Virtual Event, March 28 - April 1, 2021, Proceedings, Part II*, volume 12657 of *Lecture Notes in Computer Science*, pages 639–649. Springer.

Tri Nguyen, Mir Rosenberg, Xia Song, Jianfeng Gao, Saurabh Tiwary, Rangan Majumder, and Li Deng. 2016. Ms marco: A human generated machine reading comprehension dataset. In *30th Conference on Neural Information Processing Systems (NIPS 2016)*, Barcelona, Spain.

Yixin Nie, Adina Williams, Emily Dinan, Mohit Bansal, Jason Weston, and Douwe Kiela. 2020. Adversarial NLI: A new benchmark for natural language understanding. In *Proceedings of the 58th Annual Meeting of the Association for Computational Linguistics*, pages 4885–4901, Online. Association for Computational Linguistics.

Colin Raffel, Noam Shazeer, Adam Roberts, Katherine Lee, Sharan Narang, Michael Matena, Yanqi Zhou, Wei Li, and Peter J. Liu. 2020. Exploring the limits of transfer learning with a unified text-to-text transformer. *Journal of Machine Learning Research*, 21(140):1–67.

Mohammed Adel Saeed, Giulio Alfarano, Khai Nguyen, Duc Pham, Raphael Troncy, and Paolo Papotti. 2021. Neural re-rankers for evidence retrieval in the FEVEROUS task. In *Proceedings of the Fourth Workshop on Fact Extraction and VERification (FEVER)*, pages 108 – 113. Association for Computational Linguistics.

Tal Schuster, Darsh Shah, Yun Jie Serene Yeo, Daniel Roberto Filizzola Ortiz, Enrico Santus, and Regina Barzilay. 2019. Towards debiasing fact verification models. In *Proceedings of the 2019 Conference on Empirical Methods in Natural Language Processing and the 9th International Joint Conference on Natural Language Processing (EMNLP-IJCNLP)*, pages 3419–3425, Hong Kong, China. Association for Computational Linguistics.

Orkun Temiz, Özgün Ozan Kılıç, Arif Ozan Kızıldağ, and Tuğba Taşkaya Temizel. 2021. A fact checking and verification system for FEVEROUS using a zero-shot learning approach. In *Proceedings of the Fourth Workshop on Fact Extraction and VERification (FEVER)*, pages 113 – 121. Association for Computational Linguistics.

James Thorne and Andreas Vlachos. 2018. Automated fact checking: Task formulations, methods and future directions. In *Proceedings of the 27th International Conference on Computational Linguistics*, pages 3346–3359, Santa Fe, New Mexico, USA. Association for Computational Linguistics.

James Thorne, Andreas Vlachos, Christos Christodoulopoulos, and Arpit Mittal. 2018a. FEVER: a large-scale dataset for fact extraction and VERification. In *Proceedings of the 2018 Conference of the North American Chapter of the Association for Computational Linguistics: Human Language Technologies, Volume 1 (Long Papers)*, pages 809–819, New Orleans, Louisiana. Association for Computational Linguistics.

James Thorne, Andreas Vlachos, Oana Cocarascu, Christos Christodoulopoulos, and Arpit Mittal. 2018b. The fact extraction and VERification (FEVER) shared task. In *Proceedings of the First Workshop on Fact Extraction and VERification (FEVER)*, pages 1–9, Brussels, Belgium. Association for Computational Linguistics.

James Thorne, Andreas Vlachos, Oana Cocarascu, Christos Christodoulopoulos, and Arpit Mittal. 2019. The FEVER2.0 shared task. In *Proceedings of the Second Workshop on Fact Extraction and VERification (FEVER)*, pages 1–6, Hong Kong, China. Association for Computational Linguistics.

Nancy X. R. Wang, Diwakar Mahajan, Marina Danilevsky, and Sara Rosenthal. 2021. SemEval-2021 task 9: Fact verification and evidence finding for tabular data in scientific documents (SEM-TAB-FACTS). In *Proceedings of the 15th International Workshop on Semantic Evaluation (SemEval-2021)*, pages 317–326, Online. Association for Computational Linguistics.

William Yang Wang. 2017. "liar, liar pants on fire": A new benchmark dataset for fake news detection. In *Proceedings of the 55th Annual Meeting of the Association for Computational Linguistics (Volume 2: Short Papers)*, pages 422–426, Vancouver, Canada. Association for Computational Linguistics.

Wenhan Xiong, Xiang Li, Srini Iyer, Jingfei Du, Patrick Lewis, William Yang Wang, Yashar Mehdad, Scott Yih, Sebastian Riedel, Douwe Kiela, and Barlas Oguz. 2021. Answering complex open-domain questions with multi-hop dense retrieval. In *International Conference on Learning Representations*.

Peilin Yang, Hui Fang, and Jimmy Lin. 2017. Anserini: Enabling the use of lucene for information retrieval research. In *Proceedings of the 40th International ACM SIGIR Conference on Research and Development in Information Retrieval*, SIGIR '17, page 1253–1256, New York, NY, USA. Association for Computing Machinery.

A System Description Summaries Submitted by Participants

A.1 Bust a move! (Bouziane et al., 2021)

We proposed a novel architecture to handle the joint retrieval and entailment over unstructured and structured information. To verify a claim, we first retrieve documents and filter the most relevant tables using BM25. Therefrom, our passage retriever extracts the relevant pieces of evidence, which can be either sentences or table cells. Finally, we obtain the verdict prediction by performing entailment using a TAPAS-based ensemble model. For retrieval, we proposed a novel training paradigm, Reinforced Adaptive Retrieval Embedding (RARE), which is inspired by reinforcement learning. It consists of re-ranking the BM25 retrieved hard-negative samples based on a snapshot of the embedding model of the last epoch. RARE samples better hard negatives, helping the model correct itself and preventing overfitting. For entailment, we proposed Noisy Entailment through Adapted Training (NEAT) that consists of two models trained on golden and noisy evidence sets, respectively. Together, they will see both relevant and irrelevant passages during training to make the ensemble more robust to noisy inputs at inference.

A.2 Papelo (Malon, 2021)

We develop a system for the FEVEROUS fact extraction and verification task that ranks an initial set of potential evidence and then pursues missing evidence in subsequent hops by trying to generate it, with a "next hop prediction module" whose output is matched against page elements in a predicted article. Seeking evidence with the next hop prediction module continues to improve FEVEROUS score for up to seven hops. Label classification is trained on possibly incomplete extracted evidence chains, utilizing hints that facilitate numerical comparison. The system achieves .281 FEVEROUS score and .658 label accuracy on the development set, and finishes in second place with .259 FEVEROUS score and .576 label accuracy on the test set.

A.3 NCU (Gi et al., 2021)

Our 3rd place FEVEROUS system is a three-stage model consisting of document retrieval, element retrieval, and verdict inference. Our document retrieval utilizes Anserini (Yang et al., 2017), an information retrieval toolkit built on Lucene. For element retrieval, we experiment two different approaches, the Anserini and the BERT model, to select relevant elements from documents retrieved in previous stage. For the third stage, we adopt the RoBERTa NLI model pre-trained on well-known NLI datasets, including SNLI, MNLI, FEVER-NLI, ANLI (Nie et al., 2020), and experiment on its variants with aggregation method to fully utilize the semantic information of retrieved elements in previous stage. Our system improves the FEVEROUS baseline in two aspects. First, while the baseline retriever pays attention to literally relevance with a combination method of entity matching and TF-IDF, we fine-tune the BERT model to integrate more semantic relevance for finding evidential elements and downstream verdict inference. Second, the baseline predictor uses the concatenation of claim and elements as input, having a constraint of maximum length. We experiment several ways to include more elements for verdict inference. These improvements allow us to achieve 0.29 feverous score on the development set and 0.25 feverous score on the blind test set, both outperforming the FEVEROUS baseline.

A.4 EURECOM_Fever (Saeed et al., 2021)

It is clear that enhancing evidence retrieval plays a vital role in any fact-checking system. In our submission, we focus on enhancing the identification of Wikipedia pages by utilizing advances in the information retrieval (IR) community, where neural ranking models have been proposed for better data retrieval (Mitra et al., 2017). We extend the baseline by providing a two-stage re-ranking process in the spirit of simple IR systems: (a) first, numerous pages to a given query are retrieved from a corpus using entity-matching and TF-IDF (Chen et al., 2017) and (b) second, the pages are scored and reranked using a more computationally-demanding method. Given that neural ranking methods have shown success in the IR community (Guo et al., 2020), we used one as part of our extension to the baseline, where a re-ranker provides a score for every (query, table) pair. We then retain the tables with the top scores. The re-ranker is based on a pre-trained BERT model that is fine-tuned on the passage re-ranking task of the MS MACRO (Nguyen et al., 2016) dataset to minimize the binary cross-entropy loss. This extension to the baseline was enough to beat it, exhibiting that having higher recall with a computationally-demanding method would be more effective for evidence retrieval than standard mechanisms.

A.5 Martin Funkquist (Funkquist, 2021)

The proposed system consists of three main parts: document retrieval, evidence retrieval and label prediction. The first part retrieves the most relevant documents using TF-IDF vector similarity scores between the claim and the title and body text of the documents. Then evidence is retrieved from these documents using similarity scores between TF-IDF vectors to retrieve the textual evidence and similarity scores between dense vectors created by fine-tuned TaPaS models to retrieve tabular evidence. Finally, the evidence is passed through a dense neural network to produce a veracity label, where the input is vectors created by a pre-trained RoBERTa for the sentence evidence and a TaPaS model for the table evidence.

A.6 Albatross

For the retrieval part, we experimented with Spacy NER based on Transformers and FastText matching instead of TFIDF. We also analyzed performance change across parameters like page count, table count, etc in the TFIDF module of baseline implementation. For verdict prediction, we fine tuned several publicly available NLI models on the competition data. We also tried a majority vote strategy for creating the test predictions using the various verdict prediction models that we had trained.

A.7 METUIS (Temiz et al., 2021)

We propose a pipeline that retrieves documents by using Anserini indexing on top of the Wikipedia dump. After the document retrieval, evidence related to the claim is selected by using Bert-Large-Cased Question Answering model, and the results of the QA model are sorted by using Universal Sentence Encoder score, which measures the similarity between the claim and the document portion. The final verdict of the claim is determined by the XLNET natural language inference model, which compares the evidence and the claim. Other than the sentence evidence, the cell evidence is obtained by TAPAS Table Question Answering model and by looking at the match score between the entities of the claim and the cell values. The pipeline is fully unsupervised, and all the models used in the pipeline require no pretraining.

B Further result tables

Team Name	Label Accuracy	Evidence Precision	Evidence Recall	F1	FEVEROUS Score
Textual-only					
Bust a move	0.54	0.06	0.57	0.11	0.35
Papelo	0.60	0.06	0.35	0.10	0.28
NCU	0.56	0.11	0.48	0.17	0.32
Z team	0.47	0.06	0.57	0.11	0.29
EURECOM_Fever	0.51	0.15	0.49	0.23	0.29
Baseline	0.50	0.13	0.43	0.20	0.27
Saturday_Night_Fever	0.50	0.12	0.43	0.19	0.26
Martin Funkquist	0.40	0.07	0.49	0.13	0.22
Albatross	0.49	0.10	0.43	0.16	0.26
METUIS	0.44	0.05	0.17	0.08	0.12
ChaCha	0.39	0.02	0.13	0.03	0.05
seda_kaist	0.39	0.02	0.13	0.03	0.05
qmul_uou_iiith	0.41	0.02	0.05	0.03	0.03
Tabular-only					
Bust a move	0.58	0.07	0.36	0.12	0.23
Papelo	0.63	0.07	0.44	0.13	0.33
NCU	0.49	0.07	0.35	0.12	0.20
Z team	0.43	0.07	0.36	0.12	0.16
EURECOM_Fever	0.44	0.09	0.28	0.13	0.14
Baseline	0.47	0.07	0.22	0.11	0.12
Saturday_Night_Fever	0.46	0.07	0.22	0.11	0.11
Martin Funkquist	0.30	0.04	0.16	0.06	0.04
Albatross	0.34	0.01	0.04	0.01	0.02
METUIS	0.41	0.03	0.09	0.04	0.05
ChaCha	0.41	0.02	0.13	0.04	0.05
seda_kaist	0.42	0.02	0.13	0.04	0.05
qmul_uou_iiith	0.51	0.03	0.04	0.03	0.02
Combined					
Bust a move	0.59	0.11	0.30	0.16	0.22
Papelo	0.50	0.10	0.27	0.14	0.19
NCU	0.52	0.13	0.33	0.18	0.23
Z team	0.62	0.11	0.30	0.16	0.22
EURECOM_Fever	0.49	0.18	0.19	0.18	0.15
Baseline	0.46	0.15	0.16	0.16	0.13
Saturday_Night_Fever	0.49	0.15	0.17	0.16	0.14
Martin Funkquist	0.65	0.09	0.12	0.10	0.09
Albatross	0.34	0.08	0.01	0.02	0.01
METUIS	0.29	0.06	0.04	0.05	0.01
ChaCha	0.48	0.05	0.05	0.05	0.03
seda_kaist	0.46	0.04	0.03	0.04	0.02
qmul_uou_iiith	0.27	0.03	0.02	0.02	0.01

Table 6: Results of the blind test phase of the FEVEROUS challenge, only considering samples that require exclusively textual evidence (top), tabular evidence (middle), and both (bottom), respectively.

Team Name	Label Accuracy	Evidence Precision	Recall	F1	FEVEROUS Score
		Numerical Reasoning (740)			
Bust a move	0.55	0.09	0.22	0.13	0.11
Papelo	0.62	0.11	0.32	0.16	0.21
NCU	0.46	0.10	0.20	0.13	0.10
Z team	0.41	0.09	0.22	0.13	0.08
EURECOM_Fever	0.42	0.09	0.20	0.13	0.07
Baseline	0.38	0.08	0.16	0.11	0.07
Saturday_Night_Fever	0.44	0.08	0.16	0.11	0.07
Martin Funkquist	0.32	0.04	0.10	0.06	0.01
Albatross	0.31	0.02	0.05	0.03	0.02
METUIS	0.33	0.03	0.06	0.04	0.04
ChaCha	0.41	0.02	0.07	0.03	0.03
seda_kaist	0.41	0.02	0.07	0.03	0.02
qmul_uou_iiith	0.51	0.03	0.03	0.03	0.02
		Multi-hop Reasoning (1195)			
Bust a move	0.55	0.09	0.20	0.12	0.14
Papelo	0.48	0.07	0.13	0.09	0.10
NCU	0.46	0.12	0.21	0.15	0.14
Z team	0.59	0.09	0.20	0.12	0.13
EURECOM_Fever	0.47	0.18	0.16	0.17	0.12
Baseline	0.44	0.13	0.15	0.14	0.11
Saturday_Night_Fever	0.48	0.14	0.15	0.15	0.12
Martin Funkquist	0.65	0.09	0.18	0.12	0.14
Albatross	0.38	0.10	0.11	0.10	0.09
METUIS	0.32	0.05	0.01	0.02	0.00
ChaCha	0.47	0.03	0.03	0.03	0.01
seda_kaist	0.46	0.03	0.03	0.03	0.01
qmul_uou_iiith	0.23	0.03	0.01	0.02	0.01
		Entity Disambiguation (200)			
Bust a move	0.40	0.07	0.34	0.11	0.20
Papelo	0.41	0.05	0.14	0.08	0.10
NCU	0.49	0.09	0.27	0.14	0.20
Z team	0.38	0.07	0.35	0.11	0.18
EURECOM_Fever	0.41	0.13	0.26	0.17	0.17
Baseline	0.42	0.10	0.21	0.14	0.12
Saturday_Night_Fever	0.40	0.12	0.22	0.15	0.12
Martin Funkquist	0.37	0.07	0.25	0.11	0.12
Albatross	0.43	0.08	0.17	0.11	0.10
METUIS	0.37	0.04	0.06	0.05	0.04
ChaCha	0.38	0.02	0.06	0.03	0.01
seda_kaist	0.37	0.02	0.05	0.03	0.01
qmul_uou_iiith	0.24	0.02	0.01	0.01	0.01
		Search terms not in Claim (195)			
Bust a move	0.28	0.05	0.33	0.09	0.15
Papelo	0.26	0.02	0.09	0.03	0.02
NCU	0.38	0.07	0.24	0.11	0.12
Z team	0.26	0.05	0.35	0.09	0.11
EURECOM_Fever	0.33	0.08	0.23	0.12	0.10
Baseline	0.38	0.06	0.19	0.09	0.12
Saturday_Night_Fever	0.30	0.07	0.20	0.10	0.11
Martin Funkquist	0.27	0.05	0.25	0.08	0.09
Albatross	0.48	0.05	0.17	0.07	0.12
METUIS	0.37	0.02	0.03	0.02	0.01
ChaCha	0.27	0.01	0.05	0.01	0.00
sed_kaist	0.26	0.01	0.05	0.01	0.00
qmul_uou_iiith	0.22	0.01	0.01	0.01	0.01

Table 7: FEVEROUS scores on the blind test phase, grouped into their different challenges, with samples numbers in brackets.

Evidence Selection as a Token-Level Prediction Task

Dominik Stammbach
Center for Law & Economics
ETH Zurich
dominik.stammbach@gess.ethz.ch

Abstract

In Automated Claim Verification, we retrieve evidence from a knowledge base to determine the veracity of a claim. Intuitively, the retrieval of the correct evidence plays a crucial role in this process. Often, evidence selection is tackled as a pairwise sentence classification task, i.e., we train a model to predict for each sentence individually whether it is evidence for a claim. In this work, we fine-tune document level transformers to extract all evidence from a Wikipedia document at once. We show that this approach performs better than a comparable model classifying sentences individually on all relevant evidence selection metrics in FEVER. Our complete pipeline building on this evidence selection procedure produces a new state-of-the-art result on FEVER, a popular claim verification benchmark.

1 Introduction

Automated Claim Verification is the task of determining the veracity of a claim given evidence retrieved from a knowledge base. A popular and large-scale benchmark for this task is FEVER, consisting of almost 200K synthetically generated claims derived from the introduction sections of Wikipedia sentences (Thorne et al., 2018). Input to such a system is a claim. We then search relevant documents from Wikipedia, and select the evidence sentences from the retrieved documents. Finally, we determine the veracity of the claim given the retrieved evidence, i.e., we predict one of the labels SUPPORTS, REFUTES or NOT ENOUGH INFO.

In this paper, we propose a new angle to think about evidence selection. Unlike the sentence-level approaches taken in previous work, we extract all evidence sentences from a Wikipedia document at once. This procedure outperforms a comparable sentence-level baseline in FEVER. The code and models described in this paper are publicly available.[1]

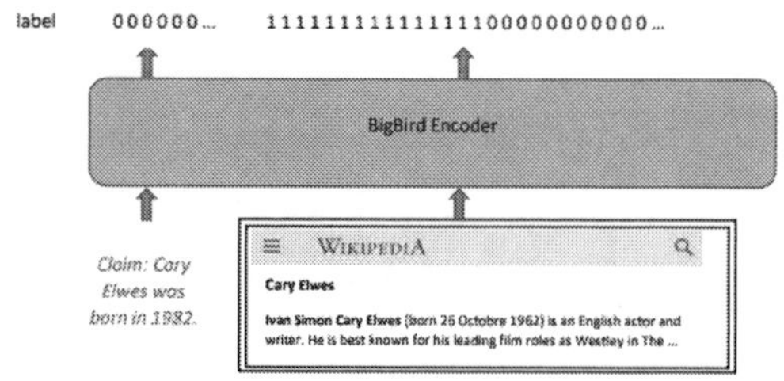

Figure 1: Selecting evidence from <claim, article> pairs, while predicting a score for each token.

Consider the claim *Cary Elwes was born in 1982*. The FEVER task consists of extracting the annotated evidence from Wikipedia and to predict the right label. For this claim, we would have to retrieve the page about *Cary Elwes* from which we have to select the following evidence sentence: *Cary Elwes, born 26 October 1962, is an English actor and writer*. Because the evidence contradicts the claim, the claim is REFUTED. FEVER Score, the official metric, is a combination of returning the correct evidence and predicting the correct label.

Past work considered evidence selection to be a pairwise sentence classification task. For example, the page about *Cary Elwes* contains four sentences. A model would predict each <claim, sentence> pair individually. Our intuition is that more context helps to decide whether a given sentence is evidence – where more context is having access to the complete article. Hence, we predict a score for each token in a document and aggregate token scores on a sentence level. We show a visualization of our approach in Figure 1. Input to our system are <claim, article> pairs. We then fine-tune a transformer to predict 1 for each token belonging to annotated evidence for a claim, and to predict 0 for all other tokens. At test time, we average scores for

[1] https://github.com/dominiksinsaarland/document-level-FEVER

Proceedings of the Fourth Workshop on Fact Extraction and VERification (FEVER) at EMNLP 2021, pages 14–20
November 10, 2021.

all tokens on a sentence level. If the resulting average is higher than 0.5, we consider the sentence to be evidence. Because Wikipedia articles are often longer than the maximum sequence length allowed in standard Transformers (e.g. Devlin et al., 2018; Liu et al., 2019), we use BigBird, which uses sparse attention to accommodate long sequences (Zaheer et al., 2020).

This perspective on evidence selection is more related to, e.g., answer span extraction in question answering (Rajpurkar et al., 2016; Kwiatkowski et al., 2019). Beltagy et al. (2020) and Zaheer et al. (2020) have both shown that long document encoders significantly improve model performance in question answering tasks with lots of context. We explore whether this holds for claim verification in FEVER as well. For example, consider the claim *St. Anger is the first studio album by Metallica.* One evidence sentence for this claim is *It was released in June 2003 as the lead single from their eighth studio album of the same name .* which can be found in the Wikipedia page *St. Anger (Song)*. Without additional context, it is not possible to resolve *their eight studio album*, and therefore it is difficult to select this sentence as evidence. However, the first sentence of this article states *[...] is a song by American heavy metal group Metallica .*, and thus resolves *their*. Having access to the whole document makes it straightforward to correctly predict this example.

To summarize: We propose a new perspective on evidence retrieval in automated claim verification.[2] We treat evidence selection as a token-level prediction task and extract all evidence from a Wikipedia article at once. This approach improves all relevant evidence retrieval metrics in FEVER compared to a RoBERTa baseline. Finally, we fine-tune a claim verification model using evidence retrieved by the proposed method which results in a new state-of-the-art result in FEVER.

2 Methods and Related Work

In this section, we describe our methods and we place our modeling decisions in the context of previous FEVER systems. To begin with, there exists a plethora of related work on FEVER – The most notable arguably is the FEVER baseline system itself. Thorne et al. (2018) perform (i) coarse-grained TF-IDF-based document retrieval, followed by (ii) more fine-grained evidence retrieval and eventually (iii) a model prediction of whether the extracted evidence entails the claim. Most subsequent systems broadly follow this pipeline while improving the individual building blocks with more tailor-made solutions. And so do we – in this work, we specifically provide a new perspective on evidence selection.

Document Retrieval: Many FEVER systems query the MediaWiki API to retrieve relevant evidence documents (introduced by Hanselowski et al., 2019). Given the importance of having retrieved the relevant candidate documents, more recent systems started to combine the MediaWiki API with TF-IDF or bm25 (Stammbach and Ash, 2020; Jiang et al., 2021).

We also take the union of documents retrieved via MediaWiki API and TF-IDF scores. These documents are the starting point of our system.

Evidence Selection: After having retrieved documents, the relevant sentences have to be selected from the documents. This step is usually perceived to be a pairwise sentence classification task. For each <claim, sentence> pair, a model predicts whether the sentence is evidence for the claim. Alternatively, this stage can be considered re-ranking of the evidence (Jiang et al., 2021). Most systems use Transformer-based architecture for sentence retrieval (e.g. Malon, 2018; Soleimani et al., 2020; Jiang et al., 2021).

The novelty of our work lies in the evidence selection stage. As visualized in Figure 1, we approach evidence selection as a token-level prediction task. We fine-tune BigBird to predict an evidence score for each token in a document individually and average[3] these scores on sentence-level. Hence, inputs to our system are <claim, article> pairs and output is a score for each sentence.

Document-level context has already been introduced in earlier FEVER systems, e.g. Malon (2018) prepends page titles to sentences to help resolve co-references. Additionally, document-level context improves evidence selection for scientific claim verification (Li et al., 2021) – our approach models both implicitly.

[2]In fact, the authors in (Wadden et al., 2020) also explored paragraph-level evidence selection using Longformer (Beltagy et al., 2020) for scientific claim verification. They add a [CLS] token (with global attention) to each sentence and the model predicts whether this token is evidence. Their system *LongChecker* ranks on top of the SciFact leaderboard at the time of submission of this work.

[3]The median and max lead to almost identical results.

Furthermore, our approach is computationally more efficient. Assuming BigBird is as efficient for a <claim, article> pair as RoBERTa is for a <claim, sentence> pair (which is not quite the case), we reduce training and inference time by the factor of the mean sentence length of Wikipedia articles[4].

Multi-hop Retrieval: Some systems follow hyperlinks present in a Wikipedia article to explore additional documents (see e.g. Nie et al., 2018; Stammbach and Neumann, 2019). We do the same and model hyperlink documents in the same way as described in (Stammbach and Neumann, 2019).

Sparse Attention: Vanilla Transformer-based architectures (introduced in Vaswani et al., 2017) calculate the full attention matrix A which includes all pairwise interactions between tokens in a sequence. Because A is quadratic in time and memory complexity, these systems only work on modestly long input, i.e., the cutoff is usually made at 512 subwords. A substantial amount of introduction sections in Wikipedia are longer, so we fall back to BigBird which implements sparse attention patterns, allowing for sequence lengths up to 4096 tokens.

BigBird only computes neighboring interactions between tokens, global interactions for a subset of tokens (by default the [CLS] and [SEP] token), and random interactions between a token and randomly sampled other tokens in the sequence. Thus, the full attention matrix is not computed anymore, which resolves the quadratic time and memory complexity. Zaheer et al. (2020) have shown that BigBird's attention pattern is equivalent in performance to e.g. BERT on short sequence lengths and outperforms BERT on all tasks requiring longer sequence lengths.

Claim verification: This is the last step, where most related work takes a textual entailment approach. To account for all retrieved evidence in the previous stage, the selected sentences are concatenated (see e.g. Thorne et al., 2018).

There is no annotated evidence for non-verifiable claims. Hence, early systems extracted evidence for these claims using the Sentence Selection module (Thorne et al., 2018). More recent systems create a noisy claim verification dataset by predicting evidence for all claims in the training set. The verification model is then trained on this noisy dataset (Stammbach and Ash, 2020; Jiang et al., 2021). This arguably minimizes distribution mismatch during training and inference and can lead to substantially higher label accuracy.

We take this approach as well and extract evidence for all claims in the training set. We then concatenate the five highest scoring evidence sentences for each claim and sort them in descending order according to the assigned sentence score. This constitutes our noisy training set, on which we fine-tune DeBERTa-V2-XL pre-trained on MNLI[5] (He et al., 2021).

3 Results

3.1 Sentence Selection Results

We present evidence selection results on the FEVER development set in Tables 1 and 2. We compare results of our sentence selection method to a RoBERTa checkpoint making a decision for each sentence individually.

We show evidence precision, recall, F1 and FEVER Score assuming access to oracle labels. In the first half of the tables, we show metrics for evidence scoring > 0.5, i.e. our model is confident that this is an evidence sentence. In Table 1, we see that BigBird achieves remarkable gains in both precision and recall, resulting in a 2% point increase in F1 compared to a RoBERTa checkpoint with the same amount of parameters. Assuming oracle claim verification labels for both selection methods, our approach still results in a 1% higher FEVER Score. BigBird-large maintains recall while gaining another 5% points in precision.

In the second half of the tables, we show results assuming re-ranking.[6] Comparing RoBERTa and BigBird in this setting, we again observe an increase of 1% in recall and FEVER Score assuming oracle labels. BigBird-large again improves recall over BigBird-base. We also present an oracle upper bound (last row) to explore what is possible given our retrieved Wikipedia pages: The oracle assigns 1 to each annotated evidence sentence and 0 to all other sentences. Surprisingly, if we measure FEVER Scores assuming oracle labels, the FEVER Score of the oracle is less than 1% point higher than our BigBird-large model.

[4]if an article contains N sentences, pairwise sentence classification requires N computation steps, whereas our approach takes only one step.

[5]larger models perform better – DeBERTa has been shown to work well on MNLI and is the largest model we could fit on a single 32GB GPU

[6]This is standard in FEVER – only recall matters and the five highest scoring evidence sentences are submitted.

Experiment	Pr (%)	Rc (%)	F1 (%)	FEVER Score (%)
Roberta-base	71.25	83.21	76.72	88.74
Bigbird-base	73.57	84.57	78.69	89.71
Bigbird-large	**79.16**	84.52	**81.75**	89.68
Roberta-base top5	25.06	89.30	39.14	92.86
Bigbird-base top5	24.86	90.33	38.99	93.55
Bigbird-large top5	25.49	**90.79**	39.81	**93.86**
Oracle	98.39	97.58	92.19	94.81

Table 1: Evidence Retrieval

Experiment	Pr (%)	Rc (%)	F1 (%)	FEVER Score (%)
Roberta-base	53.17	86.81	65.95	91.20
Bigbird-base	56.9	88.15	69.13	92.1
Bigbird-large	**69.98**	88.22	**78.05**	92.15
Roberta-base top5	24.51	91.94	38.7	94.62
Bigbird-base top5	26.87	92.55	41.6	95.03
Bigbird-large top5	26.03	**93.62**	40.73	**95.74**
Oracle	98.50	97.76	96.02	96.88

Table 2: Multi-hop Evidence Retrieval

In Table 2, we show analogous results for additionally incorporating retrieved multi-hop evidence sentences. Consequently, precision drops while recall and FEVER Score assuming oracle labels increase for all settings. We observe the same trends where BigBird-base outperforms an equivalent RoBERTa model in precision and recall, leading to a 3% point increase in F1 and a 0.8% point increase in FEVER Score. Again, the large model achieves similar recall than the base model, but makes remarkable gains in precision. In the re-ranking setting, BigBird (both base and large) achieve higher recall and FEVER Score than RoBERTa, with more striking differences between the two BigBird checkpoints. Lastly, if we again assume an oracle selecting evidence, this oracle would only achieve a FEVER Score 1% higher than our BigBird-large model. Thus, we conclude our approach achieves close to what is possible in evidence selection given the retrieved documents.

3.2 Leaderboard Results

Our final submission consists of the evidence retrieved by BigBird-large, including multi-hop evidence. We submit the five highest scoring evidence sentences for each claim. Our claim verification model is also trained on this input and assigns a veracity label to each claim. In Appendix A, we compare our submission to other high ranking systems on the leaderboard of the FEVER test set.

4 Conclusion

We present a novel approach to evidence retrieval. Instead of considering sentence selection as a pairwise sentence task, we extract all evidence sentences from a Wikipedia article at once by predicting for each token whether it is part of an evidence sentence or not. Our method outperforms a comparable RoBERTa checkpoint trained on <claim, sentence> pairs in every metric regarding evidence retrieval in FEVER, while being less computationally expensive. Hence, we consider our method for evidence selection to be an unambiguous improvement over previous approaches. We believe most FEVER systems (and possibly other claim verification tasks) would benefit from the method proposed in this work. We have shown that our system performs only 1% point worse than an oracle in terms of FEVER Score assuming gold veracity labels. Hence, we reason that our evidence selection method reflects strong performance given our initial set of retrieved documents. Finally, our full pipeline leads to a new state-of-the-art on the blind FEVER test set at the time of submission.

We consider our work only as the starting point in the incorporation of document-level transformers to automated claim verification. Avenues for future work could include e.g. taking a more SQuAD-like approach where only start and end tokens of evidence spans are predicted, or where we predict a special [CLS] token for each sentence, while having the whole article as input. Given re-ranked documents (such that the combined sequence length is < 4096), it might also be interesting to concatenate all of them and extract evidence at once from all documents for a given claim. Or predict the veracity directly from these documents, without having to extract evidence at all.

References

Iz Beltagy, Matthew E. Peters, and Arman Cohan. 2020. Longformer: The long-document transformer.

Jacob Devlin, Ming-Wei Chang, Kenton Lee, and Kristina Toutanova. 2018. Bert: Pre-training of deep bidirectional transformers for language understanding. *arXiv preprint arXiv:1810.04805*.

Andreas Hanselowski, Hao Zhang, Zile Li, Daniil Sorokin, Benjamin Schiller, Claudia Schulz, and Iryna Gurevych. 2019. Ukp-athene: Multi-sentence textual entailment for claim verification.

Pengcheng He, Xiaodong Liu, Jianfeng Gao, and Weizhu Chen. 2021. Deberta: Decoding-enhanced bert with disentangled attention.

Kelvin Jiang, Ronak Pradeep, and Jimmy Lin. 2021. Exploring listwise evidence reasoning with t5 for fact verification. In *Proceedings of the 59th Annual Meeting of the Association for Computational Linguistics and the 11th International Joint Conference on Natural Language Processing (Volume 2: Short Papers)*, pages 402–410, Online. Association for Computational Linguistics.

Tom Kwiatkowski, Jennimaria Palomaki, Olivia Redfield, Michael Collins, Ankur Parikh, Chris Alberti, Danielle Epstein, Illia Polosukhin, Matthew Kelcey, Jacob Devlin, Kenton Lee, Kristina N. Toutanova, Llion Jones, Ming-Wei Chang, Andrew Dai, Jakob Uszkoreit, Quoc Le, and Slav Petrov. 2019. Natural questions: a benchmark for question answering research. *Transactions of the Association of Computational Linguistics*.

Xiangci Li, Gully Burns, and Nanyun Peng. 2021. A paragraph-level multi-task learning model for scientific fact-verification.

Yinhan Liu, Myle Ott, Naman Goyal, Jingfei Du, Mandar Joshi, Danqi Chen, Omer Levy, Mike Lewis, Luke Zettlemoyer, and Veselin Stoyanov. 2019. Roberta: A robustly optimized bert pretraining approach.

Christopher Malon. 2018. Team papelo: Transformer networks at FEVER. In *Proceedings of the First Workshop on Fact Extraction and VERification (FEVER)*, pages 109–113, Brussels, Belgium. Association for Computational Linguistics.

Yixin Nie, Haonan Chen, and Mohit Bansal. 2018. Combining fact extraction and verification with neural semantic matching networks. *CoRR*, abs/1811.07039.

Pranav Rajpurkar, Jian Zhang, Konstantin Lopyrev, and Percy Liang. 2016. Squad: 100,000+ questions for machine comprehension of text. In *Proceedings of the 2016 Conference on Empirical Methods in Natural Language Processing*, pages 2383–2392. Association for Computational Linguistics.

Amir Soleimani, Christof Monz, and Marcel Worring. 2020. Bert for evidence retrieval and claim verification. In *Advances in Information Retrieval*, pages 359–366, Cham. Springer International Publishing.

Dominik Stammbach and Elliott Ash. 2020. e-fever: Explanations and summaries forautomated fact checking. In *Proceedings of the 2020 Truth and Trust Online Conference (TTO 2020), Virtual, October 15-17, 2020*, pages 32–43. Hacks Hackers.

Dominik Stammbach and Guenter Neumann. 2019. Team DOMLIN: Exploiting evidence enhancement for the FEVER shared task. In *Proceedings of the Second Workshop on Fact Extraction and VERification (FEVER)*, pages 105–109, Hong Kong, China. Association for Computational Linguistics.

James Thorne, Andreas Vlachos, Christos Christodoulopoulos, and Arpit Mittal. 2018. FEVER: a large-scale dataset for fact extraction and VERification. In *Proceedings of the 2018 Conference of the North American Chapter of the Association for Computational Linguistics: Human Language Technologies, Volume 1 (Long Papers)*, pages 809–819, New Orleans, Louisiana. Association for Computational Linguistics.

Ashish Vaswani, Noam Shazeer, Niki Parmar, Jakob Uszkoreit, Llion Jones, Aidan N Gomez, Ł ukasz Kaiser, and Illia Polosukhin. 2017. Attention is all you need. In I. Guyon, U. V. Luxburg, S. Bengio, H. Wallach, R. Fergus, S. Vishwanathan, and R. Garnett, editors, *Advances in Neural Information Processing Systems 30*, pages 5998–6008. Curran Associates, Inc.

David Wadden, Shanchuan Lin, Kyle Lo, Lucy Lu Wang, Madeleine van Zuylen, Arman Cohan, and Hannaneh Hajishirzi. 2020. Fact or fiction: Verifying scientific claims. In *Proceedings of the 2020 Conference on Empirical Methods in Natural Language Processing (EMNLP)*, pages 7534–7550, Online. Association for Computational Linguistics.

Manzil Zaheer, Guru Prashanth Guruganesh, Avi Dubey, Joshua Ainslie, Chris Alberti, Santiago Ontanon, Philip Minh Pham, Anirudh Ravula, Qifan Wang, Li Yang, and Amr Mahmoud El Houssieny Ahmed. 2020. Big bird: Transformers for longer sequences.

A Leaderboard at Time of Submission

In Table 3, we show results of the leaderboard for the blind FEVER test set at time of submission of this work. Even though our submission does not achieve the highest label accuracy, it still improves by 0.9% points the FEVER score compared to the second best entry. FEVER Score by default is upper-bounded by the retrieved evidence, and we attribute the mis-match in FEVER Score and label accuracy to our method of selecting evidence sentences. Compared to the third best entry, our system scores higher in every metric.

B Hyperparameters

In Table 4, we list the hyper-parameters used for training the models used in this paper. We did not tune them for the Sentence Selection model, but used the same training data and hyper-parameters as in (Stammbach and Ash, 2020), from where we also have the Roberta-base model against which we compare our results in Table 1 and 2. We experimented with batchsizes 8, 16 and 32 for the RTE model, where batchsize 16 yielded best development set results.

C Additional Training and Evaluation Tricks

Excluding Long Wikipedia Pages: We exclude Wikipedia articles during training and evaluation which contain more than 1500 tokens (split by whitespace). Manual inspection of the training and development set yields that these lengthy articles are mostly verbose lists and do not contain annotated evidence. Including these articles would imply that we could not train with batchsize 4 (and 8 gradient accumulation steps), but would need to train on batchsize 2 and 16 gradient accumulation steps (due to memory requirements).

Masking: We mask the predictions for tokens in the claim during training (and ignore these predictions during fine-tuning). We also set the label of the [CLS] token to 1 if a Wikipedia article contains at least 1 evidence sentence, else the label of the [CLS] token is 0. The [CLS] token is not masked during computation of the loss.

Down-sampling Negative Examples We downsample articles not containing any annotated evidence. We downsample lengthier articles more frequently, i.e. we keep 10% lengthy articles and 25% *short* articles. This speeds up training time.

Model Input: We add a special <EOS> token at the end of each sentence. We add the [CLS] token at the beginning of each <claim, article> pair, a [SEP] token between the claim and the article and a [SEP] token at the end of each Wikipedia article, i.e. model input for sentence selection consists of

[CLS] claim [SEP] sentence_1 [EOS] sentence_2 [EOS] ... [SEP]

Figure 2: Model Input for Sentence Selection Model

Down-weighting Hyperlink Evidence: We follow (Stammbach and Neumann, 2019) and retrieve hyperlink pages for each evidence sentence e_i selected by our model in a first pass. We then predict for each such retrieved page whether it contains evidence, by additionally prompting e_i next to the claim in the model input. We down-weight scores for examples retrieved in this manner to be 0.0001 (barely above confidence threshold) if the score is > 0. If the score is negative, it remains unchanged. We find that our model would otherwise rank these sentences higher than *more important* evidence retrieved in the first pass.

author	evidence F1	LA	FEVER Score
nudt_nlp	38.9	77.4	74.4
(Jiang et al., 2021)	39.6	**79.4**	75.9
ours	**40.0**	79.2	**76.8**

Table 3: Leaderboard Entries at Time of Submission

parameter	Sentence Selection	RTE
checkpoint	bigbird-roberta-large	deberta-v2-xlarge-mnli
learning rate	2e-5	3e-6
(effective) batch size	32	16
number of epochs	2	2
max_length	1536	256
max_grad_norm	1.0	1.0
weight_decay	0.0	0.0
warmup_steps	0	0
FP16_training	True	True
adam_epsilon	1e-8	1e-8
dropout	0.1	0.1

Table 4: Hyper-parameters Used during Training

Graph Reasoning with Context-Aware Linearization for Interpretable Fact Extraction and Verification

Neema Kotonya[*1], **Thomas Spooner**[2], **Daniele Magazzeni**[2], and **Francesca Toni**[1]
[1]Department of Computing, Imperial College London
[2]J.P. Morgan AI Research
nk2418@ic.ac.uk, {thomas.spooner,daniele.magazzeni}@jpmorgan.com, ft@ic.ac.uk

Abstract

This paper presents an end-to-end system for fact extraction and verification using textual and tabular evidence, the performance of which we demonstrate on the FEVEROUS dataset. We experiment with both a multi-task learning paradigm to jointly train a graph attention network for both the task of evidence extraction and veracity prediction, as well as a single objective graph model for solely learning veracity prediction and separate evidence extraction. In both instances, we employ a framework for per-cell linearization of tabular evidence, thus allowing us to treat evidence from tables as sequences. The templates we employ for linearizing tables capture the context as well as the content of table data. We furthermore provide a case study to show the interpretability our approach. Our best performing system achieves a FEVEROUS score of 0.23 and 53% label accuracy on the blind test data.[1]

1 Introduction

Fact checking has become an increasingly important tool to combat misinformation. Indeed the study of automated fact checking in NLP (Vlachos and Riedel, 2014), in particular, has yielded a number of valuable insights in recent times. These include task formulations such as matching for discovering already fact-checked claims (Shaar et al., 2020), identifying neural fake news (Zellers et al., 2020), fact verification in scientific (Wadden et al., 2020) and public health (Kotonya and Toni, 2020b) domains, and end-to-end fact verification (Thorne et al., 2018), which is the subject of the FEVEROUS benchmark dataset (Aly et al., 2021).

A majority of automated fact checking studies only consider text as evidence for verifying claims. Recently, there have been a number of works which look at fact-checking with structured and semi-structured data, mainly in the form of tables and knowledge bases (Chen et al., 2020) — but fact-checking from both structured and unstructured data has been largely unexplored. Given the sophistication in the presentation of fake news, it is important to develop fact checking tools for assessing evidence from a wide array of evidence sources in order to reach a more accurate verdict regarding the veracity of claims.

In this work, we propose a graph-based representation that supports both textual and tabular evidence, thus addressing some of the key limitations of past architectures. This approach allows us to capture relations between evidence items as well as claim-evidence pairs, borrowing from the argumentation and argument mining literature (Cabrio and Villata, 2020; Vecchi et al., 2021), as well as argument modeling for fact verification (Alhindi et al., 2018).

We experiment with two formulations for graph learning. For the first, we employ a multi-task learning paradigm to jointly train a graph attention network (Velickovic et al., 2018) for both the task of evidence extraction — which we model as a node selection task — and a graph-level veracity prediction task. In the second, we explicitly separate the verification and extraction tasks, where standard semantic search is used for evidence extraction, and veracity prediction is treated as a graph-level classification problem.

For veracity prediction we predict a label for each claim, one of SUPPORTS, REFUTES, or NOT-ENOUGH-INFO (NEI), which is conditioned on all relevant evidence, hence the intuition to frame veracity prediction as a graph-level prediction task. In both formulations, we employ context-aware table linearization templates to produce per-cell sequence representations of tabular evidence and thus construct evidence reasoning graphs where nodes

* Work done while the author was an intern at J.P. Morgan AI Research.

[1]This system was not submitted to the shared task competition, but instead to the after competition leader board under the name **CARE** (**C**ontext **A**ware **RE**asoner).

Proceedings of the Fourth Workshop on Fact Extraction and VERification (FEVER) at EMNLP 2021, pages 21–30
November 10, 2021. ©2021 Association for Computational Linguistics

have heterogeneous evidence types (i.e., representing sentences and tables on the same evidence reasoning graph).

Contributions. The three main contributions of the paper are summarized below:

1. Provide **insightful empirical analysis** of the new FEVEROUS benchmark dataset.
2. Propose a novel framework for interpretable fact extraction using templates to derive **context-aware per-cell linearizations**.
3. Present a **graph reasoning model** for fact verification that supports both structured and unstructured evidence data.

Both the joint model and separately trained models exhibit a significant improvement over the FEVEROUS baseline, as well as significant improvements for label accuracy and evidence recall. Our separated approach to fact extraction and verification achieves a FEVEROUS score of 0.23 and label accuracy of 53% on the blind test data.

2 Related Work

Graph Reasoning for Fact Verification. Several works explore graph neural networks (GNN) for fact extraction and verification, both for fine-grained evidence modelling (Liu et al., 2020; Zhong et al., 2020) and evidence aggregation for veracity prediction (Zhou et al., 2019). Furthermore, graph learning has also been leveraged to build fake news detection models which learn from evidence from different contexts; e.g., user-based and content-based data (Liu et al., 2020; Lu and Li, 2020). There are also non-neural approaches to fake news detection with graphs (Ahmadi et al., 2019; Kotonya and Toni, 2019). However, to the best of our knowledge, this work is the first to employ a graph structure to jointly reason over both text and tabular evidence data in both single task learning (STL) and multi-task learning (MTL) settings.

Table Linearization. A number of approaches have been adopted in NLP for table linearization. For example, Gupta et al. (2020) study natural language inference in the context of table linearizations, in particular they are interested to see if language models can infer entailment relations from table linearizations. The linearization approach employed by Schlichtkrull et al. (2021) is also used for automated fact verification. However, they linearize tables row- and column-wise, whereas we focus on cells as evidence items in the FEVEROUS dataset are annotated at table-cell level.

3 Data Analysis

Further to the FEVEROUS dataset statistics discussed by the task description paper (Aly et al., 2021), we perform our own data exploration. We present insights from our data analysis of the FEVEROUS dataset, which we use to inform system design choices.

Table types. Wikipedia tables can be categorized into one of two classes: infoboxes and general tables. Infoboxes are fixed format tables which typically appear in the top right-hand corner of a Wikipedia article. General tables can convey a wider breadth of information (e.g., election results, sports match scores, the chronology of an event) and typically have more complex structures (e.g., multiple headers). List items can also be considered as a special subclass of tables, where the number of items is analogous to the number of columns and the nests of the list signify table rows.

Evidence types. The first observation we make is that, similar to the FEVER dataset (Thorne et al., 2018), a sizeable portion of the training instances rely on evidence items which are extracted from the first few sentences of a Wikipedia article. The most common evidence items are the first and second sentences in a Wikipedia article, which appear in 36% and 18% of evidence sets, respectively. The four most frequent evidence cells all come from the first table, with 49% of first tables listed as evidence in the train and dev data being infoboxes. Further, the vast majority of cell evidence items are non-header cells, but these only account for approximately 5.1% of tabular evidence in the train and dev datasets. A summary of these findings is provided in Table 1 for the most common evidence types in the training data.

Evidence item co-occurrences. We investigate the most common evidence pairs, both in individual evidence sets and also in the union of all evidence sets relating to a claim. The most common evidence pair in the training data is (SENTENCE_0, SENTENCE_1), which accounts for 3.2% of evidence co-occurrences. The most common sentence-table cell co-occurrence is (CELL_0_2_1, SENTENCE_0). The most common table cell pair is

Evidence type	% Evidence sets
List items	1.6%
Sentences	67.7%
All tables	58.2%
Infoboxes	26.5%
General tables	33.9%

Table 1: Prevalence of evidence types in the training data by number of evidence sets in which they appear.

(CELL_0_2_0, CELL_0_2_1). All of the ten most common co-occurrences either contain one of the first four sentences in an article or evidence from one of the first two tables.

NEI label. Lastly, we choose to explore instances of the NEI class. We sample 100 instances of NEI claims from the training data and note their qualitative attributes. We pay particular attention to this label as it is the least represented in the data. Unlike the FEVER score, the FEVEROUS metric requires the correct evidence, as well as the label, to be supplied for an NEI instance for credit to awarded. Our analysis is summarized in Table 2. We categorize mutations, using the FEVEROUS annotation scheme, as one of three types: entity substitution, including more facts than available in the provided evidence (i.e., including additional propositions), and paraphrasing or generalizing. We use *Other* to categorize claims with a mutation not captured by one of these three categories.

Mutation Type	% Sample
Entity Substitution	21%
More facts than in evidence	42%
Paraphrasing or generalizing	36%
Other	1%

Table 2: We sample 100 NEI instances and categorize them according to the type of lexical mutation which results in the claim being unverifiable.

We note that a number of NEI examples are mutations of SUPPORTS or REFUTES examples. For example the claim in Table 3 is a mutation of a SUPPORTS instance where entity substitution (humans $\rightarrow$ reptiles) has been used to make the first clause unverifiable, hence changing the label to NEI.

Claim
Nucleoporin 153, a protein which in **reptiles** is encoded by the NUP153 gene, is an essential component of the basket of nuclear pore complexes (NPCs) in vertebrates, and required for the anchoring of NPCs.
Evidence
Nucleoporin 153 (Nup153) is a protein which in **humans** is encoded by the NUP153 gene. It is an essential component of the basket of nuclear pore complexes (NPCs) in vertebrates, and required for the anchoring of NPCs.

Table 3: NEI example where the evidence is highlighted according to the part of the claim to which it refers. The text in **bold** is the substitution which resulted in the label changing from SUPPORTS to NEI.

4 Methods

Our proposed method for fact verification is an end-to-end system comprising three modules:

(1) A robust document retrieval procedure (see Section 4.1).

(2) An evidence graph construction and intermediate evidence filtering process (see Section 4.2).

(3) A joint veracity label prediction and evidence selection layer that reasons over the evidence graph (see Section 4.3).

An illustration of the complete pipeline is provided in Figure 1, and details of each processing stage are provided in the following sections.

4.1 Document Retrieval

For document retrieval, we employ an entity linking and API search approach similar to that of Hanselowski et al. (2018). The WikiMedia API[2] is used to query Wikipedia for articles related to the claim, using named entities and noun phrases from the claim as search terms. These retrieved Wikipedia page titles form our candidate document set. Named entities that are not retrieved by the API are then extracted from the claim as a handful of these identify pages which are present in

[2] https://www.mediawiki.org/wiki/API

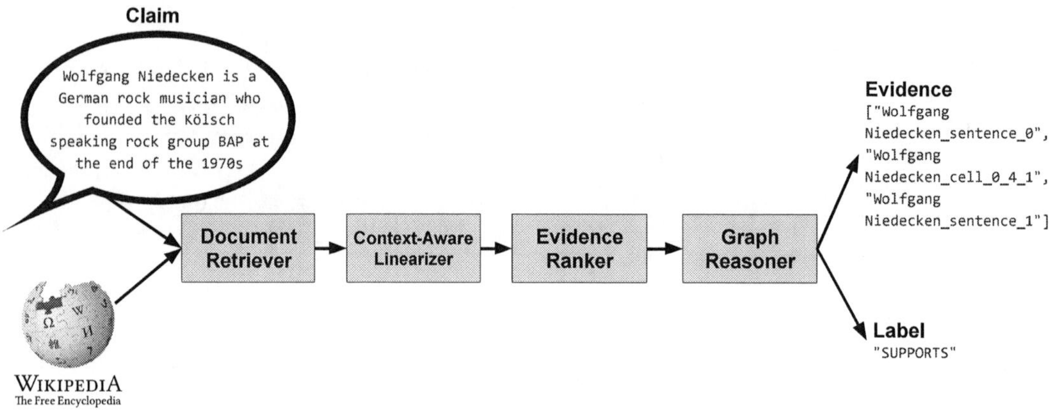

Figure 1: Our fact verification pipeline. We employ two graph reasoning approaches: STL where the evidence extraction and modelled separately, and MTL where further evidence filtering is performed jointly with veracity prediction by the Graph Reasoner.

the Wikipedia dump (e.g., **/wiki/Lars_Hjorth** is present in the provided Wikipedia evidence dump, but is not returned by the WikiMedia API). In the same vein, we discard titles which are returned by the API, but are not in the Wikipedia dump. TF-IDF and cosine similarity are employed to score and rerank the retrieved Wikipedia articles with respect to their similarity to the claim.

As in the approach of Hanselowski et al. (2018), the seven highest ranked pages are chosen at test time. For completeness, we also experiment with approaches to document retrieval which select pages based on a threshold score (Nie et al., 2019). Ultimately, we find these methods yield lower precision.

4.2 Evidence Reasoning Graph

Similar to other fact verification systems (Augenstein et al., 2019; Hidey et al., 2020), we jointly train our model for both the evidence selection and veracity prediction tasks. In contrast to these approaches, however, we employ a graph reasoning module for the joint learning of the two tasks. We choose this approach to exploit the permutation invariance of evidence with respect to a claim, as there is no canonical ordering of evidence. Our graph formulation differs from previous graph-based fact verification systems in that we construct a *heterogeneous graph to model both tabular and sequence evidence data.*

In the following sections we will describe two specific approaches that are taken for the fact verification task: (1) where we condition the graph model to learn both node-level, fine-grained evidence selection and graph-level veracity label prediction simultaneously, and (2) where we only learn graph-level veracity prediction.

Linearizing Tabular Data. We linearize both table and list evidence data and generate from these linearizations a contextualized sequence representation which captures information about each cell as well as its surrounding page elements. This is accomplished using templates that distinguish explicitly between infoboxes and general tables. For the latter, we engineer the templates to handle two particular complexities that are present only in general tables: (1) nested headers, and (2) table cells which span multiple rows and multiple columns (see Figure 2). Furthermore, we also employ templates for producing context-rich representations of item lists (see Table 4 for more details).

Club	Season	League		
		Division	Apps	Goals
Santa Cruz	2019	Série C	7	1
Athletico Paranaense	2020	Serie A	0	0
	2021		0	0
	Total		0	0
Guarani (loan)	2020	Série B	5	0

Figure 2: Example of a complex general table taken from **/wiki/Elias_Carioca**. This table contains both multi-row cells and multi-column cells, some of which are headers. They are shown highlighted.

Graph Structure. We construct a fully connected graph $G = (V, E)$, where each node $n_i \in V$ represents a claim-evidence pair, similar to previ-

Evidence Type	Linearization		Example from FEVEROUS dataset
Infoboxes			
Headers	TABLE **has** CELL_I_J [in SUBHEADER]	**is**	Brewster Productions has Genres . **[/wiki/Brewster_Productions]**
Non-headers	CELL_I_0 **of** TABLE [in SUBHEADER] CELL_I_J		Current ranking of Barbora Krejčíková in Singles is No. 65 (16 November 2020) . **[/wiki/Barbora_Krejcikova]**
General tables			
Headers	TABLE **has** CELL_I_J [in SUBHEADER]		The 1964 United States Senate election in Maine has Party . **[/wiki/1908_Clemson_Tigers_football_team]**
Non-headers	TABLE/PAGE **has** SUBHEADER_0 CELL_I_0 **in** SUBHEADER_J **of** CELL_I_J		2014 Ladies European Tour has Rank 9 in Player of Florentyna Parker . **[/wiki/2014_Ladies_European_Tour]**
List items			
Without subheaders	TITLE **includes** ITEM_I_J		Site includes Location, a point or an area on the Earth's surface or elsewhere. **[/wiki/Site]**
With subheaders	SUBHEADERS **for** TITLE **includes** ITEM_I_J		The Player Honours for Park Sang-in includes K-League Best XI: 1985 **[/wiki/Park_Sang-in]**

Table 4: Templates for encoding tabular evidence. CELL_I_0, SUBHEADER_0, SUBHEADER_J, SUBHEADERS, TABLE, TITLE and PAGE are all context elements. The content of the evidence item is highlighted . In each case ITEM_I_J denotes list item content and CELL_I_J denotes table cell content.

ous evidence graphs for automated fact checking (Zhao et al., 2020; Zhou et al., 2019). Self-loops are also included in G for each node in order to improve evidence reasoning, so the set of edges for the graph is $E = \{(n_i, n_j) \mid n_i, n_j \in V\}$.

At test time, we take the Wikipedia pages output by the document retrieval module, segment each Wikipedia page into its constituent page items (i.e., sentences, table cells, table captions and list items), and refer to these as evidence items. These evidence items are then filtered. Using an ensemble of pre-trained S-BERT sentence embeddings (Reimers and Gurevych, 2019), we perform semantic search with the claim as our query. Cosine similarity is then used to rank the evidence items. For the joint and single training approaches, we select a different number of evidence nodes; in particular, a larger graph is used with the former. For training, we select nodes to occupy the graph according to the following rule-set:

(1) If gold evidence, include as a node.

(2) For claims that require a single evidence item, include the top four candidates returned using our semantic search approach as nodes.

(3) For claims with more than one gold evidence item, retrieve the same number of candidates as gold items.

The union of these sets form the collection of nodes, V, that occupy the evidence graph G.

Node Representations. For the initial node representations, similar to Liu et al. (2020) and Zhao et al. (2020), we represent evidence nodes with the claim to which they refer as context. The claim is concatenated with a constructed context-rich evidence sequence e_i. When constructing the sequences, e_i, we consider the unstructured evidence items (i.e, sentences and table captions) and the structured table and list items separately.

For sentences and table captions the evidence sequence is generated by concatenating the evidence item with the page title which serves as context.

For table cells and list items we perform a per cell linearization, where this linearization forms the evidence sequence for table and list item evidence items (see Table 4 for the templates used). For each evidence item, we feed this claim-evidence sequence pair to a RoBERTa encoder (Liu et al., 2019), and each node $\mathbf{n}_i \in V$ in an evidence graph has the pooled output of the last hidden state of the [CLS] token, $\mathbf{h}_i^0$ as its initial state:

$$\mathbf{n}_i = \mathbf{h}_i^0 = \text{RoBERTa}_{\text{CLS}}(c, e_i). \quad (1)$$

4.3 Evidence Selection and Veracity Prediction

Training graphs. We train two graph networks, one for joint veracity prediction and evidence extraction, and the second solely for the veracity prediction task.

Oversampling NEI Instances. As discussed in Section 3, the FEVEROUS dataset suffers from a significant class imbalance with respect to the NEI instances. Similar to the baseline approach, we employ techniques for generating new NEI instances in order to address this issue. Concretely, we use two data augmentation strategies in order to increase the number of NEI at train time: (1) evidence set reduction, and (2) claim mutation. For the first case, we randomly sample SUPPORTS and REFUTES instances and drop evidence. Given the distribution of entity substituted and non-entity substituted mutations — as discovered in our data analysis (see Section 3) — we make the choice to include in the training data: 15,000 constructed NEI examples made using the first approach, and 5,946 NEI examples constructed using the second. This means that a total of 92,237 NEI examples were used for model training.

STL: Separate Verification and Extraction. For the first model, we perform the tasks of fact extraction and verification of evidence selection and veracity prediction separately. We make use of an ensemble semantic search method for extracting top evidence items for claims. We employ S-BERT[3] to encode the claim and the evidence items separately. We then compute cosine similarity for the claim evidence pair.

The 25 highest ranking tabular evidence items were chosen, and the top-scoring 5 sentences (and captions) for each claim were selected as the nodes of our evidence reasoning graph at test time. This is the evidence limit stated by the FEVEROUS metric.

When constructing the evidence graph at test time, we choose to exclude header cells and list items evidence types as nodes as they account for a very small portion of evidence items (see Section 3), and experimentation shows that the evidence extraction model has a bias to favour these evidence elements over sentences. We use two GAT layers in our graph reasoning model, with: a hidden layer size of 128, embeddings size of 1024, and a global attention layer for node aggregation. The logits generated by the model are fed directly to a categorical cross entropy loss function, and the veracity label output probability distribution $\mathbf{p}_i$, for each evidence graph $G_i \in \mathcal{G}$, is computed using the relation

$$\mathbf{p}_i = \text{softmax}(\text{MLP}(\mathbf{W}\mathbf{o}_i + \mathbf{b})), \quad (2)$$

where

$$\mathbf{o}_i = \sum_{n_i \in V}^{n_i} \text{softmax}\left(h_{\text{gate}}(\mathbf{x}_n)\right) \odot h_{\mathbf{\Theta}}(\mathbf{x}_n). \quad (3)$$

MTL: Joint Verification and Extraction. We also experiment with a joint training or multi-task learning (MTL) approach in order to explore if simultaneously learning the veracity label and evidence items can lead to improvements in the label accuracy metric and also evidence prediction recall and precision. For this approach, we construct larger evidence graphs at test time, including the thirty-five highest ranked evidence items according to the S-BERT evidence extraction module. The intention is for the graph network to learn a binary classification for each claim-evidence pair in the network.

For the multi-task learning model, we increase the dimensions of our graph network by feeding our initial input graphs to two separate GAT components (in order to increase the model's capacity for learning the more complex multi-task objective), the outputs of which, $\mathbf{h}_a$ and $\mathbf{h}_b$, are concatenated to form representation $\mathbf{h}$ over which we compute global attention, where the combined representation takes the form:[4]

$$\mathbf{h} = [\mathbf{h}_a; \mathbf{h}_b]. \quad (4)$$

[3]We use the 'msmarco-distilbert-base-v4' and 'paraphrase-mpnet-base-v2" pretrained models.

[4]We denote the concatenation of vectors $\mathbf{x}$ and $\mathbf{y}$, by $[\mathbf{x}; \mathbf{y}]$.

The binary cross entropy loss is then used for the node-level evidence selection task, and, as with the separated model, we use categorical cross entropy to compute the graph-level veracity prediction, as shown in (2) and (3). The resulting joint graph neural network is then trained with the linear-additive objective

$$\mathcal{L}_{\text{joint}} = \lambda \mathcal{L}_{\text{evidence}} + \mathcal{L}_{\text{label}}, \qquad (5)$$

taking the form of a Lagrangian with multiplier $\lambda \geq 0$, where

$$\mathcal{L}_{\text{evidence}} = \text{sigmoid}(\text{MLP}(\mathbf{W}_i \mathbf{h} + \mathbf{b})). \qquad (6)$$

As with the previous approach, we feed the model logits to our loss functions and use an Adam optimizer to train the network, and set $\lambda = 0.5$.

4.4 Hyper-parameter Settings

For all models, we make use of a ROBERTA-LARGE model which is pre-trained on a number of NLI datasets including NLI-FEVER (Nie et al., 2020). We use a maximum sequence length of 512 for encoding all claim-evidence concatenated pairs. We experiment with the following learning rates [1e-5, 5e-5, 1e-4], ultimately choosing the learning rate underlined. Training was performed using batch size of 64. We train the single objective model for 20k steps, choosing the weights with the minimum veracity prediction label loss, and train the joint model for 20k steps, taking the model with highest recall for evidence extraction. The Adam optimizer is used in training for both approaches.

5 Results

We report the results of the entire fact extraction and verification pipeline, as well as the evaluation of the pipeline's performance for intermediate stages of the fact verification system, e.g., document retrieval and evidence selection.

Document retrieval. Our method for DR shows significant improvement on the TF-IDF+DrQA approach used by the baseline. In particular we find that our document retrieval module sees gains from querying the Wikipedia dump for pages related to entities which are not retrieved by the WikiMedia API. However, we do note that our approach struggles to retrieve Wikipedia pages in cases relating to specific events which can only be inferred through reasoning over the claim.

For example, consider the following claim from the development dataset: *"2014 Sky Blue FC season number 18 Lindsi Cutshall (born October 18, 1990) played the FW position."*. In this case, the document selection process returns *"Sky Blue FC"*, *"Lindsi Cutshall"*, and *"2015 Sky Blue FC season"*, but does not return the gold evidence page *"2014 Sky Blue FC season"* which is required for verification of the claim.

We report recall@k for $k = \{3, 5, 7\}$ where k is the number of Wikipedia page documents retrieved by the module. Our approach shows significant improvements over the baseline (see Table 5).

Method	Rec@3	Rec@5	Rec@7
Baseline	0.58	0.69	–
Ours	0.65	0.73	**0.80**

Table 5: Document retrieval results measured by Recall@k, where k is the number of documents retrieved. Results reported for the dev set.

Evidence selection and veracity prediction. For evidence selection and veracity prediction, we observe that the approach trained for the single objective of veracity prediction marginally outperforms the jointly trained module (see Table 6). We hypothesize that the difficulty of learning to select the correct evidence nodes along with predicting veracity might be the cause of this. It is possible that performance of the joint model could be improved with better evidence representation or through the use of a different graph structure, e.g., by incorporating edge attributes.

Method	Recall	LA
Baseline	29.51	53.22
STL	**37.20**	**62.89**
MTL	36.25	62.21

Table 6: System performance of the dev set for evidence recall and label accuracy.

Finally, we submitted our blind test results for STL, which is our best performing method, to the after-competition FEVEROUS leaderboard. Our system outperforms the baseline significantly on both the FEVEROUS metric and also label accuracy as reported in Table 7. Furthermore, our results on the blind test data show almost no degradation from development to test set with respect to the evidence recall which remains at 37%. So the cause of our reduced FEVEROUS score between the development and test data is mainly due to a decrease in label accuracy from 63% on the development data to 53% for the test data. We are confident that this could be improved with better label accuracy for the NEI class.

Method	Dev		Test	
	LA	FS	LA	FS
Baseline	53.22	19.28	47.60	17.70
Ours	**62.81**	**25.71**	**53.12**	**22.51**

Table 7: Results for label accuracy (**LA**) and FEVEROUS score (**FS**) for the full pipeline on both the development and blind test datasets.

5.1 Case Study and System Interpretability

We present an example of a claim from the development dataset, which requires both tabular and textual evidence to be verified. We show how it is labelled by our pipeline (see Table 8). For this example, our evidence selection module correctly identifies all three evidence items required to fact-check the claim. Furthermore, two of the three evidence items receive the highest relevance scores from our evidence selection module. Of the irrelevant evidence items retrieved for this claim, eleven out of twenty-two come from an unrelated Wikipedia page ("Scomadi Turismo Leggera"). The correct label of SUPPORTS is also predicted for this instance.

In order to explore the interpretability system predictions, for this same instance, we analyse the node attention weights for the first GAT layer, they are shown in parenthesis for each predicted evidence item in Table 8. We can see that the two evidence nodes with the highest values both correspond to items in the gold evidence set. However the third gold evidence item, SCOMADI_SENTENCE_15, has a much lower weight than a number of items which are not in the gold evidence set.

Claim "In 2019, Scomadi, a private limited company with limited liability, was bought by a British owner which changed Scomadi's management structure."

Evidence
Scomadi_cell_0_0_1,
Scomadi_sentence_14, Scomadi_sentence_15.

Predicted Evidence

(1) Scomadi_cell_0_0_1	*(0.1794)*,
(2) Scomadi_sentence_14	*(0.1203)*,
(3) Scomadi_table_caption_0	*(0.0871)*,
(4) Scomadi_cell_0_3_1	*(0.0685)*,
(5) Scomadi_cell_0_7_1	*(0.0561)*,
(6) Scomadi_cell_0_2_1	*(0.0472)*
(7) Scomadi_cell_0_8_1	*(0.0405)*
(8) Scomadi_sentence_15	*(0.0360)*,
(9) Scomadi_sentence_11	*(0.0324)*,
(10) Scomadi_sentence_0	*(0.0292)*,
(11) Scomadi_cell_0_6_1	*(0.0266)*,
(12) Scomadi_cell_0_5_1	*(0.0243)*,
(13) Scomadi_cell_0_1_1	*(0.0224)*,
(14) Scomadi_cell_0_4_1	*(0.0208)*.

Label SUPPORTS
Predicted Label SUPPORTS

Table 8: Example claim from the development dataset which requires extracting both tabular and textual evidence in order for it to be verified. For brevity we only show the top fourteen (out of twenty-five) extracted evidence items, correctly predicted evidence is highlighted .

6 Conclusion and Future Work

In this work, we have demonstrated two novel approaches for fact extraction and verification that support both structured and unstructured evidence. These architectures were motivated by literature in argumentation, and also by the empirical analysis presented in Section 3. Our results show significant improvement over the shared task baseline for both the joint and separated models, with the latter generating a marginal improvement on the FEVEROUS metric compared with the former. Overall, we conclude that the use of graph-based reasoning in fact verification systems could hold great promise for future lines of work.

We hypothesize that exploring varied task formulations could potentially yield strong improvements in model performance, for example: constructing reasoning graphs on an evidence set level, or using the FEVER dataset to augment the NEI claims used during training, or further fine-tuning sentence embeddings on the FEVEROUS dataset. Furthermore, we believe further insights could be gained by evaluating our table linearization approach on other datasets related to fact verification over tabular data. In addition to this, we hope to conduct further experiments with our graph based approach using structured and unstructured evidence independently, to further investigate which aspect of our approach led to the improvement on the FEVEROUS score.

Incorporating prior knowledge or constraints into the training procedure would also be an interesting direction. Finally, we believe that our graph-based approach lends itself well to the extraction of veracity prediction *explanations* (Kotonya and Toni, 2020a), obtained from evidence extracted from our underpinning graphs as justifications for claims. The ability to provide evidence for a claim, and to justify this, would better enable the integration of these techniques in practical systems.

Disclaimer This paper was prepared for informational purposes by the Artificial Intelligence Research group of JPMorgan Chase & Co and its affiliates ("J.P. Morgan"), and is not a product of the Research Department of J.P. Morgan. J.P. Morgan makes no representation and warranty whatsoever and disclaims all liability, for the completeness, accuracy or reliability of the information contained herein. This document is not intended as investment research or investment advice, or a recommendation, offer or solicitation for the purchase or sale of any security, financial instrument, financial product or service, or to be used in any way for evaluating the merits of participating in any transaction, and shall not constitute a solicitation under any jurisdiction or to any person, if such solicitation under such jurisdiction or to such person would be unlawful.

References

Naser Ahmadi, Joohyung Lee, Paolo Papotti, and Mohammed Saeed. 2019. Explainable fact checking with probabilistic answer set programming. In *Proceedings of the 2019 Truth and Trust Online Conference (TTO 2019), London, UK, October 4-5, 2019*.

Tariq Alhindi, Savvas Petridis, and Smaranda Muresan. 2018. Where is your evidence: Improving fact-checking by justification modeling. In *Proceedings of the First Workshop on Fact Extraction and VERification (FEVER)*, pages 85–90, Brussels, Belgium. Association for Computational Linguistics.

Rami Aly, Zhijiang Guo, Michael Schlichtkrull, James Thorne, Andreas Vlachos, Christos Christodoulopoulos, Oana Cocarascu, and Arpit Mittal. 2021. Feverous: Fact extraction and verification over unstructured and structured information.

Isabelle Augenstein, Christina Lioma, Dongsheng Wang, Lucas Chaves Lima, Casper Hansen, Christian Hansen, and Jakob Grue Simonsen. 2019. MultiFC: A real-world multi-domain dataset for evidence-based fact checking of claims. In *Proceedings of the 2019 Conference on Empirical Methods in Natural Language Processing and the 9th International Joint Conference on Natural Language Processing (EMNLP-IJCNLP)*, pages 4685–4697, Hong Kong, China. Association for Computational Linguistics.

Elena Cabrio and Serena Villata, editors. 2020. *Proceedings of the 7th Workshop on Argument Mining*. Association for Computational Linguistics, Online.

Wenhu Chen, Hongmin Wang, Yunkai Zhang Jianshu Chen, Hong Wang, Shiyang Li, Xiyou Zhou, and William Yang Wang. 2020. Tabfact : A large-scale dataset for table-based fact verification. In *International Conference on Learning Representations (ICLR)*, Addis Ababa, Ethiopia.

Vivek Gupta, Maitrey Mehta, Pegah Nokhiz, and Vivek Srikumar. 2020. INFOTABS: Inference on tables as semi-structured data. In *Proceedings of the 58th Annual Meeting of the Association for Computational Linguistics*, pages 2309–2324, Online. Association for Computational Linguistics.

Andreas Hanselowski, Hao Zhang, Zile Li, Daniil Sorokin, Benjamin Schiller, Claudia Schulz, and Iryna Gurevych. 2018. UKP-athene: Multi-sentence textual entailment for claim verification. In *Proceedings of the First Workshop on Fact Extraction and VERification (FEVER)*, pages 103–108, Brussels, Belgium. Association for Computational Linguistics.

Christopher Hidey, Tuhin Chakrabarty, Tariq Alhindi, Siddharth Varia, Kriste Krstovski, Mona Diab, and Smaranda Muresan. 2020. DeSePtion: Dual sequence prediction and adversarial examples for improved fact-checking. In *Proceedings of the 58th Annual Meeting of the Association for Computational Linguistics*, pages 8593–8606, Online. Association for Computational Linguistics.

Neema Kotonya and Francesca Toni. 2019. Gradual argumentation evaluation for stance aggregation in automated fake news detection. In *Proceedings of the 6th Workshop on Argument Mining*, pages 156–166, Florence, Italy. Association for Computational Linguistics.

Neema Kotonya and Francesca Toni. 2020a. Explainable automated fact-checking: A survey. In *Proceedings of the 28th International Conference on Computational Linguistics*, pages 5430–5443, Barcelona, Spain (Online). International Committee on Computational Linguistics.

Neema Kotonya and Francesca Toni. 2020b. Explainable automated fact-checking for public health claims. In *Proceedings of the 2020 Conference on*

Empirical Methods in Natural Language Processing (EMNLP), pages 7740–7754, Online. Association for Computational Linguistics.

Yinhan Liu, Myle Ott, Naman Goyal, Jingfei Du, Mandar Joshi, Danqi Chen, Omer Levy, Mike Lewis, Luke Zettlemoyer, and Veselin Stoyanov. 2019. Roberta: A robustly optimized bert pretraining approach.

Zhenghao Liu, Chenyan Xiong, Maosong Sun, and Zhiyuan Liu. 2020. Fine-grained fact verification with kernel graph attention network. In *Proceedings of the 58th Annual Meeting of the Association for Computational Linguistics*, pages 7342–7351, Online. Association for Computational Linguistics.

Yi-Ju Lu and Cheng-Te Li. 2020. GCAN: Graph-aware co-attention networks for explainable fake news detection on social media. In *Proceedings of the 58th Annual Meeting of the Association for Computational Linguistics*, pages 505–514, Online. Association for Computational Linguistics.

Yixin Nie, Songhe Wang, and Mohit Bansal. 2019. Revealing the importance of semantic retrieval for machine reading at scale.

Yixin Nie, Adina Williams, Emily Dinan, Mohit Bansal, Jason Weston, and Douwe Kiela. 2020. Adversarial NLI: A new benchmark for natural language understanding. In *Proceedings of the 58th Annual Meeting of the Association for Computational Linguistics*, pages 4885–4901, Online. Association for Computational Linguistics.

Nils Reimers and Iryna Gurevych. 2019. Sentence-BERT: Sentence embeddings using Siamese BERT-networks. In *Proceedings of the 2019 Conference on Empirical Methods in Natural Language Processing and the 9th International Joint Conference on Natural Language Processing (EMNLP-IJCNLP)*, pages 3982–3992, Hong Kong, China. Association for Computational Linguistics.

Michael Sejr Schlichtkrull, Vladimir Karpukhin, Barlas Oguz, Mike Lewis, Wen-tau Yih, and Sebastian Riedel. 2021. Joint verification and reranking for open fact checking over tables. In *Proceedings of the 59th Annual Meeting of the Association for Computational Linguistics and the 11th International Joint Conference on Natural Language Processing (Volume 1: Long Papers)*, pages 6787–6799, Online. Association for Computational Linguistics.

Shaden Shaar, Nikolay Babulkov, Giovanni Da San Martino, and Preslav Nakov. 2020. That is a known lie: Detecting previously fact-checked claims. In *Proceedings of the 58th Annual Meeting of the Association for Computational Linguistics*, pages 3607–3618, Online. Association for Computational Linguistics.

James Thorne, Andreas Vlachos, Christos Christodoulopoulos, and Arpit Mittal. 2018. FEVER: a large-scale dataset for fact extraction and VERification. In *Proceedings of the 2018 Conference of the North American Chapter of the Association for Computational Linguistics: Human Language Technologies, Volume 1 (Long Papers)*, pages 809–819, New Orleans, Louisiana. Association for Computational Linguistics.

Eva Maria Vecchi, Neele Falk, Iman Jundi, and Gabriella Lapesa. 2021. Towards argument mining for social good: A survey. In *Proceedings of the 59th Annual Meeting of the Association for Computational Linguistics and the 11th International Joint Conference on Natural Language Processing (Volume 1: Long Papers)*, pages 1338–1352, Online. Association for Computational Linguistics.

Petar Velickovic, Guillem Cucurull, Arantxa Casanova, Adriana Romero, Pietro Liò, and Yoshua Bengio. 2018. Graph attention networks. In *6th International Conference on Learning Representations, ICLR 2018, Vancouver, BC, Canada, April 30 - May 3, 2018, Conference Track Proceedings*. OpenReview.net.

Andreas Vlachos and Sebastian Riedel. 2014. Fact checking: Task definition and dataset construction. In *Proceedings of the ACL 2014 Workshop on Language Technologies and Computational Social Science*, pages 18–22, Baltimore, MD, USA. Association for Computational Linguistics.

David Wadden, Shanchuan Lin, Kyle Lo, Lucy Lu Wang, Madeleine van Zuylen, Arman Cohan, and Hannaneh Hajishirzi. 2020. Fact or fiction: Verifying scientific claims. In *Proceedings of the 2020 Conference on Empirical Methods in Natural Language Processing (EMNLP)*, pages 7534–7550, Online. Association for Computational Linguistics.

Rowan Zellers, Ari Holtzman, Hannah Rashkin, Yonatan Bisk, Ali Farhadi, Franziska Roesner, and Yejin Choi. 2020. Defending against neural fake news.

Chen Zhao, Chenyan Xiong, Corby Rosset, Xia Song, Paul Bennett, and Saurabh Tiwary. 2020. Transformer-xh: Multi-evidence reasoning with extra hop attention. In *International Conference on Learning Representations*.

Wanjun Zhong, Jingjing Xu, Duyu Tang, Zenan Xu, Nan Duan, Ming Zhou, Jiahai Wang, and Jian Yin. 2020. Reasoning over semantic-level graph for fact checking. In *Proceedings of the 58th Annual Meeting of the Association for Computational Linguistics*, pages 6170–6180, Online. Association for Computational Linguistics.

Jie Zhou, Xu Han, Cheng Yang, Zhiyuan Liu, Lifeng Wang, Changcheng Li, and Maosong Sun. 2019. GEAR: Graph-based evidence aggregating and reasoning for fact verification. In *Proceedings of the 57th Annual Meeting of the Association for Computational Linguistics*, pages 892–901, Florence, Italy. Association for Computational Linguistics.

FaBULOUS: Fact-checking Based on Understanding of Language Over Unstructured and Structured information

Mostafa Bouziane*, **Hugo Perrin***, **Amine Sadeq*** and **Thanh Nguyen***
Aurélien Cluzeau and **Julien Mardas**
Buster.Ai
contact@buster.ai

Abstract

As part of the FEVEROUS shared task, we developed a robust and finely tuned architecture to handle the joint retrieval and entailment on text data as well as structured data like tables. We proposed two training schemes to tackle the hurdles inherent to multi-hop multi-modal datasets. The first one allows having a robust retrieval of full evidence sets, while the second one enables entailment to take full advantage of noisy evidence inputs. In addition, our work has revealed important insights and potential avenue of research for future improvement on this kind of dataset. In preliminary evaluation on the FEVEROUS shared task test set, our system achieves 0.271 FEVEROUS score, with 0.4258 evidence recall and 0.5607 entailment accuracy.

1 Introduction

In the past year, concerns about the spread of misinformation have risen dramatically. Around 54% of people claim that they have seen fake news on COVID-19 in a week (Reuters Institute for the Study of Journalism) resulting in a global lack of trust in our political institutions and the media. Considering the amount of data there is on the Internet, the need for a trustworthy, efficient, automated fact-checking tool is undeniable.

Research has made great stride in automating fact verification, driven for instance by the successive FEVER datasets and challenges (Thorne et al., 2018a) (Thorne et al., 2018b), for which new techniques have been developed for both retrieval (Xiong et al., 2021) and entailment (Liu et al., 2019b). The retrieval part has been handled through hard sample mining and an adjusted embedding based model training. This allows very fast inference, leveraging approximate nearest neighbors searches on large dimension embeddings. Given the dataset size, this is necessary to achieve fast enough running times. On the entailment end, one of the state-of-the-art approaches is called KGAT (Liu et al., 2019b). This method leverages graph structure over the evidences to allow for both more accurate entailment as well as provide interpretability to the result. However, this method was designed for text, and is therefore not suitable for out of the box handling of structured data. This is where our interest can go towards methods like TAPAS (Eisenschlos et al., 2020), which is suitable for structured data. It was developed for Tabfact (Chen et al., 2019), on which it exhibits excellent performance.

However, while the previous FEVER challenges (Thorne et al., 2018a) (Thorne et al., 2018b), and other well-known reference datasets like HotpotQA (Yang et al., 2018) only focused on text, the FEVEROUS dataset introduced multi-modality through added structured data. This brings the dataset closer to real-world data and the task closer to fact verification in a practical setting. Many difficulties inherently arise from the diverse nature of the data, and we want to shed some light on both the data and how to reason on it. Our method achieved the top result on the FEVEROUS shared task and gave us insights on how to progress further by exploring the nature of the data and where our pipeline fails.

We also developed the Reinforced Adaptive Retrieval Embedding (RARE) and Noisy Entailment through Adapted Training (NEAT) methods to address certain hurdles inside the training itself.

In this paper, we aim to share both the insights we gained on the FEVEROUS dataset (Aly et al., 2021) during the workshop competition, as well as how we designed the top scoring pipeline of the competition. We will first present the dataset, what we learned from it, as well as the issues we encountered while designing an algorithm for it and how we devised our approach. In the second section, we will explain how our pipeline works and the tweaks

* Equal Contribution

Proceedings of the Fourth Workshop on Fact Extraction and VERification (FEVER) at EMNLP 2021, pages 31–39
November 10, 2021. ©2021 Association for Computational Linguistics

we made to the classical pipeline defined by the baseline method (Aly et al., 2021). Following, we will present the unique training methods that were used to ensure both stable predictions as well as state-of-the-art performance in both retrieval and entailment.

In short, our contributions with this paper are the following:

- Top scoring pipeline on the FEVEROUS shared task
- New training paradigms for fact verification for both retrieval (RARE) and entailment (NEAT) methods
- Insights on why previous state-of-the-art approaches fails on this kind of data, how we fixed part of the issues and the proposed paradigm shift proposal for further research.

2 Dataset Insights

The dataset has been designed to introduce multimodality (Aly et al., 2021). This has been done by adding structured data, i.e. text data which has an underlying structure to support it, like tables and lists. As we say one of these clues is not like the others, and we will explain what make cells so unlike sentences, as well the particularities involving the label annotation philosophy.

The difficulty with those is that their entries are not self-contained. Indeed, the value of a cell in a table depends on other values of the table. For instance, in Table 1, while the values of certain cells might be the same, they differ in terms of context, as one cell value of 0.5 is a number of carrots per day in one case and a number of children per year in the other case.

In order to understand the value of a given cell, you might need to access values of headers and other values of the same row/column. This makes the retrieval particularly hard as it might miss the value or the header which are needed for the full set to be retrieved. In addition, linearising the table might not be enough, as the header to retrieve might be on a different row altogether. This could also cause oversampling of a certain row or column. This issue of context can be solved more easily for entailment as you can keep the extra information present of all headers available. Indeed, we can reconstruct the full table from the retrieved cells for entailment, as long as the model for entailment allows dealing with the full table size. As it was the case with the TAPAS (Eisenschlos et al., 2020) method we used for entailment, one important part might be to find the right position embedding space to encode that structure.

Another peculiar aspect of the data that proved hard to tackle was the handling of refuting evidence sets. We have found that often refuting relies on small details which have been changed. The issue with this is that training for retrieval will most of the time converge towards trying to get as much information out of the selected evidence as possible. It will therefore not rank the small information overlap of the evidence refuting as high as needed for the evidence retrieval and as a consequence not get the full accurate result. An iterative approach to build up supporting, refuting and non relevant evidence sets might prove successful to address this. As described in Figure 1, we would build a set of supporting evidence up until we verify everything, find a refuting evidence or reach a termination heuristic, and then re-rank evidences properly based on their entailment usefulness. This paradigm would fit the way the dataset has been annotated. The main drawback to this is the need to entangle the entailment and retrieval in one model that may not scale with data as easily as the embedding-based retrieval models that rely on cosine similarity.

Same goes for Not Enough Information (NEI) examples, where the piece of information missing might be very small. Hence making the difference between "support" and "NEI" is hard for classical approaches. An example of this can be found in Appendix A where the claim is not completely covered by supporting evidences and therefore does not count as supported. In the setup of Figure 1, NEI labels would appear naturally from not verifying the full claim.

Finally, it is noteworthy to point out that the document retrieval is relying heavily on name entities, which makes BM25 quite good at it. An easy way to improve it would be to disambiguate the nicknames, abbreviations and the likes to make it more able to find certain pages.

3 Our Pipeline

As depicted in Figure 2, for the full pipeline, we first perform document retrieval, then passage retrieval and finally entailment. On a single GPU machine described in appendix B, inference takes

Figure 1: Example of an iterative retrieval and entailment process. Ideally we would take the candidates from retrieval, eliminate the non-supporting passages, and retrieve again, à la Multi-hop Dense Retriever (Xiong et al., 2021).

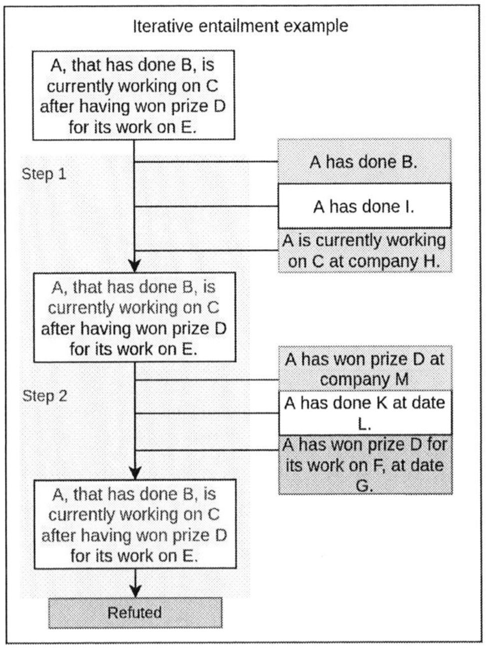

Organisation	Carrots/day	Children/year
Hogwarts	0.5	0.98
Phoenix Order	0.98	0.5

Table 1: Table example. It displays an example of table that might be hard to make sense of without columns and rows contexts.

less than 10 seconds per sample, which translates to under 20 hours for the full dev and test sets.

For each claim to verify, we first retrieve documents using BM25 and filter the tables of those documents to only keep the most relevant ones according to BM25. From these documents we can extract sentence and cell passages, on which, in turn, we run our passage retriever to get the most relevant passages. Using input normalisation techniques, we feed this to the ensemble entailer model which predicts the entailment class. This full pipeline achieves a significant improvement of 53% improvement over the FEVEROUS baseline (Aly et al., 2021). We will detail in the next subsections each sub-part of the pipeline with its respective performance.

Figure 2: Full pipeline diagram of our solution to the FEVEROUS Shared Task. The mentioned SQL database is the one available on the FEVEROUS dataset page

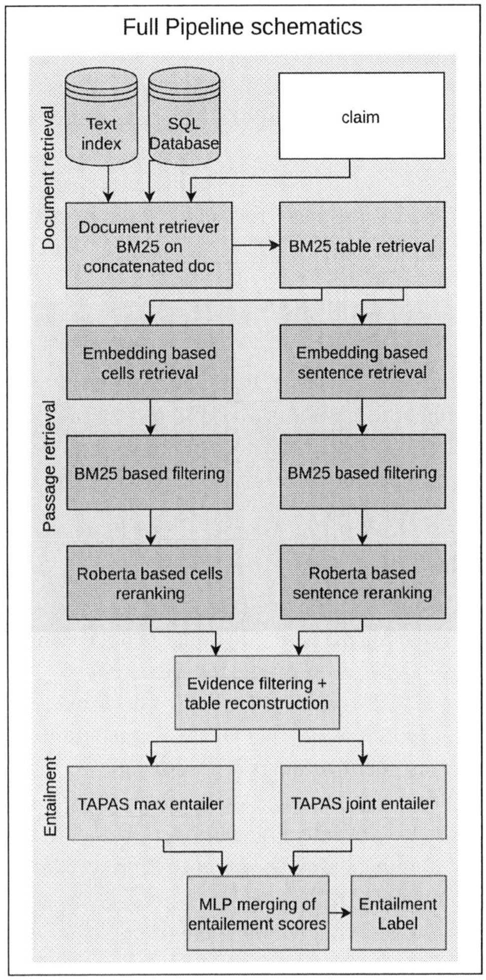

3.1 Document retrieval

For document retrieval, we use BM25 by indexing the documents. We tested indexing with (i) the page title only, (ii) the page and the beginning of the document and (iii) indexing the page title concatenated with all the passages of the document, and the latter performed best with Mean Average Precision (MAP) at depth (here the number of top retrieved documents) 3 of 81.8% (Table 2). Here the MAP is computed for full sets of evidence present rather than just one piece of evidence. For just one evidence, the MAP@3 is around 92%. We intentionally decided to stop at three documents retrieved, as taking more documents was counterproductive for the passage selection for which dropped significantly when using five or more pages instead of three.

Additionally, we also filter the tables by taking the seven best tables according to BM25 as well. Here we take all tables present in the retrieved documents, and we index the linearised and concatenated tables as strings for BM25. Thereby, eliminate a lot of potential cell candidates and improved cell MAP of cells by 10% afterwards. Grid search showed us that seven tables proved to be the ideal number in our pipeline, as we achieved around 92% MAP@7 for the retrieved tables (see Table 2).

3.2 Passage retrieval

After the documents have been retrieved, we derive relevant passages therein using the following pipeline: the embedding-based retrieval, the BM25 re-filtering, and finally a re-ranking step. We apply the following processes on cells and sentences independently.

Embedding-based retrieval

One main challenge we face when we retrieve the top k documents is scaling to large documents. A simple approach to get the top passages consists of using BM25 here also. However, the drawback of this approach would be that we lose the multi-hop aspect of the dataset. Also, we want to catch the passages with semantics similar to the query, while BM25 would only find term matches. We propose training a Multi-hop Dense Retriever (MDR) (Xiong et al., 2021).

The page passages contain in some cases, words in different languages. To tackle this, we decided to use a language-agnostic embedding model LaBSE (Feng et al., 2020) that has proven to be efficient in this kind of tasks. After training the model, the passages from the documents retrieved at last step are scored with cosine similarity in an iterative manner as suggested in the MDR paper and then ranked by their relevance. We then keep only the best passages with top k value adjusted based on the passage type.

BM25 re-filtering

While analysing the results of our embedding-based retrieval model, we found out that it is not robust to the presence of named entities in passages. In this case, it struggles to put the right pieces of evidence on top, as it tends to choose the ones that are close in terms of semantics and context. To tackle this problem, we run BM25 on top of the retrieved passages. That way, we keep the relevant semantics, and only push to the top those that actually contain the right named entities. Using this strategy, we succeeded to achieve improvements of around 11% on MAP@50 on sentences, and 22% on MAP@200 on cells. This effectively re-ranks the filtered passages from the embedding-based retrieval. We provide an example where it helped in Appendix C.

Re-ranking

Finally, we re-rank the remaining passages and only keep the top five sentences and top 25 cells. In order to do this, we trained a RoBERTa (Liu et al., 2019a) model with the same training data as the passage retrieval embedding model. We will give more details in Section 4. The model is trained to output a score between 0 and 1, given a pair input consisting of the query and the passage claim we want to re-rank, with 0 being non-matching and 1 being matching. This allowed a significantly more robust MAP on the train and dev set, even though it only gives a minor boost in performance for the MAP after re-ranking evaluation. Indeed, we barely gain anything in terms of cell ranking, and around 1% for sentence ranking but that ends up giving an almost absolute 3% boost to the combined MAP (for which we evaluate if the full set containing the cells and sentences is retrieved), which is around 7.5% relative improvement. The re-ranking is, however, not being trained in a multi-hop manner, which might explain why it does not show a more significant performance increase. We decided against using a multi-hop approach for computational budgeting reasons, as it would have required us to evaluate the network on $\frac{n!}{(n-k)!}$ pairs instead of just n, with n the number of pieces of evidence retrieved at the last step.

Step	MAP @ depth	depth
Document retrieval	0.818	3
Table retrieval	0.92	7
Sentence retrieval	0.715	50
Sentence retrieval	0.543	5
Cell retrieval	0.555	200
Cell retrieval	0.341	25
Total retrieved	0.376	30
Sentence re-ranked	0.566	5
Cell re-ranked	0.342	25
Total re-ranked	0.404	30

Table 2: Table of retrieval results on the dev set.

3.3 Entailment

For entailment on retrieved pieces of evidence, we propose using an Multi-Layer Perceptron (MLP) ensemble to combine two models: TAPAS Max and TAPAS Joint. The name TAPAS Max is derived from the use of the max pooling layer described in Section 3.3.1, whereas TAPAS Joint is derived from the way we join the two modalities, as explained in Section 3.3.2. Both models use a TAPAS (Herzig et al., 2020; Eisenschlos et al., 2020) backbone pre-trained on TabFact (Chen et al., 2019). While the two models share the same backbone architecture, the ways they process sentences and cells are significantly different. The following subsections explain how each model encodes the pieces of evidence and then aggregates the information.

3.3.1 TAPAS Max

Given a claim, retrieved evidences include sentences, cells and headers. TAPAS Max preprocesses the sentences as tables with the document title and the sentence. For cells and headers, TAPAS Max recreates the table from the Wiki database and crops them to only the retrieved rows and columns. Table evidences are afterwards encoded in parallel via the TAPAS backbone. Since the number of pieces of table evidence is not known a priori for each claim, TAPAS Max aggregates the encoded tables in latent space as a fixed-size feature vector using a Max Pooling Layer. Finally, a classification head assigns the claim label "SUPPORTS", "REFUTES" or "NEI" based on the aggregated feature vector.

3.3.2 TAPAS Joint

The idea of TAPAS Joint is to aggregate all pieces of evidence in a single joint table in advance. For sentences, TAPAS Joint also considers each sentence as a table of document title and the sentence itself. For cells and headers, TAPAS Joint groups pieces of evidence by the table and truncates them to the right rows and columns. Afterwards, table evidences are outer-joined as a single joint table. Experiments have shown that table joining is order-sensitive, i.e., sentence, tables... are preferred to stand before other tables. Once having a single joint table, for each claim, encoding and classification parts are similar to the TAPAS Max without the Max Pooling aggregation.

3.4 Entailment Ensemble Model

As stated above, after training, we ensemble the scores of the TAPAS Max and the TAPAS Joint. We experimented with two strategies:

- Max confidence: we choose the label corresponding to the maximum score.
- MLP ensemble: we train a MLP model on the dev set to aggregate the scores.

The tables 3, 4 below show the performance of each model alone on dev 3 and test 4 sets, and the performance of the ensembled ones on the same datasets. We reach the best performance on label accuracy and FEVEROUS score using the MLP (hidden layer size of 32, and a ReLU activation function) ensemble.

Model	Accuracy	FEVEROUS score
TAPAS Max	56.23 %	0.2461
TAPAS Joint	58.02 %	0.2560
Max confidence	58.82 %	0.2574
MLP ensemble	65%	0.3046

Table 3: Entailment models performance on dev set: label accuracy & FEVEROUS score (Accuracy is computed only on the claims for which we find the right evidences with the same retrieval output).

Model	Accuracy	FEVEROUS score
TAPAS Joint	53.24 %	0.2267
Max confidence	55.04 %	0.2344
MLP ensemble	63.64 %	0.2710

Table 4: Entailment models performance on test set: label accuracy & FEVEROUS score (Accuracy is computed only on the claims for which we find the right evidences with the same retrieval output)

4 Training methodology

In this section, we will give additional detail on our training methodology and how it helped us achieve state-of-the-art performance on the FEVEROUS dataset.

4.1 Passage retrieval

For passage retrieval, we propose a novel approach we call Reinforced Adaptive Retrieval Embedding paradigm (RARE). Building upon the training scheme of MDR (Xiong et al., 2021), we not only use BM25 to retrieve $m_i \in \mathbb{N}$ passages, as we did in (Bouziane et al., 2020), we then compute embeddings based on an earlier copy of the model and re-rank the negative samples based on their embedding cosine similarities to the embedding of the query, and we keep the top $m_f \leq m_i, m_f \in \mathbb{N}$ for negative sampling (Figure 3). Here m_f stands for m filtered and m_i for m initial. It has to be noted that this re-ranking is not done during the first epoch, but is rather only done using the frozen weights of the latest epoch, starting from the second epoch. This is a direct analogue of what is called re-targeting in the reinforcement learning setting that has been used numerous times (Mnih et al., 2013).

Using this training scheme allows getting better hard negatives for the learning process as it helps the algorithm to naturally correct itself where it is wrong, and doing so in a manner that will not overfit on handcrafted hard samples. Ideally, we would want to re-index the complete database and directly perform retrieval on it using cosine similarity search. Unfortunately in the case of the FEVEROUS dataset, the amount of data to re-index with embeddings was too large to be tractable, hence why we had to do it the proposed way. Using a large threshold for BM25 increases the probability of having high recall of both the samples it should retrieve, as well as the samples on which it would make mistakes on.

As proven efficient in reinforcement learning (Mnih et al., 2013), updating the sampling weights only once per epoch becomes very important in order to avoid undesired local minima. This principle of training is also used for re-ranking, where it, alas, has less effectiveness improving performance. This extended training scheme is one of the key contributions that were needed to achieve state-of-the-art performance on the FEVEROUS dataset.

Figure 3: RARE training scheme. We sample with BM25, then use the frozen model to get better hard negatives that we use for our training loop to train the embedding creation of the algorithm, which we use to update current weights M_c. Once per epoch, we copy those weights to frozen weights M_s in order to use them for sampling.

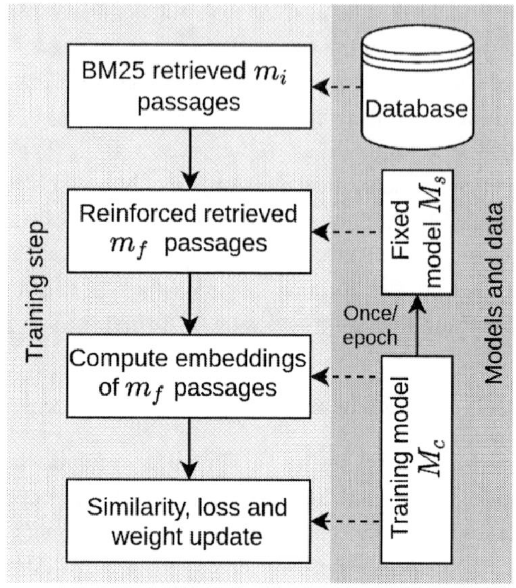

4.2 Entailment

NEAT

For the entailment, the main challenge is to use multiple inputs (cells and sentences) to predict the true label. Furthermore, this model should be robust to noisy inputs, because the retrieved passages in the pipeline can potentially contain irrelevant pieces of evidence for the query, which can make it harder for the model to perform well. To account for this, we propose Noisy Entailment through Adapted Training (NEAT). This method consists in training TAPAS Max and TAPAS Joint with a large TAPAS (Herzig et al., 2020) backbone on gold passages sets as well as the results of the passage retriever. This leads to the input containing both the relevant pieces of evidences and irrelevant passages together. This joint optimisation allowed us to gain crucial points when evaluating the models on the gold dev set and on the noisy one.

Model	Gold dev	Noisy dev	Test
TAPAS Max	80 %	51 %	49.31 %
TAPAS Joint	84 %	58 %	53.24 %

Table 5: Entailment models accuracy on dev (gold and noisy) and test set.

As depicted in Table 5, TAPAS joint outperforms TAPAS Max on both the dev and test sets. When looking at the error analysis, we found out that TAPAS Max struggles to deal with noisy inputs. On one hand, the more noisy evidences we add to the gold sets, the more performance decreases. On the other hand, TAPAS Joint seemed to generalise well on both gold and noisy dev sets. For the test set, we can see that the performances of the two models are not that far apart.

Ensembling

While having close global accuracy, one of the model had an easier time with NEI examples and the other with refuting examples. From that point on, ensembling them as described in Section 3 by training the MLP seemed natural. We take the scores of each model applied on dev set as an input (i.e input of dimension 6) and we output the score for each entailment class. This strategy gave us a boost of around 6% accuracy and 4 points FEVEROUS score on the test set.

Dealing with NEI

The NEIs (Not Enough Info) class represents only 3% of the train set, which makes it hard for the model to learn the right patterns and focus more on "SUPPORT" and "REFUTE" classes. Indeed, the confusion matrix in Figure 4 shows that our performance on NEIs is very low (1.5% precision performance on NEI). To solve that, future works could employ data augmentation strategies, so as to create NEI examples to balance the dataset, and thereby force the model to be equally good on the three classes. The following two strategies are examples of how samples could be generated:

- Create NEIs by concatenating the claim with a random passage from the answering pages that is not in the gold evidence sets.
- Create NEIs by removing one or more evidences from the gold evidence sets.

Figure 4: Confusion matrix of the TAPAS Max model. We can point out that it is very decent on the "SUPPORT" and "REFUTE" labels. The misclassification of NEIs does not seem to go towards one of the other labels in particular and it does not seem the model tries to predict NEI too much, but when it does, it mostly is for examples that are refuting and which do not have much evidence to begin with.

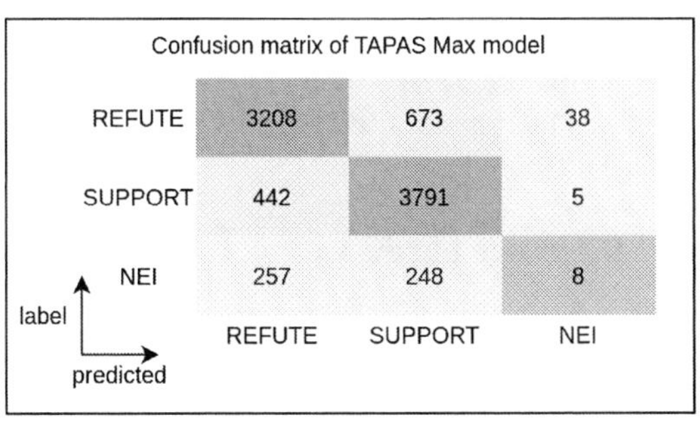

Our models struggle to converge using these augmentations, necessitating more investigation on new sampling strategies or compatible models.

5 Conclusion

Overall, this multi-modal task creates a plethora of new challenges to overcome and opens exciting avenues of research for the future of automated fact verification.

Our design improved on the classical retrieve-then-entail approach by giving special treatment to both modalities before putting them in a common multi-hop entailment model, that is necessary for multi-hop entailment. Thereby, we reached improvement of the state-of-the-art for that specific task.

Through novel and adapted training schemes, we overcame certain challenges like maximising the full set evidence recall, and allowing to have entailment work with a fixed number of evidence, discarding irrelevant pieces of evidence for its decision. This paradigm allows us to re-think the future of entailment on this type of real-world dataset, so as to see it as a selection mechanism too.

A direct consequence of this is the belief that doing entailment in an interpretable way will boost both the evidence recall and accuracy. Indeed, using the interpretation will allow deriving the passages that were useful for entailment and not those that were matching the most in terms of information overlap. This might prove to be the only way to get the right evidence set even when the refuting evidence set only deals with a small detail of the claim.

The way the dataset is constructed gives rise to the idea of an iterative process that starts with finding evidence, then performing entailment and then going back to retrieve more. Such an approach would provide a more natural way of distinguishing between NEI and SUPPORT labels and allow for reasonable runtimes. Ultimately, this will be accompanied by both more interpretable entailment and better scalability. This will in turn make the algorithm even more useful in the real world as a tool against misinformation and a general researching tool for fact verification.

Finally, a model that can deal with multiple modalities more universally and scalably is a question left for the future, making room for new research possibilities.

Those intuitions are entailed by both the insights

we gained on this new dataset, and the fact that our best effort with a more classic approach could not yield human-level results on this complex problem.

Acknowledgements

The authors want to thank the reviewers and contributors of the Buster.Ai team.

Additional elements were taken from the formatting instructions of the *International Joint Conference on Artificial Intelligence* and the *Conference on Computer Vision and Pattern Recognition.*

References

Rami Aly, Zhijiang Guo, Michael Schlichtkrull, James Thorne, Andreas Vlachos, Christos Christodoulopoulos, Oana Cocarascu, and Arpit Mittal. 2021. Feverous: Fact extraction and verification over unstructured and structured information.

Mostafa Bouziane, Hugo Perrin, Aurélien Cluzeau, Julien Mardas, and Amine Sadeq. 2020. Team buster. ai at checkthat! 2020 insights and recommendations to improve fact-checking. In *CLEF (Working Notes)*.

Wenhu Chen, Hongmin Wang, Jianshu Chen, Yunkai Zhang, Hong Wang, Shiyang Li, Xiyou Zhou, and William Yang Wang. 2019. Tabfact: A large-scale dataset for table-based fact verification. *arXiv preprint arXiv:1909.02164*.

Julian Martin Eisenschlos, Syrine Krichene, and Thomas Müller. 2020. Understanding tables with intermediate pre-training. *arXiv preprint arXiv:2010.00571*.

Fangxiaoyu Feng, Yinfei Yang, Daniel Cer, Naveen Arivazhagan, and Wei Wang. 2020. Language-agnostic bert sentence embedding. *arXiv preprint arXiv:2007.01852*.

Jonathan Herzig, Paweł Krzysztof Nowak, Thomas Müller, Francesco Piccinno, and Julian Martin Eisenschlos. 2020. Tapas: Weakly supervised table parsing via pre-training. *arXiv preprint arXiv:2004.02349*.

Yinhan Liu, Myle Ott, Naman Goyal, Jingfei Du, Mandar Joshi, Danqi Chen, Omer Levy, Mike Lewis, Luke Zettlemoyer, and Veselin Stoyanov. 2019a. Roberta: A robustly optimized BERT pretraining approach. *CoRR*, abs/1907.11692.

Zhenghao Liu, Chenyan Xiong, and Maosong Sun. 2019b. Kernel graph attention network for fact verification. *CoRR*, abs/1910.09796.

Volodymyr Mnih, Koray Kavukcuoglu, David Silver, Alex Graves, Ioannis Antonoglou, Daan Wierstra, and Martin A. Riedmiller. 2013. Playing atari with deep reinforcement learning. *CoRR*, abs/1312.5602.

Oxford University Reuters Institute for the Study of Journalism. Digital news report 2021. `https://reutersinstitute.politics.ox.ac.uk/digital-news-report/2021`. Accessed: 2021-08-04.

James Thorne, Andreas Vlachos, Oana Cocarascu, Christos Christodoulopoulos, and Arpit Mittal. 2018a. The fact extraction and VERification (FEVER) shared task. In *Proceedings of the First Workshop on Fact Extraction and VERification (FEVER)*, pages 1–9, Brussels, Belgium. Association for Computational Linguistics.

James Thorne, Andreas Vlachos, Oana Cocarascu, Christos Christodoulopoulos, and Arpit Mittal. 2018b. The FEVER2.0 shared task. In *Proceedings of the Second Workshop on Fact Extraction and VERification (FEVER)*.

Wenhan Xiong, Xiang Li, Srini Iyer, Jingfei Du, Patrick Lewis, William Yang Wang, Yashar Mehdad, Scott Yih, Sebastian Riedel, Douwe Kiela, and Barlas Oguz. 2021. Answering complex open-domain questions with multi-hop dense retrieval. In *International Conference on Learning Representations*.

Zhilin Yang, Peng Qi, Saizheng Zhang, Yoshua Bengio, William W. Cohen, Ruslan Salakhutdinov, and Christopher D. Manning. 2018. HotpotQA: A dataset for diverse, explainable multi-hop question answering. In *Conference on Empirical Methods in Natural Language Processing (EMNLP)*.

A Not Enough Information example

- **Claim:** The Alexander Faribault House is a historic house museum in 12 First Avenue, Faribault, MN built by Alexander Faribault, a local tradesman and philanthropist.

- **Evidence 1:** Alexander Faribault House The Alexander Faribault House is a historic house museum in Faribault, Minnesota, United States.

- **Evidence 2:** Alexander Faribault House The local address of the house is 12 First Avenue, Faribault, MN.

- **Evidence 3:** Alexander Faribault House It was built by fur trader Alexander Faribault in the Greek Revival style.

B Inference hardware

- **GPU:** NVIDIA RTX 3090 with 24 GB of VRAM, 1950 MHz boost and 10496 CUDA cores. The GPU driver version was 465.19.01, and CUDA version was 11.3.

- **CPU:** Intel i9 10920X with 12 cores and 24 threads, running at stock clocks.
- **RAM:** 64 GB of DDR4 with CAS 16 latency running at 3000 MHz, in 4 times 16 GB configuration.

C Re-filtering with BM25 example

- **Claim:** Raffaele Celeste Rosso, born on September 19, 1927 in San Michele Mondovì, was active from 1948 to 1994 under Durium Label.

Passage id	Rank retriever	Rank re-filtered
cell 0 1 1	1	1
cell 0 6 1	9	2

Table 6: Re-filtering example. In this case, we see that the cell 0 6 1 is not retrieved at the top but gets re-ranked higher by BM25 which is more sensitive to the exact date matching than the embedding cannot entirely catch.

- **cell 0 6 1:** Nini Rosso Years active Nini Rosso 1948 - 1994
- **cell 0 1 1:** Nini Rosso Born Nini Rosso Raffaele Celeste Rosso (1927-09-19) September 1

Team Papelo at FEVEROUS: Multi-hop Evidence Pursuit

Christopher Malon
NEC Laboratories America
Princeton, NJ 08540
malon@nec-labs.com

Abstract

We develop a system for the FEVEROUS fact extraction and verification task that ranks an initial set of potential evidence and then pursues missing evidence in subsequent hops by trying to generate it, with a "next hop prediction module" whose output is matched against page elements in a predicted article. Seeking evidence with the next hop prediction module continues to improve FEVEROUS score for up to seven hops. Label classification is trained on possibly incomplete extracted evidence chains, utilizing hints that facilitate numerical comparison. The system achieves .281 FEVEROUS score and .658 label accuracy on the development set, and finishes in second place with .259 FEVEROUS score and .576 label accuracy on the test set.

1 Introduction

The 2021 FEVEROUS (Fact Extraction and VERification Over Unstructured and Structured Information) task (Aly et al., 2021) introduces several challenges not seen in the 2018 FEVER task (Thorne et al., 2018). Tabular information, lists, and captions now appear as evidence, in addition to natural text sentences. Most claims now require multiple pieces of supporting evidence to support or refute them. Even claims that cannot be fully verified now require the submission of supporting evidence for aspects of the claim that can be verified. Counting and numerical reasoning skills are needed to verify many claims.

Annotators for FEVEROUS differed in their interpretation of what constituted necessary evidence, and often added duplicate evidence that should be in an alternative reasoning chain to a main reasoning chain. For this reason it is dangerous to target a precise, minimal set of evidence as in FEVER for high evidence F1 (Malon, 2018), and we instead fill the full set of five sentences and 25 table cells permitted for submission.

Thus we focus on solving the evidence retrieval problem and first assemble a set of preliminary set of relevant facts. Several of these facts may be combined to determine the veracity of the claim. Yang et al. (2018) define multi-hop reasoning as reasoning with information taken from more than one document to arrive at an answer, so using the preliminary evidence set could already be multi-hop reasoning, but from the perspective of retrieval we consider retrieving the initial evidence set to be a first "hop." Where multi-hop reasoning is required, it may be necessary to retrieve additional documents after reading the preliminary evidence, which could not be searched for using the claim alone. We support this functionality by predicting whether evidence chains are complete and generating additional search queries based on the preliminary evidence. This next hop prediction module can be applied as many as seven times to update the evidence chains, each time improving the FEVEROUS score.

On the final evidence chains, the label ("supports", "refutes", or "not enough information") is predicted by a module trained on extracted evidence chains. Because "not enough information" (NEI) labels are scarce, we alternatively can decide whether to give an NEI label based on whether the next hop prediction module is still seeking more evidence for the claim. Inputs are carefully represented to facilitate numerical comparisons for the final label decision and to allow the use of other contextual information by every module. The described system attains a FEVEROUS score of .281 on the development set with label accuracy of .658.

2 Context and structured information

Downstream classifiers usually classify page elements in isolation, but the meaning of these elements sometimes is not clear without contextual information. In the FEVER task, attaching a prefix to each sentence consisting of the page title

Proceedings of the Fourth Workshop on Fact Extraction and VERification (FEVER) at EMNLP 2021, pages 40–49
November 10, 2021. ©2021 Association for Computational Linguistics

Type	Example
Sentence	[Mississippi River] When measured from its traditional source at Lake Itasca, the Mississippi has a length of 2,320 miles (3,730 km).
List item	[Temple Tower] LIST CONTEXT Cast VALUE Marceline Day as Patricia Verney
Table cell	[Temple Tower] VALUE Release date {{ KEY Temple Tower VALUE April 13, 1930 }}
Table cell	[L-arabinose operon] CAPTION Catabolism of arabinose in E. coli {{ KEY Substrate VALUE L-arabinose }} KEY Enzyme(s) VALUE AraA KEY Function VALUE Isomerase KEY Reversible VALUE Yes KEY Product VALUE L-ribulose

Table 1: Example representations of various page elements.

in brackets improved performance (Malon, 2018), for example by providing hints about what pronouns might refer to. We continue this practice for FEVEROUS.

For list elements, we take the page element immediately preceding the list as context. This often is a sentence indicating what is in the list. Then the list element is represented by "[*title*] CONTEXT *context* VALUE *list item*", so that the list element and what the list is about may be seen simultaneously.

For table cells, we represent the entire row containing the cell. If a cell in a row above has an `is_header` attribute, the cells are prefixed with "KEY *header*". This is followed by the actual value from the current row, in the form "VALUE *header*". Thus each cell in a row looks like a combination of key/value pairs (or simply values if there is no header). This representation is similar to the one used by Schlichtkrull et al. (2020). All the cells in a row would look alike if we simply followed this procedure, so we distinguish the key/value pair corresponding to the current cell by enclosing it in double braces. Finally, the title is prepended, and if there is a caption, it is prepended as "CAPTION *caption*". Examples of the table cell, list element, and sentence formats are shown in Table 1.

3 Preliminary evidence retrieval

We follow the baseline system (Aly et al., 2021) to select an initial set of documents for downstream analysis. This module retrieves documents whose titles match named entities that appear in the claim, plus documents with a high TF-IDF score against the claim, up to five total documents.

Following Thorne and Vlachos (2021), we also considered the use of GENRE (Cao et al., 2021) to identify more Wikipedia page titles from entities that were not quite exact matches. (We preferred an exact match if present.) The use of these entities actually drove FEVEROUS score down, perhaps by crowding out the TF-IDF documents, so we reverted to the baseline approach.

Given a set of documents, we rank page elements using models trained to predict the set of evidence elements. One model is trained on sentences, list elements, and table captions, and the other is trained on table cells. We use a RoBERTa base model (Liu et al., 2019) and follow a training approach similar to the Dense Passage Retriever (Karpukhin et al., 2020). Given a positive training pair consisting of a claim c and a piece of evidence e, we collect six negative pairs (c, x_i). For four of the negatives we take x_i to be the highest TF-IDF matches returned by the baseline system that are not part of the gold evidence. For the other two negatives we take x_i to be part of the gold evidence for a different claim, randomly chosen. The multiple choice classification head of RoBERTa outputs a scalar $f(c, x)$ for each pair, and the batch of seven pairs is trained as one example with the cross-entropy loss

$$-\log \frac{e^{f(c,e)}}{e^{f(c,e)} + \sum_{i=1}^{6} e^{f(c,x_i)}} \quad (1)$$

just as in the Dense Passage Retriever. At test time, we run the model on examples of a single claim/evidence pair and collect the scalar $f(c, x)$. These outputs are ranked across all potential evidence to collect five sentences and 25 table cells. Every sentence in the retrieved documents is ranked, but only the top three tables retrieved by the baseline TF-IDF ranker are considered for extracting table cells.

The baseline system extracts sentences and other non-cell elements by TF-IDF similarity to the claim, and table cells with a RoBERTa base sized model that performs sequence tagging on linearized tables. Table 2 compares the recall of our system

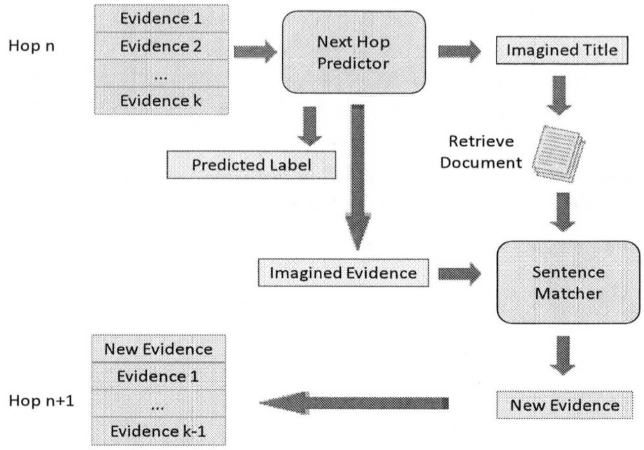

Figure 1: Applying the next hop prediction module to update evidence.

System	Recall
Baseline sentences	.5265
Ranking sentences	.3875
Baseline cells	.2741
Random cells	.2808
Ranking cells	.5028

Table 2: Page element recall.

(top 25 cells and five non-cell page elements) to these modules. This is computed by taking the union of all page elements (cells or non-cells) in all evidence chains in all claims, and considering the fraction that belong to one of our predicted evidence sets for the corresponding claims. We recall more relevant table cells, but surprisingly, fewer relevant sentences. In development, we mistakenly benchmarked the ranking models on a set which made gold evidence available for ranking even if it was not in a retrieved document, and on this basis, it appeared that ranking the sentences was advantageous. Therefore we used not only the table cell ranking module but also the sentence ranking module in our submitted system.

4 Next hop prediction

The use of the evidence ranking model is not sufficient to solve problems that require more difficult kinds of multi-hop reasoning. Though evidence chains are typically rooted in entities and concepts that appear in the claim, as one progresses down the chain it may be necessary to retrieve information about an entity mentioned in a previous piece of evidence. Such information would be difficult to query based on the claim alone.

To support this scenario, we introduce a next hop prediction module, as shown in Figure 1. Hop 1 consists of the evidence retrieved by the evidence ranking module. Given an evidence set produced in hop n, the next hop prediction module attempts to imagine information that is still needed but not retrieved yet. It generates a string consisting of the title of the needed article and the sentence or table cell (in the same format as before) that it wants to retrieve from that article. If available, the article with that title is retrieved; otherwise, sentences from previously retrieved articles will be searched. Then we choose one sentence and two table cells with the best word overlap against the imagined evidence. The bottom ranked elements of the evidence set for hop n are pushed out, and these chosen elements are pushed to the top of the evidence set for hop $n + 1$. The evidence ranking module was found not to be helpful in ranking newly retrieved evidence, often because it strayed too far from the original claim.[1]

The next hop prediction module is implemented by a T5 base sized model (Raffel et al., 2020). T5 consists of a text-to-text encoder-decoder transformer architecture, and its pre-training mixes mul-

[1]We also tried running the evidence ranking model after locating a bridge sentence based on overlap and prepending it to the candidates.

tiple unsupervised objectives on the Colossal Clean Crawled Corpus with supervised NLU tasks including abstractive summarization, question answering, GLUE text classification, and translation, cast into a text to text format. We train the model for three epochs on maximum sequence length 512, using Huggingface default parameters (Wolf et al., 2020). In our task, each input begins with the task identifier "missing: " and a list of the pages retrieved already, followed by the string `[HYP]` and then the claim being classified. Then the elements of the current evidence set (each beginning with a page title in brackets) are concatenated.

Training is based on the gold evidence chains in the training set, and the set of documents retrieved by the baseline model. Every example with evidence from a missing document is used as an example, with the current evidence set being the gold evidence in the retrieved documents and the target evidence being the first piece of evidence from a missing document. For half of the remaining examples (those with no missing documents) including all NEI examples with multiple pieces of evidence, a piece of evidence is randomly left out from the current evidence set, and that evidence is to be predicted as the target. In the other examples, the word "none" is to be predicted, indicating that the evidence chain is complete.

The target output strings are the word "supports" or "refutes," followed by the target evidence in the usual format or "none." For NEI examples, "supports" is to be predicted, indicating a partial evidence chain with no contradictions yet. Thus the log likelihood objective on the target output string amounts to a multi-task objective, combining a prediction of missing evidence with a prediction of the label based on partial information. Because missing evidence should be helpful for label prediction, we hope that co-training on the task of label prediction improves the features used to generate the missing evidence.

The existence of distracting evidence distinguishes the training setting from the testing setting. At test time, the module is always queried with a full set of five sentences and 25 cells, some of which may be irrelevant. For comparison, we trained a model with extracted evidence instead of gold evidence, but the model trained on gold chains achieved more complete chains in fewer hops.

Table 3 describes the performance of the next hop predictor on the development set. "Improved," "Same," and "Worse" count the number of examples where the number of pieces of gold evidence successfully predicted increased, stayed the same, or decreased compared to the previous hop. "Complete" indicates the number of examples for which a complete evidence set is predicted. "FEVEROUS score" is the downstream result of the label classification module (see next section) based on the evidence predicted. Each subsequent hop (up to five) improves the fraction of evidence retrieved, and the FEVEROUS score is monotonically improving up to at least seven hops. This implies that the module knows when to stop and output "none," or else its predictions would eventually overwrite needed evidence from the initial retrieval.

An example of next hop prediction is given in the appendix.

5 Label classification

After the next hop predictor has been run for seven hops, our system uses a label classification module to predict the final label. Another T5 base model is used for this problem, but here we train on the extracted evidence sets (including irrelevant evidence, and missing some gold evidence) that are collected for the training set. Input strings are the same as for the next hop predictor module. The target strings are just "supports," "refutes," or "neutral." As NEI instances only make up 3% of the training set, this label is never learned and the outputs are either "supports" or "refutes."[2]

The label accuracy of this approach on the development set is compared to other approaches that are trained with gold evidence or a RoBERTa model in Table 4. We see that a RoBERTa model has trouble learning in the presence of irrelevant evidence, but is confused by the distractions if only trained on gold evidence chains. In contrast, a T5 model can train and perform successfully on real extracted evidence chains. Consistent with our observations, Jiang et al. (2021) recently established a new state of the art on FEVER using T5 trained on lists of real extracted evidence.

Math hints. As numbers are represented as (possibly several) strings of digits, each with its own pre-trained embedding, it is difficult for the model to answer numerical comparison questions. Also, the model may not precisely know the relationship between a number as a word ("fourteen") and its

[2]In the training set we assign "supports" labels to NEI instances. See below.

Hops	Changes	Improved	Same	Worse	Complete Evidence	FEVEROUS Score
1	—	—	—	—	2661	.271
2	1245	249	7581	60	2722	.276
3	572	77	7768	45	2737	.280
4	391	44	7811	35	2745	.280
5	271	19	7835	36	2748	.281
6	202	13	7846	31	2744	.281
7	166	11	7861	18	2745	.281

Table 3: Performance of the next hop prediction module. FEVEROUS score is based on applying the downstream label classification module after the given hop.

Model	Train/Dev	Label accuracy
RoBERTa	Gold on Gold	.829
RoBERTa	Gold on Extracted	.550
RoBERTa	Extracted on Extracted	.495
T5	Gold on Gold	.848
T5	Gold on Extracted	.572
T5	Extracted on Extracted	.661
T5	Extracted+Math on Extracted+Math	.658

Table 4: Label classification models.

Truth	Supports	NEI	Refutes
Supports	.3403	.5179	.1418
NEI	.0918	.7146	.1936
Refutes	.0822	.4559	.4619
Supports	.6471	.0000	.3529
NEI	.4431	.0000	.5569
Refutes	.2341	.0000	.7659

Table 5: Confusion (development set) when training with (top) and without (bottom) extracted NEI labels.

numerical form ("14").

We attach hints to the beginning of each premise (list of concatenated evidence) as follows. Numbers in the claim or premise appearing in word form (up to twenty, and multiples of ten, one hundred, and one thousand) are converted to their numerical form, and we attach strings such as "four equals 4" for each conversion. Then we collect all numbers (including decimals and integers with commas) with a regular expression, and sort them (along with the number words) from least to greatest, forming a string such as "LEAST 0 less than 1 less than 30 less than 2017 GREATEST". After these prefixes, the original premise begins. It can be clearly recognized because it begins with a title inside brackets.

The NEI class. The NEI class did not have enough examples to be learned reliably in the standard training procedure, but represents 19% of examples in the final test set. To address this, the baseline system upsampled the NEI class by leaving out sentences or entire tables from gold evidence chains to create more NEI examples. For our system, our training data consists of extracted evidence chains rather than gold evidence chains. In addition to the natural NEI examples, we labeled any extracted chain that was still missing information as NEI, gave other extracted chains that were complete their original "supports" or "refutes" label, and trained a T5 base model with the resulting labels. In the resulting training set, 58% of examples were NEI, 20% were refutes, and 23% were supports.

As seen in the confusion matrix of Table 5, the T5 model could not learn the NEI class well and was biased towards NEI even on supporting or refuting examples. Even if 19% of true labels were NEI, as in the test set, the decrease in accuracy on supporting and refuting classes is too great to justify trying to predict this label. Therefore our submitted system is trained to predict only "supports" or "refutes" and never NEI.

An interesting alternative would be to use the existence of an evidence prediction from the next hop predictor after the final hop to indicate whether an example should be NEI. Following this approach, only 4.4% of NEI examples would be predicted as NEI, compared to 2.8% of supporting and 2.9% or refuting examples, so again including the NEI predictions would yield a net loss.

6 Conclusion

Team Papelo's system for FEVEROUS achieves .281 FEVEROUS score on the development set, with .658 label accuracy and .348 evidence recall. The largest increase in performance over the baseline comes from the label classifier, which uses a different model architecture and is trained on extracted evidence chains including irrelevant evidence. We also achieve better evidence recall through our table cell ranking module, which was trained with a multiple choice cross entropy loss similar to DPR. Additional gains are achieved by our multi-hop evidence retrieval. These modules can only be effective when given good representations of the context of sentences, list items and table cells, which we have carefully constructed.

On the test set we achieve a slightly lower .259 FEVEROUS score. This is largely due to the decrease of label accuracy to .576, reflecting an introduction of an additional 13% of NEI examples compared to the development set (Aly et al., 2021), which our system will always misclassify. The evidence recall of .346 is comparable to the development set.

Already the next hop predictor establishes a beneficial enhancement to the original evidence and can be safely run for many hops. The use of word overlap to match the imagined evidence to actual page elements was a compromise for faster and easier development. We believe the same basic method could be made stronger if a new ranking module, with a similar architecture and training procedure to the preliminary evidence retriever, were trained to match imagined evidence to actually missing evidence. The potential for improvement here is suggested by the number of attempted changes in Table 3, which is always several times the number of evidence sets that were improved.

Additional work is needed to improve performance on particular kinds of examples. Many claims require a system to count certain pieces of retrieved evidence. This skill is taught by datasets such as DROP (Dua et al., 2019) and until recently, neural module networks have needed a stronger form of supervision to learn it (Gupta et al., 2020). A recent alternative (Saha et al., 2021) learns a neural module network with weaker supervision, but instead relies on dependency parsing of the query. To address discrete reasoning examples in FEVEROUS, it may be necessary to integrate models trained on external datasets.

References

Rami Aly, Zhijiang Guo, Michael Sejr Schlichtkrull, James Thorne, Andreas Vlachos, Christos Christodoulopoulos, Oana Cocarascu, and Arpit Mittal. 2021. FEVEROUS: fact extraction and verification over unstructured and structured information. *CoRR*, abs/2106.05707.

Nicola De Cao, Gautier Izacard, Sebastian Riedel, and Fabio Petroni. 2021. Autoregressive entity retrieval. In *International Conference on Learning Representations*.

Dheeru Dua, Yizhong Wang, Pradeep Dasigi, Gabriel Stanovsky, Sameer Singh, and Matt Gardner. 2019. DROP: A reading comprehension benchmark requiring discrete reasoning over paragraphs. In *Proceedings of the 2019 Conference of the North American Chapter of the Association for Computational Linguistics: Human Language Technologies, Volume 1 (Long and Short Papers)*, pages 2368–2378, Minneapolis, Minnesota. Association for Computational Linguistics.

Nitish Gupta, Kevin Lin, Dan Roth, Sameer Singh, and Matt Gardner. 2020. Neural module networks for reasoning over text. In *International Conference on Learning Representations*.

Kelvin Jiang, Ronak Pradeep, and Jimmy Lin. 2021. Exploring listwise evidence reasoning with t5 for fact verification. In *Proceedings of the 59th Annual Meeting of the Association for Computational Linguistics and the 11th International Joint Conference on Natural Language Processing (Volume 2: Short Papers)*, pages 402–410, Online. Association for Computational Linguistics.

Vladimir Karpukhin, Barlas Oguz, Sewon Min, Patrick Lewis, Ledell Wu, Sergey Edunov, Danqi Chen, and Wen-tau Yih. 2020. Dense passage retrieval for open-domain question answering. In *Proceedings of the 2020 Conference on Empirical Methods in Natural Language Processing (EMNLP)*, pages 6769–6781, Online. Association for Computational Linguistics.

Yinhan Liu, Myle Ott, Naman Goyal, Jingfei Du, Mandar Joshi, Danqi Chen, Omer Levy, Mike Lewis, Luke Zettlemoyer, and Veselin Stoyanov. 2019. Roberta: A robustly optimized BERT pretraining approach. *CoRR*, abs/1907.11692.

Christopher Malon. 2018. Team papelo: Transformer networks at FEVER. In *Proceedings of the First Workshop on Fact Extraction and VERification (FEVER)*, pages 109–113, Brussels, Belgium. Association for Computational Linguistics.

Colin Raffel, Noam Shazeer, Adam Roberts, Katherine Lee, Sharan Narang, Michael Matena, Yanqi Zhou, Wei Li, and Peter J. Liu. 2020. Exploring the limits of transfer learning with a unified text-to-text transformer. *Journal of Machine Learning Research*, 21(140):1–67.

Amrita Saha, Shafiq R. Joty, and Steven C. H. Hoi. 2021. Weakly supervised neuro-symbolic module networks for numerical reasoning. *CoRR*, abs/2101.11802.

Michael Sejr Schlichtkrull, Vladimir Karpukhin, Barlas Oguz, Mike Lewis, Wen-tau Yih, and Sebastian Riedel. 2020. Joint verification and reranking for open fact checking over tables. *CoRR*, abs/2012.15115.

James Thorne and Andreas Vlachos. 2021. Evidence-based factual error correction. In *Proceedings of the 59th Annual Meeting of the Association for Computational Linguistics and the 11th International Joint Conference on Natural Language Processing (Volume 1: Long Papers)*, pages 3298–3309, Online. Association for Computational Linguistics.

James Thorne, Andreas Vlachos, Christos Christodoulopoulos, and Arpit Mittal. 2018. FEVER: a large-scale dataset for fact extraction and VERification. In *Proceedings of the 2018 Conference of the North American Chapter of the Association for Computational Linguistics: Human Language Technologies, Volume 1 (Long Papers)*, pages 809–819, New Orleans, Louisiana. Association for Computational Linguistics.

Thomas Wolf, Lysandre Debut, Victor Sanh, Julien Chaumond, Clement Delangue, Anthony Moi, Pierric Cistac, Tim Rault, Remi Louf, Morgan Funtowicz, Joe Davison, Sam Shleifer, Patrick von Platen, Clara Ma, Yacine Jernite, Julien Plu, Canwen Xu, Teven Le Scao, Sylvain Gugger, Mariama Drame, Quentin Lhoest, and Alexander Rush. 2020. Transformers: State-of-the-art natural language processing. In *Proceedings of the 2020 Conference on Empirical Methods in Natural Language Processing: System Demonstrations*, pages 38–45, Online. Association for Computational Linguistics.

Zhilin Yang, Peng Qi, Saizheng Zhang, Yoshua Bengio, William Cohen, Ruslan Salakhutdinov, and Christopher D. Manning. 2018. HotpotQA: A dataset for diverse, explainable multi-hop question answering. In *Proceedings of the 2018 Conference on Empirical Methods in Natural Language Processing*, pages 2369–2380, Brussels, Belgium. Association for Computational Linguistics.

A Example of next hop prediction

Table 6 shows an example where a complete evidence chain is retrieved after 7 hops. The large number of hops is needed because the top-ranked supplementary evidence does not contain the missing information. The imagined needed evidence stays the same until satisfactory evidence is retrieved (after exhausting the higher-ranked evidence) in hop 6. Then the next imagined evidence addresses another part of the reasoning chain. With that, contradictory supplementary evidence is retrieved successfully (northwest versus southwest) and the label for the whole claim is fully supported. Although all five initially retrieved sentences have been replaced before this hop, they are not needed.

Once an example has a complete reasoning chain, its retrieval usually stops long before the seventh hop, by predicting no imagined evidence.

B Example of math hints

Table 7 gives an example of a claim correctly classified with math hints but not without. Although math hints improved some examples, overall label accuracy decreased slightly, perhaps because the length of the hints could push necessary evidence beyond the 512 tokens read by the label classifier.

Claim	Cann River, a river that descends 1,080 metres (3,540 ft) over its 102 kilometres (63 mi) course rises northwest of Granite Mountain and is traversed by the Monaro Highway (which also parallels the former Bombala railway line in several locations) in its upper reaches.
Label	REFUTES
Ground Truth Evidence	[Cann River] The Cann River rises southwest of Granite Mountain in remote country on the eastern boundary of the Errinundra National Park and flows generally east, then south, then east, then south through the western edge of the Coopracambra National Park and through the Croajingolong National Park, joined by seventeen minor tributaries before reaching its mouth with Bass Strait, at the Tamboon Inlet in the Shire of East Gippsland.
Hop 2 Imagined	[Monaro Highway] The Monaro Highway parallels the former Bombala railway line in several locations.
Hop 2 Retrieved	[Monaro Highway] In 1958, it was named the Monaro Highway in both NSW and the ACT, though the same name had been in use by the Snowy Mountains Highway until 1955. *(also two cell retrievals)*
Hop 3 Imagined	[Monaro Highway] The Monaro Highway parallels the former Bombala railway line in several locations.
Hop 4 Imagined	[Monaro Highway] The Monaro Highway parallels the former Bombala railway line in several locations.
Hop 5 Imagined	[Monaro Highway] The Monaro Highway parallels the former Bombala railway line in several locations.
Hop 6 Imagined	[Monaro Highway] The Monaro Highway parallels the former Bombala railway line in several locations.
Hop 6 Retrieved	[Monaro Highway] The road also parallels the former Bombala railway line in several locations. *(also two cell retrievals)*
Hop 7 Imagined	[Cann River] The Cann River rises northwest of Granite Mountain and is traversed by the Monaro Highway in its upper reaches.
Hop 7 Retrieved	[Cann River] The Cann River rises southwest of Granite Mountain in remote country on the eastern boundary of the Errinundra National Park and flows generally east, then south, then east, then south through the western edge of the Coopracambra National Park and through the Croajingolong National Park, joined by seventeen minor tributaries before reaching its mouth with Bass Strait, at the Tamboon Inlet in the Shire of East Gippsland. *(also two cell retrievals)*

Table 6: An example where full evidence is retrieved in seven hops.

Claim	Lamba Kheda recorded a total population of less than 3,000 with 1,100 scheduled castes in the 2011 census.
Label	REFUTES
Premise	LEAST 0.4 less than 2.6 less than 2.7 less than 6 less than 6.25 less than 7.4 less than 8.5 less than 8.7 less than 19.7 less than 28.8 less than 43.1 less than 61 less than 62 less than 82.5 less than 89.5 less than 123 less than 235 less than 289 less than 524 less than 540 less than 560 less than 1100 less than 1850 less than 1977 less than 1981 less than 2011 less than 2058 less than 3000 less than 3166 less than 3908 less than 482365 GREATEST [List of Scheduled Tribes in India] This list has been updated by the Ministry of Tribal Affairs, Government of India, to add the following three. ... [Lamba Kheda] CAPTION Demographics (2011 Census) KEY VALUE Scheduled caste {{ KEY Total VALUE 1100 }} ... [Lamba Kheda] VALUE Total {{ KEY Population (2011) VALUE 3,908 }} ...

Table 7: An example correctly classified using math hints that was misclassified without them.

Modeling Entity Knowledge for Fact Verification

Yang Liu, Chenguang Zhu, Michael Zeng
Microsoft Cognitive Services Research
1 Microsoft Way, Redmond, WA, USA
{yaliu10,chezhu,nzeng}@microsoft.com

Abstract

Fact verification is a challenging task of identifying the truthfulness of given claims based on the retrieval of relevant evidence texts. Many claims require understanding and reasoning over external entity information for precise verification. In this paper, we propose a novel fact verification model using entity knowledge to enhance its performance. We retrieve descriptive text from Wikipedia for each entity, and then encode these descriptions by a smaller lightweight network to be fed into the main verification model. Furthermore, we boost model performance by adopting and predicting the relatedness between the claim and each evidence as additional signals. We demonstrate experimentally on a large-scale benchmark dataset FEVER that our framework achieves competitive results with a FEVER score of 72.89% on the test set.

1 Introduction

The rapid development of online applications provides open and efficient platforms for spreading information. However, false information, including fake news and online rumors, have also been growing and spreading widely over the past several years. Vosoughi et al. (2018) shows that false news travels even faster, deeper and broader than the truth. To prevent harm from this false information, automatically verifying the truthfulness of textual contents is becoming an urgent need for our society. In this work, we study fact verification with the goal of automatically assessing the veracity of a textual claim given supporting evidence.

Most existing methods consider fact verification as a natural language inference task (Angeli and Manning, 2014). Usually, these systems concatenate claim and its supporting evidence sentences, and then feed them into a classification model (Nie et al., 2019). Alternatively, previous studies construct graph structures based on claim and evidence, and reason over this graph with graph neural networks (Zhou et al., 2019; Liu et al., 2020) or Transformer models (Zhong et al., 2020), which are used in top systems in the FEVER challenge (Thorne et al., 2018). While these studies focus on reasoning based on claim and evidence text, we believe entity knowledge is also important for precise fact verification. For example, given the first claim from FEVER dataset in Table 1, making the correct verification requires a model to understand what is "*Wii U*" and "*OS X*" and know the fact that they are not Microsoft and Sony platforms. Similarly, for the second claim, the knowledge that "*New York City*" is in United States can also be potentially useful for verifying the claim. This information is not included in the gold evidence provided by the dataset.

In this work, we present a fact verification model that can effectively incorporate external entity information. Given a claim and its evidence sentences, we first recognize named entities from them, linking them with Wikipedia articles, and then retrieve the lead sections of these articles as the entity descriptions. To make the most of this entity knowledge while not introducing noisy information, we propose a lightweight entity knowledge encoder module for representing external entity knowledge. Our large fact verification network then accesses this knowledge by a unidirectional attention mechanism at each encoding layer. Meanwhile, since the input evidence sentences are obtained by an upstream retrieval module, some evidence may be irrelevant to the claim. Thus, we predict and adopt this relatedness between each evidence and the claim as an auxiliary signal to train our model.

We experiment with our approach on FEVER (Thorne et al., 2018), one influential benchmark dataset for fact verification. FEVER contains over 185k labeled claims and each verifiable claim is paired with several natural language sentences from Wikipedia as their

Proceedings of the Fourth Workshop on Fact Extraction and VERification (FEVER) at EMNLP 2021, pages 50–59
November 10, 2021.

Claim #1:
Assassin's Creed has only ever been released on a **Microsoft** and **Sony** platform.
Gold Evidence:
The main video game series consists of nine games , developed by **Ubisoft**, released on **PlayStation 3**, **PlayStation 4**, **Xbox 360**, **Xbox One**, **Wii U**, **Microsoft Windows**, and **OS X** platforms .
Entity Knowledge:
Wii U: The Wii U is a home video game console developed by Nintendo as the successor to the Wii.
OS X: macOS (previously Mac OS X and later OS X) is a series of proprietary graphical operating systems developed and marketed by Apple Inc.
Verdict: REFUTED

Claim #2:
Beastie Boys was formed in **Australia**.
Gold Evidence:
The Beastie Boys were an American hip hop group from **New York City**, formed in 1981.
Entity Knowledge:
New York City: New York City (NYC), often called simply New York, is the most populous city in the United States.
Verdict: REFUTED

Table 1: Two motivating examples for fact checking and the FEVER task. Identifying the truthfulness of claims requires understanding and reasoning of entity knowledge within the claim and the evidence sentences. The bold phrases are named entities. Underlined entities are linked to their Wikipedia descriptions, which can potentially provide useful knowledge for verifying the claim.

supporting evidence. Our system achieves the state-of-the-art result on label accuracy and competitive result on FEVER score. Ablation study shows that the integration of entity knowledge and auxiliary relatedness signal can effectively improve performance. We then provide a detailed error analysis for our system. In summary, we list our contributions as follows.

- We propose to enhance fact verification models with external entity knowledge.
- We design an entity knowledge encoder module and employ unidirectional attention to effectively incorporate entity descriptions.
- Empirical results show that our approach achieves competitive performance on the FEVER dataset, and ablation study shows that incorporating entity knowledge is useful for fact verification.

2 Related Work

2.1 Fact Verification

Fact checking is a challenging task aiming to automatically verify the truthfulness of claims. A claim can be a plain text or a triple of (subject, predicate, object) (Nakashole and Mitchell, 2014), and different fact checking datasets usually provide different evidence sources. Vlachos and Riedel (2014) propose a fact verification dataset by collecting 106 labeled political claims and providing the journalists' analysis material as the evidence. Ferreira and Vlachos (2016) construct the Emergent dataset containing 300 labeled rumors and 2,595 associated news articles, collected and labelled by journalists. LIAR (Wang, 2017) is a dataset for fake news detection. It contains 2.8K labeled short statements from the web, with detailed analysis and source documents as evidence. Chen et al. (2020c) build TABFACT, a dataset collecting Wikipedia tables as the evidence for human-labeled statements.

Recently, the FEVER shared task 1.0 (Thorne et al., 2018) attracts attention from the research community. It is a challenge that requires participants to develop automatic fact verification systems to check the truthfulness of human-generated claims by extracted evidence from Wikipedia. Many systems were proposed for this challenging task. Nie et al. (2019) design a Neural Semantic Matching Network that takes the concatenation of all evidence sentences as input. They also propose a two-hop evidence enhancement process where they apply sentence selection twice to retrieve more related evidence sentences. Stammbach and Neumann (2019) propose a two-staged selection process with two different retrieval models for selecting evidence sentences. Yoneda et al. (2018) infer the veracity of each claim-evidence pair and make final prediction by aggregating multiple predicted labels. Hanselowski et al. (2018) encode each claim-evidence pair separately, and use a pooling function to aggregate features for prediction. Zhou et al. (2019) formulates claim verification as a graph reasoning task and propose a new model with graph neural networks. Liu et al. (2020) regards sentences as the nodes of a graph and uses Kernel Graph Attention Network (KGAT) to aggregate information. Zhong et al. (2020) further constructs a semantic-level graph for input claim and evidence and perform reasoning over this graph with pretrained XLNet model (Yang et al., 2019).

Similar to our work, some previous systems also

focus on using entity information for fact verification. Taniguchi et al. (2018) first extract entities from the claim and propose to use a simple entity-linking system based on text match to retrieve evidence documents. Nooralahzadeh and Øvrelid (2018) select evidence documents by finding article titles which contain the entities and noun phrases of the claim.

2.2 Modeling External Knowledge in NLP

The usage of external knowledge, like WordNet, Wikipedia and knowledge graph, has benefited many natural language processing tasks including natural language inference and fact verification. Jijkoun et al. (2005) uses WordNet to measure word similarity to obtain a better textual entailment recognizer. Chen et al. (2018) proposes a neural network model for natural language inference equipped with several external knowledge. Wang et al. (2019) finds that utilizing ConceptNet as an external knowledge source can benefit entailment model in scientific domain. Chen et al. (2020b) proposes WIKINLI, a large-scale naturally annotated dataset constructed from Wikipedia category graph. And they show that model pretrained on this dataset can achieve better performance on downstream natural language entailment tasks.

3 FEVER Challenge

In this paper, we tackle the large-scale challenge for fact extraction and verification: the FEVER Challenge (Thorne et al., 2018). It contains 185,445 claims generated by altering sentences extracted from Wikipedia.

To verify a claim in FEVER, a model typically follows a three-step pipeline framework, i.e. document retrieval, sentence selection and claim verification. In document retrieval, a system matches the claim to Wikipedia articles by extracted named entities and phrases using a search engine built on Wikipedia. In sentence selection, a system ranks the sentences from retrieved articles by their similarity scores against the claim. The similarity score can be calculated by a trainable regression model, like Enhanced LSTM (Chen et al., 2017), or pretrained language models like BERT and RoBERTa (Devlin et al., 2019; Liu et al., 2019). In claim verification, a system classifies the truthfulness of the claim based on top-ranked sentences from the previous step, also known as the evidence sentences. Like most participants in this challenge, we adopt existing approaches for document retrieval and sentence selection, while mainly focusing on the claim verification model.

4 Method

In this section, we first formalize the fact verification problem in Section 4.1 and then introduce our model for incorporating entity knowledge in Section 4.2. Finally, we present our complete solution to the FEVER Challenge including document retrieval, evidence selection and entity description collection in Section 4.3.

4.1 Problem Formulation

Given the input claim and its retrieved evidence sentences, our approach predicts the truthfulness of the claim. As defined in FEVER dataset, we frame the prediction as a three-way classification, i.e. the prediction is '*SUPPORTED*', '*REFUTED*' or '*NOT ENOUGH INFO (NEI)*'. Furthermore, we require the model to predict the relatedness of the evidence sentences as an auxiliary task.

Formally, the input to our model is $[C, E_1, E_2, E_3, \cdots, E_n]$, where C is the claim and E_i is the i-th evidence. The evidence sentences are obtained by an upstream retrieval module. The claim and each evidence are composed of a list of tokens: $C = [w_{c_1}, w_{c_2}, \cdots, w_{c_{|C|}}]$, $E_i = [w_{e_{i_1}}, w_{e_{i_2}}, \cdots, w_{e_{i_{|E_i|}}}]$. The target output is the claim truthfulness label y_c. Also, the FEVER dataset provides a relatedness label for each evidence sentence as auxiliary targets, i.e. $y_{e_i} \in \{$'RELATED', 'NOT RELATED'$\}$.

4.2 Model Architecture

The general architecture of our fact verification model is shown in Figure 1. It is a classification neural network based on RoBERTa (Liu et al., 2019), a Transformer-based model (Vaswani et al., 2017) pretrained on large corpora with a masked language modeling objective.

We concatenate the claim with evidences as input to the model. Following the default configuration of RoBERTa, we insert a [CLS] token at the start of the input; the output representation of this token is used to aggregate information from the whole sequence. And we insert a token [SEP] before each evidence sentence as an indicator of sentence boundaries. We use the output vectors of these [SEP] tokens as features for the evidence sentence after it.

The modified text is then represented as a sequence of tokens $X = [w_1, w_2, \cdots, w_n]$. Each token w_i is assigned three types of embeddings: *token embeddings* indicate the meaning of each token, *position embeddings* indicate the position of each token within the text sequence, and *segmentation embeddings* are used to discriminate between the claim and the evidence sentences[1]. These three embeddings are summed into a single input vector x_i and fed to a bidirectional Transformer with multiple layers:

$$\tilde{H}^l = \text{LN}(H^{l-1} + \text{Att}(H^{l-1}, H^{l-1})) \quad (1)$$

$$H^l = \text{LN}(\tilde{H}^l + \text{FFN}(\tilde{H}^l)) \quad (2)$$

where $H^0 = x$ are the input vectors; LN is the layer normalization operation (Ba et al., 2016); Att is the multi-head self-attention operation (Vaswani et al., 2017); the superscript l indicates the depth of the stacked layers. On the top layer, RoBERTa generates an output vector for each token with rich contextual information for fact verification.

As shown in the motivating examples in Table 1, making the correct prediction needs good understanding and reasoning of the entities in claim and evidence. Thus, we collect entity knowledge from Wikipedia and encode them by a decomposable entity encoder. The result is attended by the previous fact verification module. In the follows, we will first introduce the main fact verification module and then the entity knowledge encoder.

4.2.1 Fact Verification Module

Suppose that in the output contextual embeddings from RoBERTa, $\boldsymbol{c}$ is the vector for the [CLS] token and $\boldsymbol{e}_i$ is the vector for the i-th [SEP] token. To predict the truthfulness of the claim, we apply a three-way softmax classification layer over $\boldsymbol{c}$:

$$\hat{y}_c = \text{softmax}(\boldsymbol{c}\boldsymbol{W}_c + \boldsymbol{b}_c) \quad (3)$$

where $\boldsymbol{W}_c$ and $\boldsymbol{b}_c$ are weight and bias. We adopt the cross entropy loss for claim truthfulness classification against the ground-truth label y_c.

Since the input evidence sentences are obtained by an upstream retrieval module, some of them may be irrelevant to the claim. Therefore, as an auxiliary training task, we also predict the relatedness of each evidence sentence, which has been shown to be effective in Yin and Roth (2018).

[1]RoBERTa does not use segmentation embeddings in pretraining, but we found it is useful in finetuning.

To do that, we apply a sigmoid classification layer over each $\boldsymbol{e}_i$:

$$\hat{y}_{e_i} = \sigma(\boldsymbol{e}_i\boldsymbol{W}_e + \boldsymbol{b}_e) \quad (4)$$

where $\boldsymbol{W}_e$ and $\boldsymbol{b}_e$ are weight and bias, and σ is the sigmoid function. Likewise, we adopt cross entropy loss for this binary classification of evidence relatedness against the ground-truth label y_{e_i}.

The final loss L for our fact verification module is the weighted summation of the claim loss L_c and the evidence loss L_e:

$$L = \lambda L_c + (1 - \lambda)L_e \quad (5)$$

where λ is searched from $\{0.1, 0.3, 0.5, 0.7, 0.9\}$ based on model performance on the development set. It is set to 0.5 to achieve the best performance.

4.2.2 Decomposable Entity Knowledge Encoder

To augment fact verification model with external entity knowledge, we first identify all named entities in the claim and evidence sentences with an external named entity recognizer. We then link these entities to Wikipedia articles with a trained entity linker (more details in Section 4.3). The lead section of the corresponding Wikipedia article is used as the description of an entity.

While a straightforward approach is to append these descriptions to the input claim and evidence, it may lead to two potential issues. First, since entity descriptions are retrieved from Wikipedia articles, they could contain irrelevant noisy information and degrade the model performance. Second, many descriptions are very long and can reduce our model's efficiency in both training and inference. Therefore, we propose a decomposable entity knowledge encoder module to represent this external entity information in a compact semantic space.

We denote the fact verification module in Section 4.2.1 as T_m. We co-train a lightweight entity knowledge encoder module T_e initialized with the distilled RoBERTa-base (Sanh et al., 2019). Thus, T_e has less parameters and fewer layers than T_m and the hidden state dimension of T_e, i.e. d_e, is smaller than that of T_m, i.e. d_m.

We concatenate descriptions of entities in the claim and evidence sentences and feed the concatenated text into T_e. We denote the input hidden states to the l-th layer in T_m as H_m^{l-1} and the input hidden states to the l-th layer in T_e as H_e^{l-1}.

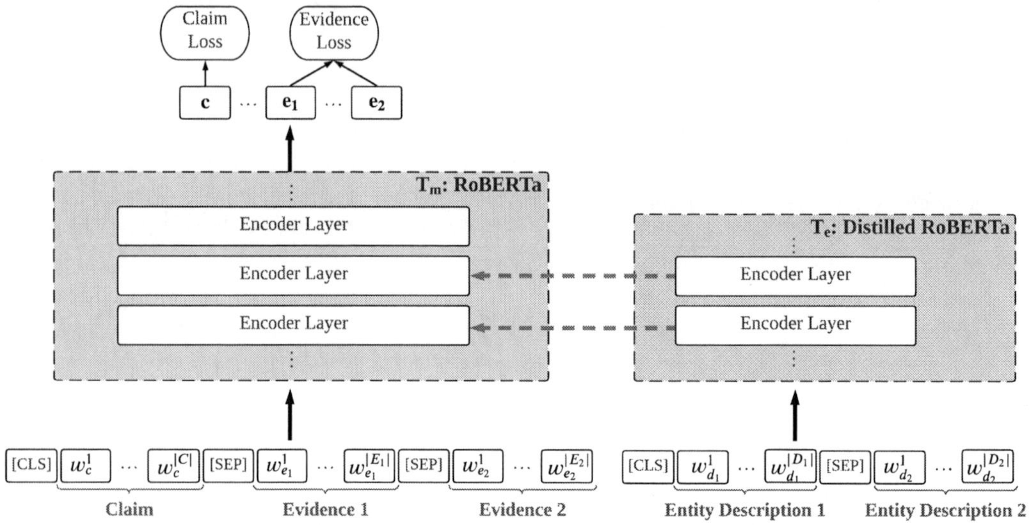

Figure 1: Architecture of our fact verification system enhanced with entity knowledge. The left part is the fact verification module based on RoBERTa and the right part is the entity encoder based on distilled RoBERTa. The dotted green arrows indicate unidirectional attention mechanism which the fact verification module uses to access outputs from the entity encoder. The final loss of our model is the combination of claim loss and auxiliary evidence loss.

Then, the fact verification module T_m employs a unidirectional attention to access outputs from T_e to adopt entity knowledge for fact verification. Since T_m and T_e have different hidden sizes, we first apply a linear transformation to the outputs of T_e:

$$\hat{h}_{e_i}^{l-1} = h_{e_i}^{l-1}\boldsymbol{W}_e^{l-1} + \boldsymbol{b}_e^{l-1} \tag{6}$$

where $h_{e_i}^{l-1}$ is the i-th output of the $(l-1)$-th layer of T_e, and $\boldsymbol{W}_e^{l-1} \in \mathbb{R}^{d_e \times d_m}$, $\boldsymbol{b}_e^{l-1} \in \mathbb{R}^{d_m}$ are weight and bias.

Then the fact verification module T_m conducts unidirectional attention to $\hat{H}_e^{l-1} = \{\hat{h}_{e_i}^{l-1}\}$, along with its self-attention, to produce the output H_m^l.

$$\begin{aligned}\tilde{H}_m^l =& \text{LN}(H_m^{l-1} \\ &+ \text{Att}(H_m^{l-1}, [H_m^{l-1}, \hat{H}_e^{l-1}])) \quad (7)\\ H_m^l =& \text{LN}(\tilde{H}_m^l + \text{FFN}(\tilde{H}_m^l)), \quad (8)\end{aligned}$$

where $[*, *]$ indicates the element-wise concatenation of two lists of vectors.

And the entity knowledge encoder T_e carries out its self-attention as in standard Transformer models.

$$\begin{aligned}\tilde{H}_e^l =& \text{LN}(H_e^{l-1} + \text{Att}(H_e^{l-1}, H_e^{l-1})) \quad (9)\\ H_e^l =& \text{LN}(\tilde{H}_e^l + \text{FFN}(\tilde{H}_e^l)) \quad (10)\end{aligned}$$

Since T_m has more encoding layers than T_e, the unidirectional attention only works on the lower layers of T_m where it has a corresponding layer in T_e.

In this way, the fact verification module can efficiently reason about the truthfulness of the claim with the compact representations of rich entity information from the entity knowledge encoder.

4.3 Complete Solution

In this section, we introduce our complete solution to the FEVER Challenge of fact verification.

Document Retrieval We adopt the same document retrieval module as in (Hanselowski et al., 2018; Liu et al., 2020). For a given claim, it first utilizes the constituency parser in AllenNLP (Gardner et al., 2018) to extract all phrases which potentially indicate entities. Then it uses these phrases as queries to find relevant Wikipedia pages through the online MediaWiki API. Then the highest-ranked results are retrieved and further filtered by a set of rules.

Evidence Selection We use the evidence selection module from Liu et al. (2020) to select related sentences from the retrieved Wikipedia pages. The module consists of a regression model based on BERT to score the claim and evidence sentence pair. For each claim, we use the top 5 ranked sentences as evidence.

Entity Descriptions We first use Flair (Akbik et al., 2019) as the NER tool to extract entities from input claim and evidence sentences. We then use the entity linking system REL (van Hulst et al., 2020) to link entities to Wikipedia articles, and take the first section of the linked article as the entity description. We limit the length of any entity description to 100 tokens, and the total length of all descriptions for one instance to 512 tokens.

Claim Verification Finally, the claim, evidence sentences and entity descriptions are fed into our model in Section 4.2 to verify the claim's truthfulness.

5 Experiments

5.1 Dataset and Evaluation Metrics

We evaluate our model on FEVER 1.0 (Thorne et al., 2018), a large-scale benchmark dataset for fact extraction and verification. Detailed statistics of FEVER are shown in Table 2. Each instance in FEVER 1.0 consists of a human-written claim, a set of ground-truth evidence sentences from Wikipedia and a label (i.e., 'SUPPORTED', 'REFUTED' or 'NOT ENOUGH INFO'), indicating the truthfulness of claim. FEVER also provides a Wikipedia dump containing 5,416,537 pre-processed articles for machine learning models to select evidence sentences.

Models are evaluated by two metrics: label accuracy and FEVER score. Label accuracy measures the accuracy of model's prediction for claim truthfulness. FEVER score considers whether both the predicted claim truthfulness and the selected evidence sentences are correct.

5.2 Implementation details

We implement our model with Huggingface Transformers (Wolf et al., 2020). The training batch size is set to 32. We use the Adam optimizer (Kingma and Ba, 2014) with a learning rate of 1e-5 and a warm-up proportion of 0.1. The main encoder is initialized with RoBERTa-large. It has 355M parameters with 24 layers and a Transformer hidden size of 1,024. The entity encoder is initialized with distilled RoBERTa-base with 82M parameters, 6 layers and a Transformer hidden size of 768. We train our models for 10 epochs and the model achieving the highest label accuracy on development set of FEVER is selected. All source codes of this work are available at `https://github.com/nlpyang/FeverEntity`.

Data Split	SUPPORTED	REFUTED	NEI
Train	80,035	29,775	35,639
Dev	6,666	6,666	6,666
Test	6,666	6,666	6,666

Table 2: Statistics of the FEVER dataset.

5.3 Baselines

We compare our system to the following top-performing systems on the FEVER shared task.

- Athene (Hanselowski et al., 2018) models each claim-evidence pair separately and applies a pooling operation for feature aggregation.
- UCL MRG (Yoneda et al., 2018) uses Convolutional Neural Network as the encoder for claim and evidence. Label aggregation is used for final prediction.
- UNC NLP (Nie et al., 2019) designs a semantic matching neural model for both sentence selection and claim verification.
- GEAR (Zhou et al., 2019) constructs a graph with each evidence sentence as a node and uses a graph neural network over this graph for prediction.
- DREAM (Zhong et al., 2020) is built upon a graph derived from semantic role labeling and embeds a graph-based module into the pretrained XLNet (Yang et al., 2019) model.
- KGAT (Liu et al., 2020) uses Kernel Graph Attention Network over a graph with evidence sentences as nodes. The model is based on the pretrained RoBERTa-large model.
- LOREN (Chen et al., 2020a) uses design a neural network that can aggregate probabilistic version of the logic rules for fact verification.

5.4 Results

Table 3 shows the results on both the development set and blind test set of FEVER. The first block in the table includes the results of systems without using pretrained models. The second block in

Method	Dev		Test	
	Label Acc.	FEVER score	Label Acc.	FEVER score
Non-pretrained Systems				
Athene	68.49	64.74	65.46	61.58
UCL MRG	69.66	65.41	67.62	62.52
UNC NLP	69.72	66.49	68.21	64.21
Pretrained Systems				
GEAR (*BERT-Base*)	74.84	70.69	71.60	67.10
DREAM (*XLNet*)	79.16	-	76.85	70.60
KGAT				
⌞ *BERT-Large*	77.91	75.86	73.61	70.24
⌞ *RoBERTa-Large*	78.29	76.11	74.07	70.38
⌞ *CorefRoBERTa-Large*	-	-	75.96	72.30
LOREN (*RoBERTa-Large*)	81.12	78.94	73.43	74.84
Our Approach				
⌞ *BERT-Large*	78.17	75.44	75.06	71.19
⌞ *RoBERTa-Large*	81.43	78.65	77.29	72.89

Table 3: Evaluation of fact verification systems on FEVER dataset. Variants of a system using different pretrained models are listed.

Entity Description	Entity Knowledge Encoder	Evidence Loss	Label Accuracy	FEVER Score
✓	✓	✓	81.43	78.65
✓	×	✓	80.89	77.93
✓	✓	×	80.15	77.30
×	×	✓	80.44	77.65
×	×	×	79.87	76.99

Table 4: Ablation study on FEVER development set. Our model is based on RoBERTa-Large in this experiment.

the table includes systems using pretrained models. The last block includes results from our framework. For a fair comparison with previous systems, we also implemented a version of our model based on BERT-Large.

As shown, our approach achieves the best performance on label accuracy and competitive results on FEVER score in both development and test set, proving the effectiveness of our entity knowledge-based approach. We also show that this improvement is consistent across different underlying pretrained models. For instance, our approach of knowledge integration outperforms KGAT when the language understanding model is initialized with either BERT-Large or RoBERTa-Large.

Ablation Study To further investigate how our proposed system improves fact verification, we conduct ablation study of different model components. Table 4 presents the result on the development set after removing different components in our model based on RoBERTa-Large.

As shown, when the entity knowledge encoder is removed and the entity description is concatenated with the claim and evidence sentences as input, the label accuracy drops 0.5%. This proves the necessity of using a separate module to represent external knowledge. When evidence loss is removed, the label accuracy drops almost 1.3%. When entity description is not used at all, the FEVER score drops 1%. When evidence loss is further removed, the FEVER score drop increases 1.6%.

These results show that our proposed entity descriptions, entity knowledge encoder and evidence loss all contribute to the effectiveness of our model.

5.5 Error Analysis

To take a deeper investigation into current fact verification systems, we manually analyze 100 randomly selected cases that are incorrectly predicted by our model. We summarize several primary error types in this section.

The first error type is the failure of inference over multiple sentences. About 44% claims in

FEVER development set have more than one gold evidence sentences. Identifying the truthfulness of these claims sometimes requires multi-sentence inference. For example, to verify the claim *"Hourglass was released 6 years after New Moon Shine."*, we need to infer over two evidence sentences: *"It built upon the success of his previous effort, New Moon Shine."* and *"Taylor's first studio album in six years was released in 1997 to glowing notices."*

Another primary error type is mistakes in semantic matching. Given the claim *"Valencia is in a country."*, although model successfully retrieved the gold evidence *"Valencia is the capital of the autonomous community of Valencia and the third largest city in Spain ..."*, it still fails to predict it correctly. We believe one possible reason is that model doesn't realize being a city of a country is synonymous with being in a country. This suggests we need more powerful language representation models to tackle fact verification.

The third error type is caused by ambiguity of concepts in the claim. For example, the claim describes *"Bones is a movie."*, and our model predicts its to be true based on retrieved evidence *"Bones is a 2001 American horror film directed ..."*. However, there are different definitions of *"Bones"* in Wikipedia and the human annotator was referring to the TV series also named *"Bones"*.

6 Conclusion

In this paper, we present a novel framework for fact verification. When assessing the truthfulness of a claim, we first identify the entities within the claim and evidence, and then retrieve external entity descriptions from Wikipedia. We design a decomposable entity knowledge encoder with unidirectional attention for effectively incorporating entity knowledge. Furthermore, we propose to use the prediction of input evidence sentences' relatedness as an auxiliary task. Experimental results show that our model achieves competitive results on the large-scale fact verification dataset FEVER. And we conduct ablation studies to showcase the effectiveness of our proposed components.

References

Alan Akbik, Tanja Bergmann, Duncan Blythe, Kashif Rasul, Stefan Schweter, and Roland Vollgraf. 2019. FLAIR: An easy-to-use framework for state-of-the-art NLP. In *Proceedings of the 2019 Conference of the North American Chapter of the Association for Computational Linguistics (Demonstrations)*, pages 54–59, Minneapolis, Minnesota.

Gabor Angeli and Christopher D. Manning. 2014. NaturalLI: Natural logic inference for common sense reasoning. In *Proceedings of the 2014 Conference on Empirical Methods in Natural Language Processing (EMNLP)*, pages 534–545, Doha, Qatar.

Jimmy Lei Ba, Jamie Ryan Kiros, and Geoffrey E Hinton. 2016. Layer normalization. *arXiv preprint arXiv:1607.06450*.

Jiangjie Chen, Qiaoben Bao, Jiaze Chen, Changzhi Sun, Hao Zhou, Yanghua Xiao, and Lei Li. 2020a. Loren: Logic enhanced neural reasoning for fact verification. *arXiv preprint arXiv:2012.13577*.

Mingda Chen, Zewei Chu, Karl Stratos, and Kevin Gimpel. 2020b. Mining knowledge for natural language inference from Wikipedia categories. In *Findings of the Association for Computational Linguistics: EMNLP 2020*, Online.

Qian Chen, Xiaodan Zhu, Zhen-Hua Ling, Diana Inkpen, and Si Wei. 2018. Neural natural language inference models enhanced with external knowledge. In *Proceedings of the 56th Annual Meeting of the Association for Computational Linguistics (Volume 1: Long Papers)*, Melbourne, Australia.

Qian Chen, Xiaodan Zhu, Zhen-Hua Ling, Si Wei, Hui Jiang, and Diana Inkpen. 2017. Enhanced LSTM for natural language inference. In *Proceedings of the 55th Annual Meeting of the Association for Computational Linguistics (Volume 1: Long Papers)*, pages 1657–1668, Vancouver, Canada.

Wenhu Chen, Hongmin Wang, Jianshu Chen, Yunkai Zhang, Hong Wang, Shiyang Li, Xiyou Zhou, and William Yang Wang. 2020c. Tabfact: A large-scale dataset for table-based fact verification. In *Proceedings of the ICLR Conference*.

Jacob Devlin, Ming-Wei Chang, Kenton Lee, and Kristina Toutanova. 2019. BERT: Pre-training of deep bidirectional transformers for language understanding. In *Proceedings of the 2019 Conference of the North American Chapter of the Association for Computational Linguistics: Human Language Technologies, Volume 1 (Long and Short Papers)*, pages 4171–4186, Minneapolis, Minnesota.

William Ferreira and Andreas Vlachos. 2016. Emergent: a novel data-set for stance classification. In *Proceedings of the 2016 Conference of the North American Chapter of the Association for Computational Linguistics: Human Language Technologies*, San Diego, California.

Matt Gardner, Joel Grus, Mark Neumann, Oyvind Tafjord, Pradeep Dasigi, Nelson F. Liu, Matthew Peters, Michael Schmitz, and Luke Zettlemoyer. 2018. AllenNLP: A deep semantic natural language processing platform. In *Proceedings of Workshop for NLP Open Source Software (NLP-OSS)*, pages 1–6, Melbourne, Australia.

Andreas Hanselowski, Hao Zhang, Zile Li, Daniil Sorokin, Benjamin Schiller, Claudia Schulz, and Iryna Gurevych. 2018. UKP-athene: Multi-sentence textual entailment for claim verification. In *Proceedings of the First Workshop on Fact Extraction and VERification (FEVER)*, pages 103–108, Brussels, Belgium.

Valentin Jijkoun, Maarten de Rijke, et al. 2005. Recognizing textual entailment using lexical similarity. In *Proceedings of the PASCAL Challenges Workshop on Recognising Textual Entailment*, pages 73–76. Citeseer.

Diederik P Kingma and Jimmy Ba. 2014. Adam: A method for stochastic optimization. *Proceedings of the ICLR Conference*.

Yinhan Liu, Myle Ott, Naman Goyal, Jingfei Du, Mandar Joshi, Danqi Chen, Omer Levy, Mike Lewis, Luke Zettlemoyer, and Veselin Stoyanov. 2019. Roberta: A robustly optimized BERT pretraining approach. *CoRR*, abs/1907.11692.

Zhenghao Liu, Chenyan Xiong, Maosong Sun, and Zhiyuan Liu. 2020. Fine-grained fact verification with kernel graph attention network. In *Proceedings of the 58th Annual Meeting of the Association for Computational Linguistics*, pages 7342–7351.

Ndapandula Nakashole and Tom M. Mitchell. 2014. Language-aware truth assessment of fact candidates. In *Proceedings of the 52nd Annual Meeting of the Association for Computational Linguistics (Volume 1: Long Papers)*, pages 1009–1019, Baltimore, Maryland.

Yixin Nie, Haonan Chen, and Mohit Bansal. 2019. Combining fact extraction and verification with neural semantic matching networks. In *Proceedings of the AAAI Conference on Artificial Intelligence*, volume 33, pages 6859–6866.

Farhad Nooralahzadeh and Lilja Øvrelid. 2018. Siriusltg: An entity linking approach to fact extraction and verification. In *Proceedings of the First Workshop on Fact Extraction and VERification (FEVER)*, pages 119–123.

Victor Sanh, Lysandre Debut, Julien Chaumond, and Thomas Wolf. 2019. Distilbert, a distilled version of bert: smaller, faster, cheaper and lighter. *arXiv preprint arXiv:1910.01108*.

Dominik Stammbach and Guenter Neumann. 2019. Team domlin: Exploiting evidence enhancement for the fever shared task. In *Proceedings of the Second Workshop on Fact Extraction and VERification (FEVER)*, pages 105–109.

Motoki Taniguchi, Tomoki Taniguchi, Takumi Takahashi, Yasuhide Miura, and Tomoko Ohkuma. 2018. Integrating entity linking and evidence ranking for fact extraction and verification. In *Proceedings of the First Workshop on Fact Extraction and Verification (FEVER)*, pages 124–126.

James Thorne, Andreas Vlachos, Christos Christodoulopoulos, and Arpit Mittal. 2018. FEVER: a large-scale dataset for fact extraction and VERification. In *Proceedings of the 2018 Conference of the North American Chapter of the Association for Computational Linguistics: Human Language Technologies, Volume 1 (Long Papers)*, pages 809–819, New Orleans, Louisiana.

Johannes M van Hulst, Faegheh Hasibi, Koen Dercksen, Krisztian Balog, and Arjen P de Vries. 2020. Rel: An entity linker standing on the shoulders of giants. In *Proceedings of the 43rd International ACM SIGIR Conference on Research and Development in Information Retrieval*, pages 2197–2200.

Ashish Vaswani, Noam Shazeer, Niki Parmar, Jakob Uszkoreit, Llion Jones, Aidan N Gomez, Ł ukasz Kaiser, and Illia Polosukhin. 2017. Attention is all you need. In *Advances in Neural Information Processing Systems*, volume 30.

Andreas Vlachos and Sebastian Riedel. 2014. Fact checking: Task definition and dataset construction. In *Proceedings of the ACL 2014 Workshop on Language Technologies and Computational Social Science*, Baltimore, MD, USA.

Soroush Vosoughi, Deb Roy, and Sinan Aral. 2018. The spread of true and false news online. *Science*, 359(6380):1146–1151.

William Yang Wang. 2017. "liar, liar pants on fire": A new benchmark dataset for fake news detection. In *Proceedings of the 55th Annual Meeting of the Association for Computational Linguistics (Volume 2: Short Papers)*, pages 422–426, Vancouver, Canada. Association for Computational Linguistics.

Xiaoyan Wang, Pavan Kapanipathi, Ryan Musa, Mo Yu, Kartik Talamadupula, Ibrahim Abdelaziz, Maria Chang, Achille Fokoue, Bassem Makni, Nicholas Mattei, et al. 2019. Improving natural language inference using external knowledge in the science questions domain. In *Proceedings of the AAAI Conference on Artificial Intelligence*, volume 33.

Thomas Wolf, Lysandre Debut, Victor Sanh, Julien Chaumond, Clement Delangue, Anthony Moi, Pierric Cistac, Tim Rault, Remi Louf, Morgan Funtowicz, Joe Davison, Sam Shleifer, Patrick von Platen, Clara Ma, Yacine Jernite, Julien Plu, Canwen Xu, Teven Le Scao, Sylvain Gugger, Mariama Drame, Quentin Lhoest, and Alexander Rush. 2020. Transformers: State-of-the-art natural language processing. In *Proceedings of the 2020 Conference on Empirical Methods in Natural Language Processing: System Demonstrations*, pages 38–45, Online.

Zhilin Yang, Zihang Dai, Yiming Yang, Jaime Carbonell, Russ R Salakhutdinov, and Quoc V Le. 2019. Xlnet: Generalized autoregressive pretraining for language understanding. In *Advances in neural information processing systems*, pages 5753–5763.

Wenpeng Yin and Dan Roth. 2018. TwoWingOS: A two-wing optimization strategy for evidential claim verification. In *Proceedings of the 2018 Conference on Empirical Methods in Natural Language Processing*, pages 105–114, Brussels, Belgium.

Takuma Yoneda, Jeff Mitchell, Johannes Welbl, Pontus Stenetorp, and Sebastian Riedel. 2018. Ucl machine reading group: Four factor framework for fact finding (hexaf). In *Proceedings of the First Workshop on Fact Extraction and VERification (FEVER)*, pages 97–102, Brussels, Belgium.

Wanjun Zhong, Jingjing Xu, Duyu Tang, Zenan Xu, Nan Duan, Ming Zhou, Jiahai Wang, and Jian Yin. 2020. Reasoning over semantic-level graph for fact checking. In *Proceedings of the 58th Annual Meeting of the Association for Computational Linguistics*, pages 6170–6180, Online.

Jie Zhou, Xu Han, Cheng Yang, Zhiyuan Liu, Lifeng Wang, Changcheng Li, and Maosong Sun. 2019. GEAR: Graph-based evidence aggregating and reasoning for fact verification. In *Proceedings of the 57th Annual Meeting of the Association for Computational Linguistics*, pages 892–901, Florence, Italy.

Verdict Inference with Claim and Retrieved Elements Using RoBERTa

In-Zu Gi[†] **Ting-Yu Fang**[†] **Richard Tzong-Han Tsai**[†‡*]

[†]Department of Computer Science and Information Engineering,
National Central University, Taiwan

[‡]Center for GIS, Research Center for Humanities and Social Sciences,
Academia Sinica, Taiwan

{inzugi0910, maple3142, thtsai}@g.ncu.edu.tw

Abstract

Automatic fact verification has attracted recent research attention as the increasing dissemination of disinformation on social media platforms. The FEVEROUS shared task introduces a benchmark for fact verification, in which a system is challenged to verify the given claim using the extracted evidential elements from Wikipedia documents. In this paper, we propose our 3rd place three-stage system consisting of document retrieval, element retrieval, and verdict inference for the FEVEROUS shared task. By considering the context relevance in the fact extraction and verification task, our system achieves 0.29 FEVEROUS score on the development set and 0.25 FEVEROUS score on the blind test set, both outperforming the FEVEROUS baseline.

1 Introduction

The large-scale dissemination of disinformation on social media platforms intended to mislead or deceive the general population has become a major societal problem (Tan et al., 2020). For example, the widespread disinformation of the Covid-19 vaccine has caused a growth of anti-vaccination sentiment online and led to declining vaccination coverage. As the best way to stop disinformation from going viral online is early verification, recent researchers have put efforts into automatic fact verification systems.

To answer the increasing demand for such systems, the FEVER (Fact Extraction and VERification) dataset (Thorne et al., 2018) was introduced and used for the shared task of the FEVER Workshop 2018. It consists of 185,445 annotated claims with a label of "SUPPORTED", "REFUTED", or "NOT ENOUGH INFO" as well as sets of evidential sentences from the given pre-processed Wikipedia pages. Among the participated teams of the shared task, Nie et al. (2019) proposed a system consisting of three connected homogeneous networks of document retrieval, sentence selection, and claim verification. Yoneda et al. (2018) proposed a four-stage system that utilizes logistic regression models for the document retrieval and sentence retrieval stages, Enhanced Sequential Inference Model (ESIM) (Chen et al., 2017) for the natural language inference stage, and Multi-Layer Perceptron (MLP) for the aggregation stage.

To explore the ability of automatic fact verification systems over both unstructured sentences and structured table-based information, Aly et al. (2021) introduces the Fact Extraction and VERification Over Unstructured and Structured information (FEVEROUS) dataset. The shared task in 2021 uses the FEVEROUS dataset and further requires a system to be able to retrieve structured information from Wikipedia as evidence for each claim, which differs from the shared task in 2018. However, these two shared tasks still share the similar setting as a fact extraction and verification problem, which makes the pipelines and methods of the early proposed systems worth referring to. All in all, the FEVEROUS shared task in 2021 challenges a system to extract evidential elements, primarily sentences and table cells, from the given 5.4M Wikipedia documents and verify as "SUPPORTS", "REFUTES", or "NOT ENOUGH INFO" for each given claim. Systems are evaluated by jointly considering how complete the relevant Wikipedia elements are retrieved and how correct the final verification verdicts are.

In this paper, we propose a three-stage system as Figure 1 shows to improve the FEVEROUS baseline in two aspects. First, while the baseline retriever pays attention to literal relevance and word frequency with a combination method of entity matching and TF-IDF, we fine-tune the BERT model (Devlin et al., 2019) to integrate the con-

* Corresponding author.

Proceedings of the Fourth Workshop on Fact Extraction and VERification (FEVER) at EMNLP 2021, pages 60–65
November 10, 2021.

text relevance for finding evidential elements and downstream verdict inference. Second, the baseline predictor uses the claim and the concatenation of retrieved elements as input, having a constraint of the maximum input length. We experiment with several ways to include more elements for verdict inference. Finally, these improvements allow us to achieve substantially higher performance than the baseline.

2 System Description

Our system is a three-stage model consisting of document retrieval, element retrieval, and verdict inference. Document retrieval aims to extract the selection of the most related Wikipedia documents when only given the claim. The claim and the set of candidate elements from the most related Wikipedia documents are then given to the subsequent element retrieval to find out the most evidential elements regarding the claim. The final stage utilizes the NLI model for verdict inference, predicting the final verdict based on the most evidential elements and the claim.

2.1 Document Retrieval

Document retrieval is to extract the most related documents from 5.4M Wikipedia documents when only given the claim. A Wikipedia document is determined as related by checking if any element from the Wikipedia document is included as evidential elements for the given claim.

Our document retrieval utilizes Anserini (Yang et al., 2018), an information retrieval toolkit built on Lucene and providing an easy-to-use interface for querying. Experiments have shown that Anserini is efficient in indexing large document collections and provides modern ranking methods that are on par with research requirements.

Based on the observation that the claim often includes the title and the introductory section of the related Wikipedia document, we take the title and the first 10 elements of each Wikipedia document, normalize them by removing the links, and then build the indices of our Wikipedia document collection. We then use our Anserini to query each claim with the indices we built and retrieve k Wikipedia documents most related to the claim as well as their relatedness scores.

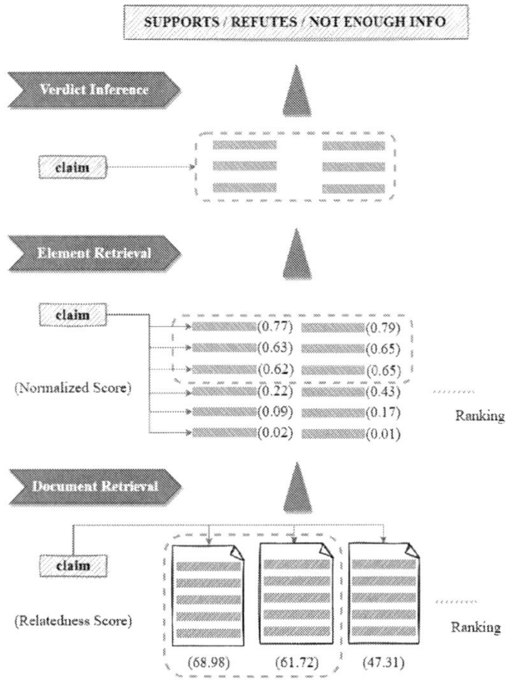

Figure 1: System Overview: Document Retrieval, Element Retrieval, and Verdict Inference.

2.2 Element Retrieval

For element retrieval, we experiment with two different approaches, the Anserini and the BERT model, to select relevant elements from documents retrieved in the previous stage. Both methods require every element to be a sequence input, including the table elements. We apply two techniques to linearize the table elements. One is converting each cell element to a sequence format of "[Header] is [Cell]." (Oguz et al., 2021), and the other is prepending the Wikipedia document title of the element in front of the converted sequence. Take the evidential cell element "Travis Hafner" as an example, we first convert it as a sequence "Player is Travis Hafner.", and then prepend the title to the sequence as "2005 Cleveland Indians season Player is Travis Hafner.".

For our Anserini in the element retrieval stage, we use every element in the entire Wikipedia documents to build the indices of another Wikipedia elements collection. Due to the mechanism of the Anserini, we first retrieve l top related Wikipedia elements when only given the claim, and apply a filter of k most related documents to utilize the benefits of the document retrieval stage and obtain the finally retrieved m elements. The afterward filter leads to the different numbers of finally retrieved m elements for each claim. To improve the performance, we separate the retrieval procedure for sentences and tables by building another two separated collections.

For the second approach experimented in the element retrieval stage, we fine-tune the BERT model as a binary classification with the ground truth elements as positive and the other elements as negative from the k most related Wikipedia documents retrieved by our Anserini in the document retrieval stage. Our BERT model takes the concatenation of the claim and the element sequence as input, and we use the output prediction to calculate the normalized relatedness scores. We rank the elements according to the normalized relatedness scores and select m Wikipedia elements top related to the claim. The normalized relatedness score between the claim c_i and the j-th element is computed as:

$$p(x = 1|c_i, j) = \frac{e^{p^+}}{e^{p^+} + e^{p^-}}$$

where $x \in \{0, 1\}$ indicates whether the j-th element is positive or negative, p^+ is the prediction scores for positive, p^- is the prediction scores for negative, and $p(x = 1|c_i, j)$ is the normalized score for p^+.

Our BERT model uses the Adam optimizer (Kingma and Ba, 2015) with a learning rate of $1e^{-5}$, a batch size of 16, and 1 training epochs due to the time constraint.

2.3 Verdict Inference

On the third stage of the FEVEROUS shared task, NLI is a task that matches the scenario of classifying the semantic relationship between the claim and the retrieved elements as "SUPPORTS", "REFUTES", or "NOT ENOUGH INFO" (NEI). Therefore, we adopt the RoBERTa (Liu et al., 2019) NLI model pre-trained on well-known NLI datasets, including SNLI, MNLI, FEVER-NLI, ANLI (Nie et al., 2020), and experiment on its variants with aggregation method on top of it to fully utilize the semantic information of retrieved elements in the previous stage.

For simplicity, we name our RoBERTa NLI model without aggregation as **RoBERTa**, RoBERTa NLI model with logical aggregation as **RoBERTa-LOG**, and RoBERTa NLI model with MLP for aggregation as **RoBERTa-MLP**. Both aggregation methods have been proved effective in Yoneda et al. (2018). Our RoBERTa takes the claim and the concatenation of all retrieved elements as input, while our RoBERTa-LOG and RoBERTa-MLP take the claim and each retrieved element as input.

Method	k	Recall
Baseline	5	0.69
Our Anserini	5	0.69
	10	0.73

Table 1: Recall is calculated by the frequency of the ground truth document occurrence in the retrieved documents. **k** indicates the number of retrieved documents.

The RoBERTa NLI models are fine-tuned with ground truth labels in FEVEROUS training set and additionally sampled NEI instances to get rid of the unbalanced labeling problem. We use the adam optimizer with a learning rate of $1e^{-6}$, a batch size of 8, a scheduler to watch on the development loss, and a total of 7 training epochs. Our RoBERTa-LOG simply merges the NLI predictions and outputs the label obtaining the highest point. For our RoBERTa-MLP, our MLP containing two fully connected layers and ReLU is trained jointly with the RoBERTa NLI models.

3 Results

3.1 Document Retrieval Results

To evaluate the performance of the document retrieval, we measure the recall metric and the results are shown in Table 1. Our document retriever achieves a document coverage of 69% when retrieving the top 5 documents and 73% when retrieving the top 10 documents. When deciding the value of k, it is a trade-off between retrieval performance and computational resources. As a result, we set $k = 5$ for the downstream element retrieval using the BERT model and at the same time experiment with different settings for the downstream element retrieval using the Anserini.

3.2 Element Retrieval Results

Table 2 shows the development set results using our Anserini. The retriever of $l = 5000$ with prepending achieves better performance than the retrievers without prepending. From the results, we observe that prepending title improves recall performance. Nevertheless, to meet the submission requirement of at most 5 sentences and 25 cells for each claim, the averagely obtained 58 elements require further

l	Prepend	k	avg-m	Recall
5000	-	5	24.4	0.35
50000	-	5	41.5	0.40
5000	✓	10	58	0.55
1000 (s)	✓	10	4.9	0.50
5000 (c)	✓	20	19.9	0.43

Table 2: Recall is calculated on an element level with our Anserini. **l** indicates the number of retrieved elements by our Anserini. (s) and (c) indicate separated retrieval for sentence and cells respectively. **Prepend** indicates whether the title is prepended to the linearized element sequence. **k** indicates the number of retrieved documents used to filter the elements. **avg-m** indicates the averagely retrieved m elements eventually after the filter of k most related documents on l elements.

Prepend	m	Sentence	Table	Overall
-	40	0.73	0.16	0.37
✓	40	0.71	0.52	0.59

Table 3: Coverage for sentence, table, and overall performance with our BERT using the 5 most related Wikipedia documents retrieved by our Anserini in the document retrieval stage. **m** indicates the number of retrieved elements. **Prepend** indicates whether the title is prepended to the linearized element sequence.

control on retrieved numbers of each element type. Experiments show that different combinations of l and k as well as separating the retrieval for sentences and tables respectively achieve comparable performance to the retriever of $l = 5000$ with prepending and provide better supervision of the number and type of the retrieved elements.

Table 3 shows the development set results using our BERT. We observe similar results with our Anserirni, which the retriever with prepending achieves better performance than the retrievers without prepending.

We use our Anserini of $l = 5000$ with prepending and our BERT with prepending to have a relatively fair comparison between our two approaches for element retrieval. Our Anserini of $l = 5000$ with prepending covers 55% of all elements, while our BERT with prepending covers 59%, showing our BERT substantially outperforms our Anserini.

3.3 Verdict Inference Results

Table 4 shows the development set results of our models trained on a training subset. We observe that the RoBERTa-LOG reaches 0.52 F_1 score and the RoBERTa-MLP reaches 0.22 F_1 score, both

Model	S	R	NEI	Overall
Baseline	0.88	0.85	0.30	0.67
RoBERTa	0.88	0.84	0.35	0.69
RoBERTa-LOG	0.74	0.68	0.14	0.52
RoBERTa-MLP	0.66	0.00	0.00	0.22

Table 4: Performance of different verdict inference methods trained on a training subset. Scores are reported on the development set in per-class F_1, with **S** represents "SUPPORTS", **R** represents "REFUTES", and **NEI** represents "NOT ENOUGH INFO". The overall score is reported using macro-averaged F_1.

are much lower than the RoBERTa. This indicates that, while each claim in the development set only requires an average of 4.6 elements to reach the golden truth label according to our analysis, it is inappropriate for our RoBERTa-LOG and RoBERTa-MLP to take all thirty elements evenly for each claim. Therefore, we choose to use our RoBERTa and simplify the input by removing potentially repeated words to allow more elements included for verdict inference.

We also test the performance of our RoBERTa with different element retrieval methods using the FEVEROUS scorer as shown in Table 5. The performance of evidence is reported with a restriction of at most 5 sentences and 25 cells as the FEVEROUS scorer limits. We observe that the quality of the upstream data is crucial to the performance of the downstream task, as our RoBERTa taking the elements from our Anserini and BERT reach 0.58 and 0.60 accuracy, respectively. Experiments also show that our RoBERTa taking the elements from our BERT is more robust than our Anserini with improvements in evidence precision, recall, and F_1 score. Our RoBERTa taking the elements from our BERT also outperforms the baseline with 0.1 improvements on FEVEROUS score.

According to our observation of the performance on all three stages, we decide our final system as the combination of our Anserini for document retrieval, our BERT for element retrieval, and our RoBERTa for verdict inference. The results of the blind test of our final system are presented in Table 6. Our final system is proved robust and outperforms the FEVEROUS baseline.

4 Error Analysis

Our system proves that performing document retrieval, element retrieval and verdict inference in the three-phase procedure is a proper pipeline for

System	FEVEROUS	Accuracy	Evidence Precision	Recall	F_1
Baseline	0.19	0.53	0.12	0.30	0.17
Ground Truth+RoBERTa	0.84	0.84	1.00	0.99	0.99
Anserini+Anserini+RoBERTa	0.22	0.58	0.09	0.32	0.14
Anserini+BERT+RoBERTa	0.29	0.60	0.10	0.42	0.17

Table 5: Performance of different element retrieval methods using our RoBERTa. Scores are reported on the development set using the FEVEROUS scorer. The Anserini uses $l = 5000$ with prepending and a filter of $k = 10$ documents. The BERT uses $k = 5$ documents retrieved from the previous stage and utilizes prepending for element retrieval.

System	FEVEROUS	Accuracy	Evidence Precision	Recall	F_1
Baseline	0.1773	0.4548	0.1017	0.2878	0.1503
Anserini+Anserini+RoBERTa	0.2215	0.5108	0.0810	0.3414	0.1310
Anserini+BERT+RoBERTa (final)	**0.2514**	**0.5229**	0.0991	0.3907	0.1581

Table 6: Performance of systems on blind test results. Our final system is Anserini for document retrieval with $k = 5$, BERT for element retrieval with prepending, and RoBERTa for verdict inference. The candidate system is Anserini for both document and separated retrieval of different element types as well as RoBERTa for verdict inference.

the fact extraction and verification shared task. For evidence retrieval (document and element retrieval), our proposed methods of the BM25-based Anserini and the context-aware BERT model considers both the presence of certain keywords and semantic context. Hence, it is able to extract related elements over unstructured sentences and structured table cells.

Nevertheless, the retrieval performance still has room for improvement in two aspects. One is to tune the balance weighting between the presence of certain keywords and the semantic context. The other is to attentively design the fine-tuning of the BERT model for element retrieval. During the fine-tuning process, we use the output from the document retrieval stage and set as negative labels for all elements from the 5 most related documents that are not annotated as evidence of the corresponding claim. While each claim has only a maximum of 3 evidence sets and an average of nearly 4 elements per set, our BERT model suffers from the unbalanced labeling problem, in which the process includes massive negative and few positive instances. The positive instances in the fine-tuning are also rather few because we use the output of the document retrieval stage that only retrieves a document coverage of 69%.

5 Conclusion

We describe our 3rd place system for the FEVEROUS shared task via the three-stage setup of document retrieval, element retrieval, and verdict inference. By considering the context relevance in the fact extraction and verification task, our system achieves 0.29 FEVEROUS score on the development set and 0.25 FEVEROUS score on the blind test set, both outperforming the FEVEROUS baseline.

References

Rami Aly, Zhijiang Guo, Michael Sejr Schlichtkrull, James Thorne, Andreas Vlachos, Christos Christodoulopoulos, Oana Cocarascu, and Arpit Mittal. 2021. FEVEROUS: fact extraction and verification over unstructured and structured information. *CoRR*, abs/2106.05707.

Qian Chen, Xiaodan Zhu, Zhen-Hua Ling, Si Wei, Hui Jiang, and Diana Inkpen. 2017. Enhanced lstm for natural language inference. *Proceedings of the 55th Annual Meeting of the Association for Computational Linguistics (Volume 1: Long Papers)*.

Jacob Devlin, Ming-Wei Chang, Kenton Lee, and Kristina Toutanova. 2019. BERT: pre-training of deep bidirectional transformers for language understanding. In *Proceedings of the 2019 Conference of the North American Chapter of the Association for Computational Linguistics: Human Language Technologies, NAACL-HLT 2019, Minneapolis, MN,*

USA, June 2-7, 2019, Volume 1 (Long and Short Papers), pages 4171–4186. Association for Computational Linguistics.

Diederik P. Kingma and Jimmy Ba. 2015. Adam: A method for stochastic optimization. In *3rd International Conference on Learning Representations, ICLR 2015, San Diego, CA, USA, May 7-9, 2015, Conference Track Proceedings*.

Yinhan Liu, Myle Ott, Naman Goyal, Jingfei Du, Mandar Joshi, Danqi Chen, Omer Levy, Mike Lewis, Luke Zettlemoyer, and Veselin Stoyanov. 2019. Roberta: A robustly optimized BERT pretraining approach. *CoRR*, abs/1907.11692.

Yixin Nie, Haonan Chen, and Mohit Bansal. 2019. Combining fact extraction and verification with neural semantic matching networks. In *The Thirty-Third AAAI Conference on Artificial Intelligence, AAAI 2019, The Thirty-First Innovative Applications of Artificial Intelligence Conference, IAAI 2019, The Ninth AAAI Symposium on Educational Advances in Artificial Intelligence, EAAI 2019, Honolulu, Hawaii, USA, January 27 - February 1, 2019*, pages 6859–6866. AAAI Press.

Yixin Nie, Adina Williams, Emily Dinan, Mohit Bansal, Jason Weston, and Douwe Kiela. 2020. Adversarial NLI: A new benchmark for natural language understanding. In *Proceedings of the 58th Annual Meeting of the Association for Computational Linguistics*. Association for Computational Linguistics.

Barlas Oguz, Xilun Chen, Vladimir Karpukhin, Stan Peshterliev, Dmytro Okhonko, Michael Schlichtkrull, Sonal Gupta, Yashar Mehdad, and Scott Yih. 2021. Unik-qa: Unified representations of structured and unstructured knowledge for open-domain question answering.

Reuben Tan, Bryan Plummer, and Kate Saenko. 2020. Detecting cross-modal inconsistency to defend against neural fake news. In *Proceedings of the 2020 Conference on Empirical Methods in Natural Language Processing (EMNLP)*, pages 2081–2106, Online. Association for Computational Linguistics.

James Thorne, Andreas Vlachos, Christos Christodoulopoulos, and Arpit Mittal. 2018. FEVER: a large-scale dataset for fact extraction and verification. In *Proceedings of the 2018 Conference of the North American Chapter of the Association for Computational Linguistics: Human Language Technologies, NAACL-HLT 2018, New Orleans, Louisiana, USA, June 1-6, 2018, Volume 1 (Long Papers)*, pages 809–819. Association for Computational Linguistics.

Peilin Yang, Hui Fang, and Jimmy Lin. 2018. Anserini: Reproducible ranking baselines using lucene. *ACM J. Data Inf. Qual.*, 10(4):16:1–16:20.

Takuma Yoneda, Jeff Mitchell, Johannes Welbl, Pontus Stenetorp, and Sebastian Riedel. 2018. UCL machine reading group: Four factor framework for fact finding (HexaF). In *Proceedings of the First Workshop on Fact Extraction and VERification (FEVER)*, pages 97–102, Brussels, Belgium. Association for Computational Linguistics.

Stance Detection in German News Articles

Laura Mascarell[1*] Tatyana Ruzsics[1*] Christian Schneebeli[1*]
Philippe Schlattner[1*] Luca Campanella[1*] Severin Klingler[1] Cristina Kadar[2]

[1] ETH Zurich, [2] Neue Zürcher Zeitung

{lmascarell,tatiana.ruzsics,christian.schneebeli,philippe.schlattner,
luca.campanella,severin.klingler}@inf.ethz.ch, cristina.kadar@nzz.ch

Abstract

The widespread use of the Internet and the rapid dissemination of information poses the challenge of identifying the veracity of its content. Stance detection, which is the task of predicting the position of a text in regard to a specific target (e.g. claim or debate question), has been used to determine the veracity of information in tasks such as rumor classification and fake news detection (Küçük and Can, 2020). While most of the work and available datasets for stance detection address short texts snippets extracted from textual dialogues, social media platforms, or news headlines with a strong focus on the English language, there is a lack of resources targeting long texts in other languages. Our contribution in this paper is twofold. First, we present a German dataset of debate questions and news articles that is manually annotated for stance and emotion detection. Second, we leverage the dataset to tackle the supervised task of classifying the stance of a news article with regards to a debate question and provide baseline models as a reference for future work on stance detection in German news articles.

1 Introduction

The automatic extraction and analysis of information from text is an important area in natural language processing that tackles a wide range of research problems such as sentiment analysis, veracity and rumor detection, emotion recognition, or fake news detection. With the rapid increase in online content and spread of misinformation, these research topics have gained attention, as it becomes crucial to identify the veracity of the information.

Stance detection is the task of predicting the position of a text (e.g. in favor or against) towards a specific target, which has shown to aid at identifying the veracity of rumors (rumor classification) and fake news (Küçük and Can, 2020). As most of the stance detection benchmarks focus on short text snippets, especially tweets, and/or English (Mohammad et al., 2016a,b; Hanselowski et al., 2018), there is a lack of annotated data to address stance detection in longer texts and in other languages.

In this paper, we present the CHeeSE dataset, a collection of manually annotated Swiss (**CH**) news articles and debate questions in German for **S**tance and **E**motion detection. Specifically, the CHeeSE dataset comprises 91 debate questions that are automatically paired with related news articles, resulting in a total of $3,693$ question and article pairs. A team of native German speakers manually annotated those pairs with the stance of the article towards the debate question, the article emotion, and the emotion of each individual paragraph. Table 1 shows an illustrative example in English of the annotations for a given question and article.

To the best of our knowledge, this is the first available dataset of German news articles annotated for this purpose. While the Fake News Challenge[1] provides document-level stance annotations for English news articles (Hanselowski et al., 2018), other datasets that consider the German language focus on shorter texts (Vamvas and Sennrich, 2020).

Finally, we perform target-specific stance detection as a supervised task using our annotated data. We then build baseline models as a reference in future work on stance detection in German news articles. Since the dataset provides both stance and emotion annotations, future work could assess the use of emotion information to improve stance detection in a multi-task setting (see discussion in Section 5). Moreover, computational journalism applications, such as news recommender systems, could leverage the dataset to mitigate the selective exposure of one-sided articles (Gao et al., 2018).

The CHeeSE dataset and the code to reproduce the baseline models are publicly available.[2]

*Equal contribution

[1] http://www.fakenewschallenge.org

[2] https://github.com/MTC-ETH/CHeeSE

Proceedings of the Fourth Workshop on Fact Extraction and VERification (FEVER) at EMNLP 2021, pages 66–77
November 10, 2021. ©2021 Association for Computational Linguistics

	Example Content	Paragraph Emotion
Question	Should the Corona measures be more strict?	
Article Title	Corona measures insufficient	
Article Text	<p>It looks bad. The number of daily cases is increasing since weeks. There is no improvement in sight.</p>	Sadness
	<p>Again, the parliament failed to respond accordingly.</p>	Anger
	<p>Yet, our health system is still stable. Let us hope for the best.</p>	Trust
Article Emotion	Sadness	
Article Stance	In Favour	

Table 1: Illustrative example in English of the provided annotations for each article and question pairs in the CHeeSE dataset: the article's stance towards the question, the article's emotion and the emotion of each paragraph.

2 Related Work

Most of the available annotated datasets for stance detection focus on short texts such as tweets. The SemEval-2016 shared task hosts a dataset of annotated English tweets and their stance towards the targets 'Atheism', 'Climate Change', 'Feminism', 'Hillary Clinton', and 'Abortion' (Mohammad et al., 2016a). Aside from English, there are available tweets datasets for Catalan and Spanish (Zotova et al., 2020), French (Lai et al., 2020), or Italian (Cignarella et al., 2020). For German, the multilingual dataset X-stance offers a collection of political questions and their corresponding comments written by candidates of elections, partly in German, partly in French and Italian (Vamvas and Sennrich, 2020).

In the journalistic domain, there are two available datasets of English news articles. The Emergent dataset is a collection of claims and their associated news articles (Ferreira and Vlachos, 2016). Similarly, the Fake News Challange detection task (FNC-1) offers a dataset of news articles and their stance towards a headline (Hanselowski et al., 2018). While the Emergent dataset performs the stance detection task on single-sentence headlines towards a specific claim, the FNC-1 is a document-level stance detection task that considers the entire news article. In our dataset, we also address stance detection at document level, but in German text.

Emotion detection datasets are also mostly concerned with short text snippets, such as tweets (Mohammad et al., 2018), news headlines (Strapparava and Mihalcea, 2007), textual dialogues (Chatterjee et al., 2019), or sentences in fairy tales (Volkova et al., 2010). In contrast, our dataset offers article- and paragraph-level annotations for emotion detection in German news articles. Paragraph-level annotations could be leveraged to identify and analyse patterns of emotion sequences (i.e. emotion flow) in news articles. While emotion flow has been explored in books (Maharjan et al., 2018) and movie synopsis (Kar et al., 2018), such analysis has not yet been applied to journalistic content.

To improve stance detection, some research approaches focus on using sentiment information, and more specifically, the polarity of the text (i.e. positive, negative, or neutral). In fact, the annual workshop on Semantic Evaluation (SemEval) organised a stance detection shared task and provided a dataset of tweets also annotated with sentiment information (Mohammad et al., 2016a).[3] However, the conclusions on whether sentiment information aids at improving stance detection are mixed. Some studies report the benefits of using such information (Li and Caragea, 2019; Sun et al., 2019), whereas others claim that the tasks are independent of each other. For example, a text with a positive sentiment could show an opposing stance towards a specific claim (Mohammad et al., 2017; Aldayel and Magdy, 2019; Sobhani et al., 2016).

3 The CHeeSE Dataset

The CHeeSE dataset is a collection of 3,693 pairs of debate questions and Swiss news articles in German that are manually annotated for stance and emotion detection. Specifically, the dataset comprises a total of 1,970 different articles paired with up to six questions (~1.87 on average) from a list of 91 questions that we manually compiled to ensure a variety of debate topics (Section 3.1).

The data comes from ~670k news articles provided by the Swiss media companies *Blick* (~536k articles),[4] *Neue Zürcher Zeitung* (~125k articles),[5] and *NZZ am Sonntag* (~9k articles).[6] The articles

[3] http://alt.qcri.org/semeval2016/task6/
[4] https://www.blick.ch
[5] https://www.nzz.ch
[6] https://nzzas.nzz.ch/

Negative Example	Issue	Preferred Formulation
Should legislation on environmental protection be relaxed to allow for the building and expansion of wind farms, solar power stations, and hydroelectric plants?	Topic too specific	Should state laws counteract climate change?
Should Saddam Hussein be executed?	Time and topic too specific	Should death penalty be legal?
Should Swiss law be changed to follow EU more restrictive firearms law?	Multiple topics	Should the firearm laws be stricter?
First case of transmission of Sars-CoV-2 identified in the uterus	News, no debate	–

Table 2: Negative examples in English of target questions and their preferred formulation.

Topic	Debate Question	Keyword Examples
Freizeit [Leisure]	Soll die Jagd als Freizeittätigkeit verboten werden? [Should hunting be banned as a leisure activity?]	Jagd, Tiere, Tierartenschutz [hunting, animals, species protection]
Digitalisierung [Digitalisation]	Verstärkt KI Vorurteile und Bias? [Does AI reinforce prejudices and bias?]	Künstliche Intelligenz, Vorurteile, Sexismus [Artificial intelligence, prejudice, sexism]
Gesellschaft [Society]	Sind Abtreibungen moralisch vertretbar? [Are abortions morally acceptable?]	Geburt, Abtreibung, Fötus [birth, abortion, fetus]
Gesellschaft [Society]	Soll die Adoption für alle ermöglicht werden? [Should adoption be possible for all?]	Adoption, Privatrecht, Gleichberechtigung [adoption, private law, equality]

Table 3: Examples of the selected debate questions to build the CHeeSE dataset and their assigned keywords.

were published between 2004 and 2020 and cover a set of 24 topics, such as science, environment, politics, religion, or society.

In this section, we describe the steps involved in the construction of the CHeeSE dataset. First, we compile a list of debate questions (Section 3.1) that we automatically pair with related articles using a two-pass ranking approach (see Section 3.2). Then, a team of native German speakers annotate the collected data with emotion and stance labels (Section 3.3). Finally, we apply a semi-automatic method to balance the stance label distribution of questions without articles in favor or against in the annotated dataset (Section 3.4).

3.1 Question Selection

We generate a list of debate questions that we later pair with news articles for the stance detection task. To do so, we organise a brainstorming session with a team of 12 participants of various backgrounds in the news media industry (e.g. journalists or data scientists). To ensure that the generated questions comprise a wide range of topics as per the IPTC topic taxonomy[7] (e.g. politics, environment, or sport), we divide the session in four iterations and four groups, where each group concerns a different set of topics. In each iteration, we rotate the group members. As a reference, the participants receive a list of controversial issues from Wikipedia[8] and the ProCon debate platform[9] and a list of negative examples with their preferred formulations (see Table 2). The participants also assign a list of keywords to each debate question as additional data to represent the questions in the stance detection task. For example, a suitable list of keywords for the English question 'should hunting be banned as a leisure activity' is 'hunting', 'animals', and 'species protection'. At the end of the session, the participants generated a total of 125 questions with their corresponding keywords. We further filter the list and eliminate duplicates or similar questions, resulting in a final list of 91 debate questions (see examples in Table 3).

3.2 Question-Article Pairs Collection

To provide a relevant dataset for the stance detection task, we focus on collecting question and article pairs that are related. That is, the article is likely to show a stance (in favor, against, or discussing) with respect to the associated question. To do so, we implement a two-pass ranking approach that re-

[7]https://iptc.org/standards/newscodes

[8]https://en.wikipedia.org/wiki/Wikipedia:List_of_controversial_issues

[9]https://www.procon.org

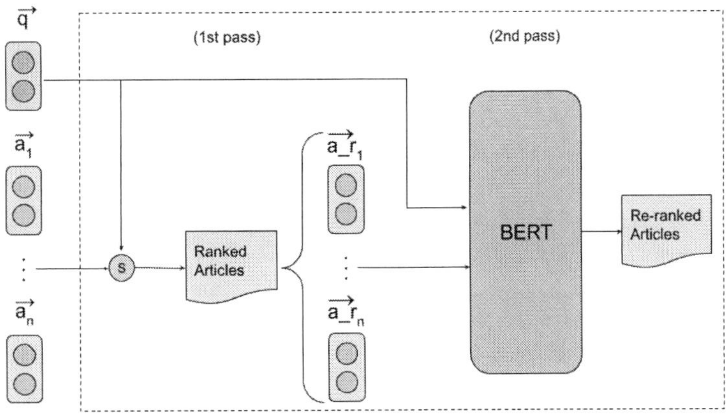

Figure 1: Two-pass ranking approach to collect related question and article pairs. For a given question and a set of news articles, in the first pass, our approach ranks the articles based on the cosine similarity scores of their tf-idf embeddings. In the second pass, it re-ranks the articles using a pre-trained German BERT model, selecting those above the probability threshold 0.75.

sembles the text ranking method used in Nogueira and Cho (2020).[10] Figure 1 illustrates our approach for a given question and the set of news articles.

The method works as follows. For each of the selected questions in section 3.1, we use our two-pass ranking approach to identify its related articles. Specifically, in the first pass, we rank the articles based on the cosine similarity scores of the tf-idf embeddings of the question and each article. Here, we represent a question as the string concatenation of the question itself and the set of its assigned keywords (see Section 3.1) and an article as the concatenation of its title and body.

In the second pass, we score and re-rank the articles according to their probability of having any stance towards the debate question (i.e. the article is in favour, against, or discussing it). As a re-ranker, we use German BERT (Devlin et al., 2019),[11] a general purpose natural language processing model for German text that we fine-tune on our re-ranking task as in Nogueira and Cho (2020).

The fine-tuning data is a set of 275 question and article pairs that we manually annotated as 'related', if the article has any stance with respect to the question, or 'unrelated', otherwise. To obtain those pairs, we first selected 11 questions from different topics through stratified sampling. For each question, we then applied the first pass of our ranking approach to rank the articles based on the cosine similarity of their tf-idf embeddings, and kept the 25 most similar articles. Note that these pairs are only used for fine-tuning and they are not part of the final CHeeSE dataset. We fine-tune the BERT model on this data for three epochs and a learning rate of 3e-05.

The BERT architecture requires a token sequence as an input. To represent a given question and article as such input sequence, we follow the method described in Devlin et al. (2019). We concatenate a question-article pair with the special token `[SEP]` and insert the special classification token `[CLS]` at the beginning of the sequence, which aggregates the features from both question and article. We truncate the input to the maximum length of 512 tokens that BERT supports.

After re-ranking the articles with BERT, we keep the highest-confidence matches. To obtain a threshold, we apply 10-fold cross-validation on the fine-tuning data. The resulting threshold of 0.75 is the average cutoff value of $(tpr + \frac{1}{fpr})/2$, where tpr and fpr are the true and false positive rates, respectively, under the ROC curve.

Our two-pass ranking approach results in a dataset of $2,096$ question and article pairs. Each article is associated with up to two questions.

Dataset extension Since manual annotations are expensive and time-consuming, we extend the collected dataset keeping in mind the annotation efforts. Articles are longer texts than questions, therefore, it is easier to annotate a new question-article pair, where only the question is new to the annota-

[10] We refer to Yates et al. (2021) for a comprehensive overview of text ranking approaches.

[11] `https://huggingface.co/dbmdz/bert-base-german-uncased`

tor. Thus, we extend the dataset by pairing more questions with the collected articles.

To do so, for each collected article after the two-pass ranking approach, we rank all questions using the German BERT classifier as in the second pass. Here, we exclude those questions that were already paired with the article. As a result, we get $1,597$ additional pairs, increasing the number of questions per article from two to five.

In the final dataset, we distinguish between the data collected after the two-pass ranking approach and this additional data, labelling them as 'two-pass' and 'two-pass-ext', respectively.

3.3 Manual Annotation Task

We design a task to manually annotate the collected question and article pairs (Section 3.2). For each pair, the annotation task is twofold: (a) annotate the stance of the article towards the question; (b) annotate the emotions of the news article.

To perform this annotation task, we recruited a team of 23 native German speakers and used a crowd-sourcing labelling tool that was implemented for this purpose (see Appendix A). In particular, the annotators, 15 women and 8 men, are university students or academics between 21 and 49 and a median of 25 years old. To ensure that each crowd-worker understood the annotation task, we closely monitored them during the labelling of their first 50 articles and notified them if they did not follow the annotation instructions as intended.

Stance Annotation To label the stance of an article towards a question, we consider the German counterpart of the English 'in favor', 'against', 'discussion', and 'unrelated', where 'discussion' indicates that the article discusses the topic of the question without taking a position, as in the FNC-1 task (Hanselowski et al., 2018). Table 4 shows an example from the CHeeSE dataset of the different stances with regards to the question 'are gene manipulations morally justifiable?'. In this table, we represent the articles with their snippet for illustrative purposes only. Note that identifying a pair as 'unrelated' is harder in our dataset than in FNC-1. The reason is that the unrelated pairs in the FNC-1 dataset are randomly matched, whereas we collect all pairs using our ranking approach, ensuring that each pair is among the most related according to their tf-idf embeddings similarity and BERT classification scores (Section 3.2).

Formally, given an article a, a question q, and the set of German stance labels *Ja, dafür* ('in favour'), *Diskutierend* ('discussion'), *Nein, dagegen* ('against'), and *Kein Bezug* ('unrelated') $\{s_1, \ldots, s_4\}$, the task is to identify the article's a stance towards the question q,

$$\text{stance}(a,q) \quad \in \{s_1, \ldots s_4\}$$

During the annotation task, three different annotators label the stance of each question-article pair. This annotation process results in 86% of question-article pairs, where at least two annotators agree on the stance. We label the remaining pairs with no annotator agreement as the German *Unklar* ('unclear'). The final inter-rater agreement (IRA) and the Fleiss' κ coefficient of inter-rater reliability (Fleiss, 1971) are 0.52 and 0.33, respectively.

Emotion Annotation The annotation task is designed to identify the emotion that is mostly represented by the text. We consider a set of eight emotions, which are the German counterpart of the basic emotions defined in Plutchik (1980)'s model: *Freude* ('joy'), *Vertrauen* ('trust'), *Angst* ('fear'), *Antizipation* ('anticipation'), *Traurigkeit* ('sadness'), *Ekel* ('disgust'), *Ärger* ('anger'), and *Überraschung* ('surprise'). The 'no emotion' label is defined as the German *Keine*.

This is a challenging annotation task for two main reasons, which negatively impact the inter-rater agreement. First, there are eight different emotion labels to choose from. Second, the text can convey an in-between emotion, also referred as 'dyads' (Plutchik, 2001). For example, 'hope', which is considered a complex emotion, is a combination of 'anticipation' and 'trust'. Indeed, we observe this phenomenon, when manually analysing the most frequent disagreeing pairs of emotions (e.g. anticipation together with trust or anger).

To mitigate this issue, we extend the annotation task as follows. We encourage the annotation of one emotion per paragraph and article and, in case of doubt, the annotators assign the emotion that the text conveys the most as primary emotion and the rest as secondary emotions. Annotators could select multiple secondary emotions. On average, they selected 0.78 and 0.43 secondary emotions at article and paragraph level, respectively.

Formally, we define a primary emotion e_p for a given text t as one of the eight emotions labels $e_p(t) \in \{e_1, \ldots e_8\}$, and the set of secondary emotions e_s as the corresponding subset of labels $e_s(t) \subset \{e_1, \ldots e_8\}$. Given an article a, which is composed of a set of paragraphs $a = \{p_1, \ldots, p_n\}$, the task

	Sind Genmanupulationen moralisch vertretbar? [Are gene manipulations morally justifiable?]
Diskutierend [Discussion]	Ein Tabu fällt: Grossbritannien erlaubt es Forschern, die Gene von Embryos zu manipulieren. Die wichtigsten Fragen und Antworten. [A taboo has been lifted: The UK allows researchers to manipulate the genes of embryos. The most important questions and answers.]
Ja, dafür [In favour]	Mäuse, die mit dem Aidserreger infiziert sind, werden virusfrei. Diesen Erfolg haben Forscher mit Medikamenten und der Genschere Crispr/Cas erzielt. [Mice infected with the AIDS virus become virus-free. Researchers have achieved this success with drugs and the gene scissors Crispr/Cas.]
Nein, dagegen [Against]	Ein chinesischer Wissenschaftler verkündet die Geburt zweier genmanipulierter Babys. Das sorgt weltweit für Entsetzen. [A Chinese scientist announces the birth of two genetically engineered babies. This is causing worldwide horror.]
Kein Bezug [Unrelated]	Das Personal in Spitälern wird besser geschult, um zu verhindern, dass Patienten Medikamente in falscher Dosierung oder gar nicht erhalten. [Hospital staff will be better trained to prevent patients from receiving the wrong dose of medication or not receiving it at all.]

Table 4: Example from the CHeeSE dataset of the four different stance annotations 'Diskutierend', 'Ja, dafür', 'Nein, dagegen', and 'Kein Bezug' with regards to the same question. The table only contains the article's snippet.

consists of (1) identifying the primary overall article emotion and secondary emotions, if any, or 'no emotion' $\neg e$, otherwise; (2) identifying the primary and secondary emotions of each paragraph, if any, or 'no emotion', otherwise.

$$\text{emotion}(a) \in \{e_p(a), \{e_p(a)\} \cup e_s(a), \neg e\},$$
$$\text{emotion}(p_1) \in \{e_p(p_1), \{e_p(p_1)\} \cup e_s(p_1), \neg e\},$$
$$\ldots$$
$$\text{emotion}(p_n) \in \{e_p(p_n), \{e_p(p_n)\} \cup e_s(p_n), \neg e\}$$

As in the stance annotation task, three different annotators label each article and paragraph. The final list of confirmed labels are those primary labels with annotator agreement. That is, those primary emotion labels that are also used as primary or secondary emotion by a different annotator. This results in 84% of the articles and 78% of the paragraphs with at least one confirmed label. We compute the IRA according to this definition as follows. For every article, we check each combination of two annotators (i.e. three pairs for three annotators). For each pair of annotators, we count them as agreement (1) if the annotators agree on the primary emotion or the primary emotion of one of the annotators matches one of the secondary emotions of the other. Otherwise, we count them as disagreement (0). We then average over all annotator pairs of all articles. The IRA of the article and paragraph annotations are 0.50 and 0.42, respectively.[12] We then annotate the rest of the articles and paragraphs without agreement as *Unklar* ('unclear').

Overall, there are 76 question and article pairs in the CHeeSE dataset, where both stance and article emotion are annotated as *Unklar*. In contrast, there are 2,588 question-article pairs, where both stance and article emotion have a confirmed label.

3.4 Balancing the Stance Class Distribution

We observe that some of the questions from the annotated data have an imbalanced stance class distribution. In particular, 17 questions have no articles in favor and 40 have no articles against (see examples in Table 5). To balance the distribution, we perform a semi-automatic method to retrieve additional articles that have a positive and negative stance towards those questions.

Our semi-automatic method works as follows. For each of the imbalanced questions, we first search for related debates on discussion platforms where users can argument in favor or against different topics, such as DebateHub.net,[13] using the question itself or the list of defined keywords (Section 3.1). Next, we group the arguments for each stance, resulting in two texts, one with arguments in favor t_{for} and another with arguments against t_{agt}. Assuming that texts sharing the same position have similar embeddings, we use their embeddings to retrieve similar articles from our data (i.e. articles that share the same stance). Specifically, we obtain the embeddings of t_{for} and t_{agt} and, for each embedding, we rank our articles based on their cosine similarity. Since our data and the arguments are in

[12] The IRA values include the articles labelled after balancing the stance class distribution (Section 3.4)

[13] https://debatehub.net

Question examples without articles in favor
Soll Werbung für Kinder verboten werden? [Should advertising to children be banned?]
Soll die 32 Stunden Arbeitswoche eingeführt werden? [Should the 32-hour work week be introduced?]
Ist ein Krieg gegen ein anderes Land gerechtfertigt? [Is war against another country justified?]

Questions examples without articles against
Sollte Sterbehilfe legal sein? [Should euthanasia be legal?]
Sollen Plastikverpackungen verboten werden? [Should plastic packaging be banned?]
Sollen Obdachlose staatlich subventioniert werden? [Should homeless people be subsidised by the state?]

Table 5: Examples of questions with no articles in favor or against after the two-pass ranking approach.

Label	Two-pass	Two-pass-ext	All
Diskutierend	620	154	774
Ja, dafür	509	193	702
Nein, dagegen	232	54	286
Kein Bezug	403	1,025	1,428
Unklar	332	171	503

Table 6: Stance class distribution in the final dataset ('All' column), consisting of the data collected after the two-pass ranking approach ('Two-pass') and its extension ('Two-pass-ext'). The question-article pairs with the *Unklar* ('unclear') label are those without annotation agreement.

different languages (mostly German and English), we use a pre-trained multilingual BERT model to obtain the embeddings.[14] Finally, we manually go through the most similar articles in each ranking and keep those that share the corresponding stance.

Our semi-automatic method reduces the number of questions with no articles against and in favour from 40 and 17 to 21 and 9, respectively, resulting in 116 additional question and article pairs in the final dataset. Table 6 shows the final distribution of the stance classes in the CHeeSE dataset. In addition, the table shows the total number of question and article pairs without annotation agreement on the stance annotation task (i.e. *Unklar* label).

4 Stance Detection Task

In the stance setting, the CHeeSE dataset provides with (a) a natural-language question and its set of related keywords; (b) a news article; (c) the stance of the article towards the question. Similar to the stance detection task defined in the FNC-1, we use the stance classes *Ja, dafür* ('for'), *Nein, dagegen* ('against'), *Diskutierend* ('discussion'), and *Kein Bezug* ('unrelated'). The target-specific stance detection task is then a multiclass classification task that consists of predicting an article's position towards its associated question.

We assess different baselines on the task using the CHeeSE dataset as a reference for future work. The proposed baselines are a bag-of-words linear classifier and a BERT-based model (Devlin et al., 2019), a multi-layer bidirectional Transformer encoder (Vaswani et al., 2017), which has shown to achieve the state-of-the-art performance on a wide range of natural language processing tasks (Radford and Narasimhan, 2018; Wu and Dredze, 2019; Peters et al., 2018). We report their class-wise F_1 and macro-averaged F_1 score, which is not affected by the majority class (Hanselowski et al., 2018).

Since the amount of training data is relatively small compared to other similar datasets, such as X-stance or FNC-1 (see Table 8), we perform five-fold cross-validation on the CHeeSE dataset, keeping the same class distribution in each fold as in the entire dataset. In our experiments, we exclude the instances annotated as *Unklar* ('unclear'), which are those with no annotator agreement.

4.1 Baseline Experiments

We evaluate two baselines: a bag-of-words linear classifier and a BERT-based model, and report their F_1 scores on the CHeeSE dataset.

Bag-of-Words Linear Classifier Our first baseline is a bag-of-words linear classifier built using fastText[15] as described in Joulin et al. (2017). We train the model for 50 epochs and a learning rate of 1 as recommended in the standard fastText settings.

Fine-tuned German BERT model As a second baseline, we fine-tune a pre-trained BERT model. Specifically, we first adapt the pre-trained German BERT model `bert-base-german-uncased` from Hugginface (Wolf et al., 2020)[16] to the stance detection task and extend it with a multiclass classification head. We then fine-tune the model on our data for four epochs and a learning rate of 3e-05.

[14] `https://huggingface.co/bert-base-multilingual-uncased`

[15] `https://github.com/facebookresearch/fastText/`

[16] `https://huggingface.co/dbmdz/bert-base-german-uncased`

Model	F_1 micro	F_1 macro	F_1 in favour	F_1 against	F_1 discussion	F_1 unrelated
Bag of words	50.8	41.9	42.8	20.5	39.9	64.3
German BERT	67.6	58.4	59.1	35.8	55.3	83.3

Table 7: Micro-averaged F_1, macro-averaged F_1 and class-wise F_1 scores for each baseline on the stance detection task. Fine-tuning the pre-trained German BERT model on the CHeeSE data outperforms the bag-of-words linear classifier.

Datasets	Lang	Training	Classification	Unrelated samples	Avg. tokens	F_1 macro
X-stance	multiple	~46k	binary	n/a	61	76.8
FNC-1	English	~61k	multiclass (4)	randomly selected	432	72.8
CHeeSE	German	~3k	multiclass (4)	two-pass ranking	843	58.2

Table 8: Overview of different stance detection benchmarks built using pre-trained BERT models on the X-stance (Vamvas and Sennrich, 2020), FNC-1 (Slovikovskaya and Attardi, 2020), and CHeeSE datasets. The benchmarks are not directly comparable as there are differences on the training sizes of the datasets, the classification task (multiclass or binary), or the nature of the unrelated samples. The 'avg. tokens' column refers to the average token length of the stance target (question or headline) and body text pairs.

Results Table 7 shows the macro-averaged and class-wise F_1 scores of the bag-of-words and the fine-tuned German BERT baselines. The results show that the pre-trained German BERT model fine-tuned on the CHeeSE data performs consistently better than the bag-of-words linear classifier. We also observe that the unrelated stance class is the easiest to correctly identify. Note that the unrelated annotations represent about 40% of all stance annotations in our dataset (see Table 6).

BERT-like models have shown to perform well in other stance detection tasks. Table 8 lists different supervised stance detection benchmarks built using BERT models. Note that there are differences on the total of predicted labels in the classification task (binary or multiclass), the nature of the unrelated samples as discussed in Section 3.3, and the training sizes; in fact, the training sizes of the X-stance and FNC-1 are considerably higher than the CHeeSE dataset. Therefore, we provide the scores as a reference rather than for comparative purposes.

5 Discussion and Future Work

The emotion of a text is closely related to sentiment analysis. Zhang et al. (2020), for example, leverage semantic-emotion knowledge in a cross-target stance detection task with positive results. However, there is insufficient research on combining emotion and stance information; perhaps due to the lack of datasets with both annotations. Since the CHeeSE dataset is annotated for both stance and emotion detection tasks, it allows the research community to further experiment in this direction.

In our experiments, we fine-tune a German pre-trained BERT model on our dataset. BERT-like models are able to deal with input sequences of up to 512 tokens. Since our dataset consists of news articles that are on average 843 and up to 4,130 tokens long, it would be interesting to assess the impact on stance detection when considering longer texts. Therefore, in future work we plan to experiment with model architectures that handle long input sequences, such as the Longformer, which processes sequences up to 4,096 tokens long and even up to 16k with the current GPUs (Beltagy et al., 2020).

The size of the CHeeSE dataset is considerably smaller than other stance datasets as shown in Table 8. Specifically, our dataset contains ~3k training instances compared to, for example, the ~61k from the FNC-1. More advanced models than our baselines could benefit from combining multiple datasets to achieve a better performance. For example, in multi-task learning, a model is simultaneously trained on related tasks, such that it learns to better generalise on the original task (Schiller et al., 2021; Hardalov et al., 2021).

We also expect the dataset to be a valuable resource in computational journalism, for example, to generate diverse news article portfolios or to provide a balanced exposure of articles' positions with recommender systems.

6 Conclusion

We presented the CHeeSE dataset, a manually annotated dataset of Swiss news articles. In contrast to most of the available datasets, which focus on short texts and/or the English language, the novelty of our dataset is that it provides document-level annotations on German news articles. Specifically, the dataset consists of a collection of German news articles automatically paired with debate questions. A team of native German speakers labelled each article and question pair with the stance of the article towards the question, the article emotion, and the emotion of each article's paragraph. We then performed target-specific stance detection as a supervised task using the CHeeSE dataset and provide baseline models as a reference in future research on stance detection in German news articles.

Acknowledgements

This project is supported by Ringier, TX Group, NZZ, SRG, VSM, viscom, and the ETH Zurich Foundation.

References

Abeer Aldayel and Walid Magdy. 2019. Assessing sentiment of the expressed stance on social media. In *Proceedings of the 2019 International Social Informatics Conference (SocInfo)*, pages 277–286, Doha, Qatar. Springer.

Iz Beltagy, Matthew E. Peters, and Arman Cohan. 2020. Longformer: The long-document transformer. *arXiv preprint arXiv:2004.05150*.

Ankush Chatterjee, Kedhar Nath Narahari, Meghana Joshi, and Puneet Agrawal. 2019. SemEval-2019 task 3: EmoContext contextual emotion detection in text. In *Proceedings of the 13th International Workshop on Semantic Evaluation*, pages 39–48, Minneapolis, Minnesota, USA. Association for Computational Linguistics.

Alessandra Teresa Cignarella, Mirko Lai, Cristina Bosco, Viviana Patti, and Paolo Rosso. 2020. Sardistance @ EVALITA2020: Overview of the task on stance detection in italian tweets. In *Proceedings of the 2020 Evaluation Campaign of Natural Language Processing and Speech Tools for Italian (EVALITA)*, Online. CEUR-WS.

Jacob Devlin, Ming-Wei Chang, Kenton Lee, and Kristina Toutanova. 2019. BERT: Pre-training of deep bidirectional transformers for language understanding. In *Proceedings of the 2019 Conference of the North American Chapter of the Association for Computational Linguistics: Human Language Technologies, Volume 1 (Long and Short Papers)*, pages 4171–4186, Minneapolis, Minnesota. Association for Computational Linguistics.

William Ferreira and Andreas Vlachos. 2016. Emergent: a novel data-set for stance classification. In *Proceedings of the 2016 Conference of the North American Chapter of the Association for Computational Linguistics: Human Language Technologies*, pages 1163–1168, San Diego, California. Association for Computational Linguistics.

J.L. Fleiss. 1971. Measuring nominal scale agreement among many raters. *Psychological Bulletin*, 76(5):378–382.

Mingkun Gao, Hyo Jin Do, and Wai-Tat Fu. 2018. Burst your bubble! an intelligent system for improving awareness of diverse social opinions. In *Proceedings of the 2018 International Conference on Intelligent User Interfaces*, pages 371–383, Tokyo, Japan. Association for Computing Machinery.

Andreas Hanselowski, Avinesh PVS, Benjamin Schiller, Felix Caspelherr, Debanjan Chaudhuri, Christian M. Meyer, and Iryna Gurevych. 2018. A retrospective analysis of the fake news challenge stance-detection task. In *Proceedings of the 27th International Conference on Computational Linguistics*, pages 1859–1874, Santa Fe, New Mexico, USA. Association for Computational Linguistics.

Momchil Hardalov, Arnav Arora, Preslav Nakov, and Isabelle Augenstein. 2021. Cross-domain label-adaptive stance detection. *arXiv preprint arXiv:2104.07467*.

Armand Joulin, Edouard Grave, Piotr Bojanowski, and Tomas Mikolov. 2017. Bag of tricks for efficient text classification. In *Proceedings of the 15th Conference of the European Chapter of the Association for Computational Linguistics: Volume 2, Short Papers*, pages 427–431, Valencia, Spain. Association for Computational Linguistics.

Sudipta Kar, Suraj Maharjan, A. Pastor López-Monroy, and Thamar Solorio. 2018. MPST: A corpus of movie plot synopses with tags. In *Proceedings of the Eleventh International Conference on Language Resources and Evaluation (LREC 2018)*, Miyazaki, Japan. European Language Resources Association (ELRA).

Dilek Küçük and Fazli Can. 2020. Stance detection: A survey. *Association for Computing Machinery*, 53(1).

Mirko Lai, Alessandra Teresa Cignarella, Delia Irazú Hernanández Farías, Cristina Bosco, Viviana Patti, and Paolo Rosso. 2020. Multilingual stance detection in social media political debates. *Computer Speech and Language*, 63:101075.

Yingjie Li and Cornelia Caragea. 2019. Multi-task stance detection with sentiment and stance lexicons. In *Proceedings of the 2019 Conference on Empirical*

Methods in Natural Language Processing and the 9th International Joint Conference on Natural Language Processing (EMNLP-IJCNLP), pages 6299–6305, Hong Kong, China. Association for Computational Linguistics.

Suraj Maharjan, Sudipta Kar, Manuel Montes-y-Gómez, Fabio A. González, and Thamar Solorio. 2018. Letting emotions flow: Success prediction by modeling the flow of emotions in books. *arXiv preprint arXiv:1805.0974*.

Saif Mohammad, Felipe Bravo-Marquez, Mohammad Salameh, and Svetlana Kiritchenko. 2018. SemEval-2018 task 1: Affect in tweets. In *Proceedings of The 12th International Workshop on Semantic Evaluation*, pages 1–17, New Orleans, Louisiana. Association for Computational Linguistics.

Saif Mohammad, Svetlana Kiritchenko, Parinaz Sobhani, Xiaodan Zhu, and Colin Cherry. 2016a. A dataset for detecting stance in tweets. In *Proceedings of the Tenth International Conference on Language Resources and Evaluation (LREC'16)*, pages 3945–3952, Portorož, Slovenia. European Language Resources Association (ELRA).

Saif Mohammad, Svetlana Kiritchenko, Parinaz Sobhani, Xiaodan Zhu, and Colin Cherry. 2016b. SemEval-2016 task 6: Detecting stance in tweets. In *Proceedings of the 10th International Workshop on Semantic Evaluation (SemEval-2016)*, pages 31–41, San Diego, California. Association for Computational Linguistics.

Saif M. Mohammad, Parinaz Sobhani, and Svetlana Kiritchenko. 2017. Stance and sentiment in tweets. *ACM Transactions on Internet Technology*, 17(3).

Rodrigo Nogueira and Kyunghyun Cho. 2020. Passage re-ranking with BERT. *arXiv preprint arXiv:1901.04085*.

Matthew E. Peters, Mark Neumann, Mohit Iyyer, Matt Gardner, Christopher Clark, Kenton Lee, and Luke Zettlemoyer. 2018. Deep contextualized word representations. In *Proceedings of the 2018 Conference of the North American Chapter of the Association for Computational Linguistics: Human Language Technologies, Volume 1 (Long Papers)*, pages 2227–2237, New Orleans, Louisiana. Association for Computational Linguistics.

Robert. Plutchik. 1980. *Emotion, a psychoevolutionary synthesis*. Harper & Row, New York, NY, USA.

Robert Plutchik. 2001. The Nature of Emotions. *American Scientist*, 89(4):344.

Alec Radford and Karthik Narasimhan. 2018. Improving language understanding by generative pre-training.

Benjamin Schiller, Johannes Daxenberger, and Iryna Gurevych. 2021. Stance detection benchmark: How robust is your stance detection? *KI-Künstliche Intelligenz*, pages 1–13.

Valeriya Slovikovskaya and Giuseppe Attardi. 2020. Transfer learning from transformers to fake news challenge stance detection (FNC-1) task. In *Proceedings of the 12th Language Resources and Evaluation Conference*, pages 1211–1218, Marseille, France. European Language Resources Association.

Parinaz Sobhani, Saif Mohammad, and Svetlana Kiritchenko. 2016. Detecting stance in tweets and analyzing its interaction with sentiment. In *Proceedings of the Fifth Joint Conference on Lexical and Computational Semantics*, pages 159–169, Berlin, Germany. Association for Computational Linguistics.

Carlo Strapparava and Rada Mihalcea. 2007. SemEval-2007 task 14: Affective text. In *Proceedings of the Fourth International Workshop on Semantic Evaluations (SemEval-2007)*, pages 70–74, Prague, Czech Republic. Association for Computational Linguistics.

Qingying Sun, Zhongqing Wang, Shoushan Li, Qiaoming Zhu, and Guodong Zhou. 2019. Stance detection via sentiment information and neural network model. *Frontiers of Computer Science*, 13(1):127.

Jannis Vamvas and Rico Sennrich. 2020. X-Stance: A multilingual multi-target dataset for stance detection. In *Proceedings of the 5th Swiss Text Analytics Conference (SwissText) & 16th Conference on Natural Language Processing (KONVENS)*, Zurich, Switzerland.

Ashish Vaswani, Noam Shazeer, Niki Parmar, Jakob Uszkoreit, Llion Jones, Aidan N. Gomez, Lukasz Kaiser, and Illia Polosukhin. 2017. Attention is all you need. In *Advances in Neural Information Processing Systems*, volume 30, page 6000–6010, Long Beach, California, USA. Curran Associates, Inc.

Ekaterina P. Volkova, Betty Mohler, Detmar Meurers, Dale Gerdemann, and Heinrich H. Bülthoff. 2010. Emotional perception of fairy tales: Achieving agreement in emotion annotation of text. In *Proceedings of the NAACL HLT 2010 Workshop on Computational Approaches to Analysis and Generation of Emotion in Text*, pages 98–106, Los Angeles, CA. Association for Computational Linguistics.

Thomas Wolf, Lysandre Debut, Victor Sanh, Julien Chaumond, Clement Delangue, Anthony Moi, Pierric Cistac, Tim Rault, Remi Louf, Morgan Funtowicz, Joe Davison, Sam Shleifer, Patrick von Platen, Clara Ma, Yacine Jernite, Julien Plu, Canwen Xu, Teven Le Scao, Sylvain Gugger, Mariama Drame, Quentin Lhoest, and Alexander Rush. 2020. Transformers: State-of-the-art natural language processing. In *Proceedings of the 2020 Conference on Empirical Methods in Natural Language Processing: System Demonstrations*, pages 38–45, Online. Association for Computational Linguistics.

Shijie Wu and Mark Dredze. 2019. Beto, bentz, becas: The surprising cross-lingual effectiveness of BERT. In *Proceedings of the 2019 Conference on*

Empirical Methods in Natural Language Processing and the 9th International Joint Conference on Natural Language Processing (EMNLP-IJCNLP), pages 833–844, Hong Kong, China. Association for Computational Linguistics.

Andrew Yates, Rodrigo Nogueira, and Jimmy Lin. 2021. Pretrained transformers for text ranking: BERT and beyond. In *Proceedings of the 2021 ACM International Conference on Web Search and Data Mining (WSDM)*, page 1154–1156, Online. Association for Computing Machinery.

Bowen Zhang, Min Yang, Xutao Li, Yunming Ye, Xiaofei Xu, and Kuai Dai. 2020. Enhancing cross-target stance detection with transferable semantic-emotion knowledge. In *Proceedings of the 58th Annual Meeting of the Association for Computational Linguistics*, pages 3188–3197, Online. Association for Computational Linguistics.

Elena Zotova, Rodrigo Agerri, Manuel Nuñez, and German Rigau. 2020. Multilingual stance detection in tweets: The Catalonia independence corpus. In *Proceedings of the 12th Language Resources and Evaluation Conference*, pages 1368–1375, Marseille, France. European Language Resources Association.

A Labelling Tool

Figure 2 shows an example of the labelling tool that we use to annotate each article and question pairs.

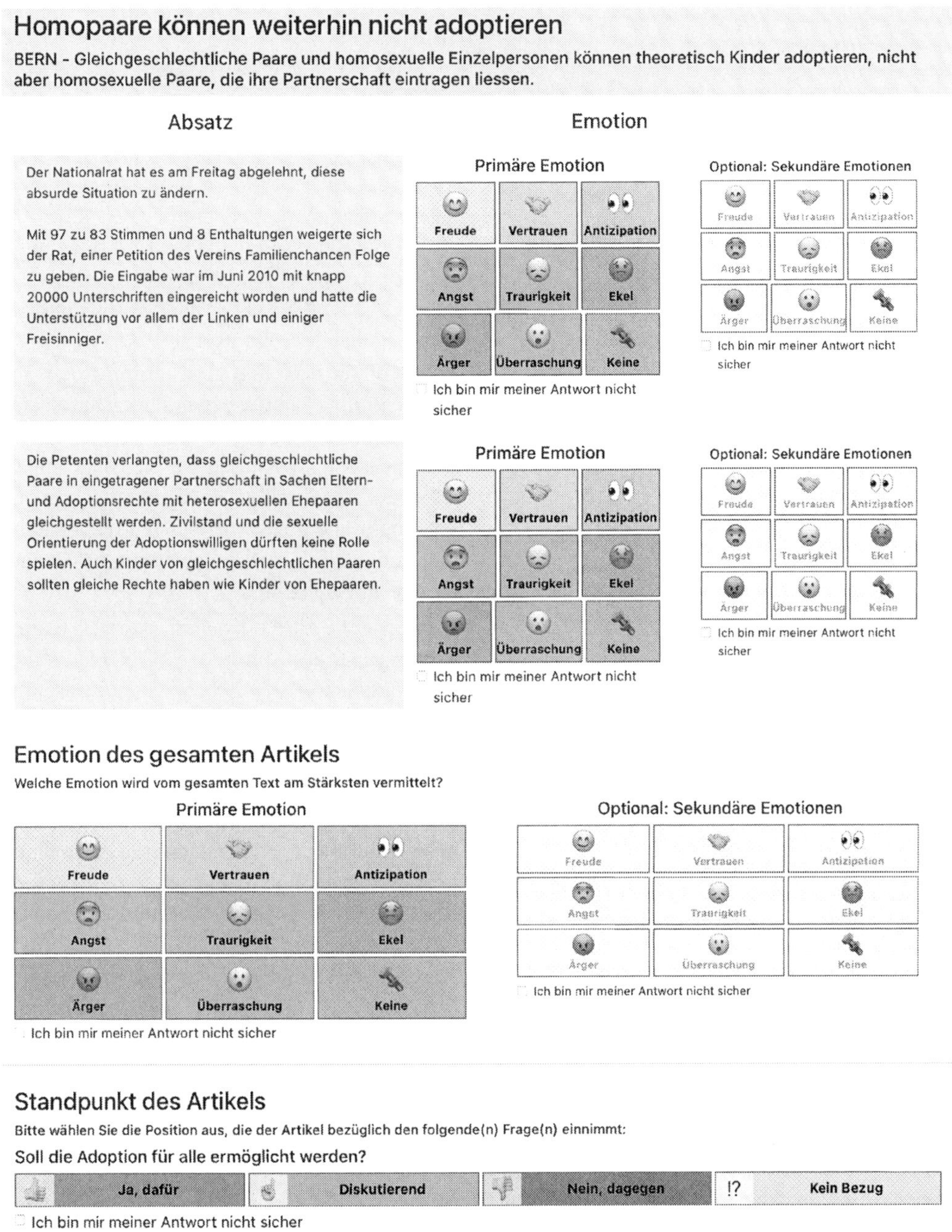

Figure 2: Example of the interface of the labelling tool that we use to annotate the CHeeSE dataset. For each article and question pair, the annotators label the emotion of each article's paragraph, the emotion of the overall article, and the stance of a debate question towards the article.

FANG-COVID: A New Large-Scale Benchmark Dataset for Fake News Detection in German

Justus Mattern[1], Yu Qiao[1], Elma Kerz[1], Daniel Wiechmann[2], Markus Strohmaier[1]
[1]RWTH Aachen University
[2]University of Amsterdam
{justus.mattern,yu.qiao}@rwth-aachen.de
elma.kerz@ifaar.rwth-aachen.de
D.Wiechmann@uva.nl
markus.strohmaier@cssh.rwth-aachen.de

Abstract

As the world continues to fight the COVID-19 pandemic, it is simultaneously fighting an 'infodemic' – a flood of disinformation and spread of conspiracy theories leading to health threats and the division of society. To combat this infodemic, there is an urgent need for benchmark datasets that can help researchers develop and evaluate models geared towards automatic detection of disinformation. While there are increasing efforts to create adequate, open-source benchmark datasets for English, comparable resources are virtually unavailable for German, leaving research for the German language lagging significantly behind. In this paper, we introduce the new benchmark dataset FANG-COVID consisting of 28,056 real and 13,186 fake German news articles related to the COVID-19 pandemic as well as data on their propagation on Twitter. Furthermore, we propose an explainable textual- and social context-based model for fake news detection, compare its performance to "black-box" models and perform feature ablation to assess the relative importance of human-interpretable features in distinguishing fake news from authentic news.

1 Introduction

The online availability and rapid dissemination of 'disinformation' and 'fake news' – cover terms for various types of false, inaccurate, or misleading information, typically related to emerging and time-sensitive events – have become a global challenge over the past 10 years (Tucker et al., 2018). Never has the scale of this challenge been clearer than in the corona crisis: as the world continues to fight the coronavirus disease 2019 (COVID-19) pandemic, it is simultaneously fighting an 'infodemic' – a flood of disinformation and spread of conspiracy theories leading to the division of society (Orso et al., 2020; Solomon et al., 2020).

In order to combat the spread and consumption of disinformation, it is of essential importance to develop diagnostic and predictive analysis models that can be used to understand how and why disinformation is created and spread as well as to uncover hidden and unexpected aspects of disinformation content. A key aspect that has a significant impact on the detection of disinformation is the existence of high-quality benchmark datasets. While there are increasing efforts to create adequate, open-source benchmark datasets for English, comparable resources are virtually unavailable for German (but see Vogel and Jiang (2019b)). Accordingly, research on disinformation detection for German is clearly lagging behind.

In order to fill the research gap, the main goal of this paper is to introduce FANG-COVID[1], an entire-article COVID-19 benchmark dataset for the German language, designed based on existing English language benchmark datasets and labeled using distant supervision.

Furthermore, we present the results of benchmark experiments on the dataset using explainable textual- and social context-based models for fake news detection and compare their performance to those of classifiers based on a fine-tuned BERT language model. Finally, we conduct feature ablation experiments to assess the relative importance of human-interpretable features in distinguishing fake news from authentic news.

This paper is structured as follows: In section 2, we provide a concise overview of existing datasets and approaches for fake news detection, focusing on work related to COVID-19 and the German language. In section 3, we introduce the FANG-COVID dataset. In section 4, we propose an explainable fake news detection system, compare its performance to a black-box model and introduce the ablation algorithm used to analyze the importance of certain features, before summarizing the results and our contribution in section 5.

[1]https://github.com/justusmattern/fang-covid

Proceedings of the Fourth Workshop on Fact Extraction and VERification (FEVER) at EMNLP 2021, pages 78–91
November 10, 2021. ©2021 Association for Computational Linguistics

2 Related Work

In recent years, with the growing recognition of the importance of understanding and detecting fake news, increasing efforts have been made to combat disinformation, resulting in the creation of large-scale annotated datasets for fake news detection for the English language (Ahmed et al., 2018; Shu et al., 2020b; Wang, 2017; Thorne et al., 2018). For the German language, first steps towards creating suitable datasets have been made (Vogel and Jiang, 2019a; Vogel et al., 2020). To date, however, existing datasets are too small to enable the development of state-of-the-art deep learning models for fake news detection. Current approaches to automatic detection of English fake news (Kula et al., 2020; Wang et al., 2018; Ruchansky et al., 2017; Qiao et al., 2020) have taken into account both textual news content and also social context based on social media data (for recent reviews of disinformation detection, see Oshikawa et al. (2020), Shu et al. (2020a), Zhou and Zafarani (2018) and Shu et al. (2017)). Language-based approaches have an advantage over knowledge-based or propagation-based approaches[2], because (1) they enable near real-time feedback (proactive rather than retroactive), i.e. they are not restricted to being applied only *a posteriori* (Potthast et al., 2017) and (2) they are scalable. In the remainder of this section, we provide a concise overview of the existing COVID-19 fake news datasets and approaches to detect disinformation regarding the virus.

2.1 COVID-19 Fake News Datasets in English

To the best of our knowledge, there exist currently four suitable and publicly available datasets for COVID-19 fake news detection in English (see Table 2 for an overview). These datasets differ with respect to the type of news source they consist of (entire articles vs. individual claims/tweets), data size, the imbalance of the class distribution (real/fake) and the type of information available for fake news detection (linguistic and/or social context).

Patwa et al. (2020) introduced the Covid19 FN dataset in connection with the CONSTRAINT shared task for Covid-19 fake news detection. This dataset consists of 5,600 correct tweets gathered from reliable sources such as government accounts, medical institutes and news channels as well as 5,100 manually fact-checked false statements from various sources such as news articles, press releases and social media posts.

FakeCovid (Shahi and Nandini, 2020) is a multilingual dataset that consists of 5,182 manually fact-checked news articles from 40 languages of which 2,116 are English and 47 are German.

ReCOVery (Zhou et al., 2020a) is a dataset containing 2,029 news articles as well as data for 140,820 tweets and the respective user profiles sharing these articles. Its labels were obtained based on the reliability of the news publisher.

Lastly, CoAID (Cui and Lee, 2020) comprises different types of news items, i.e. claims, news articles and social media posts. Specifically, it consists of 204 fake and 3,565 real fact-checked news articles referring to the pandemic, 28 wrong and 454 true claims about the virus, 926 social media posts about it and data about Tweets reposting these news, as well as data about user engagements with each tweet. With 94% of its news item representing authentic news, it is also the most imbalanced of the datasets. Veracity labels for real news articles were obtained on a publisher level, i.e. data were scraped from reliable publishers such as ScienceDaily or WHO. Fake articles were gathered using links to false articles from fact-checking websites. For claims, WHO information and additional reliable sources were used to identify statements known to be false.

Not only are the existing datasets scarce, they are also limited in terms of the amount of text and types of information they provide and, at times, are highly imbalanced, introducing inductive bias. No COVID-19 datasets are available for the German language.

2.2 COVID-19 Fake News Detection

Given the nature of the available Covid-19 datasets, most attempts to detect fake news in this domain have been language-based. The best performing approach in the CONSTRAINT shared task on the Covid19 Fake News dataset was proposed by Glazkova et al. (2020), who obtained text representations using the COVID-Twitter-BERT language model (Müller et al., 2020) that was specifically trained on 160M English tweets about the virus

[2]Knowledge-based fake news detection es techniques from information retrieval to determine the veracity/truthfulness of news item, whereas propagation-based approaches use network analysis to determine the credibility of news sources at various stages, i.e. when being created, published online and spread via social media.

Table 1: Existing datasets for Covid-19 fake news detection. Engagement refers to data about reactions to and shares of news on social media whereas user data refers to information about user profiles sharing news articles such as how frequently they post, their follower count, etc.

Dataset	Language	Size	Fake / Real	Engagement	Profiles	Data Source
Covid19 FN	English	10,700	0.47 / 0.53	-	-	Various
FakeCovid	Various	5,182	0.20 / 0.80	-	-	Articles
ReCOVery	English	2,029	0.33 / 0.67	✓	✓	Articles
CoAID	English	4,251	0.06 / 0.94	✓	-	Articles, Claims
FANG-COVID	German	41,242	0.32 / 0.68	✓	✓	Articles

and achieved an F1-score of 98.69%. High detection performance (F1-score of 96.7%) was also reached based on concatenated text representations obtained by XLNet (Yang et al., 2019) and Latent Dirichet Allocation (LDA) in a feed forward neural network (Gautam et al., 2021) (see Patwa et al. (2021) for comprehensive overview of the approaches proposed in the CONSTRAINT shared task). Experiments conducted on the FakeCovid dataset used a pretrained BERT model to represent the textual content of English news articles from FakeCovid and obtained an F1-score of 0.78 (Shahi and Nandini, 2020). For ReCOVery, the SAFE method (Zhou et al., 2020b), an approach that involves training a neural network to specifically detect discrepancies in visual and textual news content, outperformed approaches based on text-based CNN, achieving an F1-score of 0.833 for the detection of real and 0.672 for the detection of fake news. Cui and Lee (2020) conduct experiments on the CoAID dataset using various different classification models that have proven to be successful for general fake news detection. Notably, some of the best-performing models on general fake news detection datasets such as CSI (Ruchansky et al., 2017) and SAME (Cui et al., 2019) proved to be less effective on CoAID, achieving F1-scores of 0.228 and 0.340, respectively, relative to the best performing model dEFEND (Shu et al., 2019a) with an F1-score of 0.581. This further demonstrates the need for research on specific critical events like the current pandemic.

3 Introducing the FANG-COVID dataset

In this section, we provide a detailed description of the methodology used to compile the FANG-COVID dataset and present its composition. The collection and labelling of news articles was based on news publisher bias lists compiled by media professionals, following the approach taken in Kiesel et al. (2019). For gathering true news articles, we relied on three established, reputable mainstream newspapers whose quality is recognized by media experts (Wellbrock, 2011). For the collection of fake news articles, we utilized independent fact-checking organizations such as Correctiv[3] and NewsGuard[4]. The latter published a list in January 2021 containing over 30 German news sources that are classified as unreliable news publishers based on criteria such as the frequency of false information being posted, the responsible presentation of information and sources and the clear separation of opinion and fact [5]. Based on this data and further research on its listed sources via trustworthy newspapers such as *Frankfurter Allgemeine Zeitung*, *SPIEGEL* or *ZEIT*, we selected ten publishers whose articles we would label as 'fake'. An overview of the distributions of news articles and tweets across publishers is presented in Table 3. For every one of our news sources, we scraped the header, date of publication and textual content of articles that were published between February 2020 to mid March 2021 and contained one of the following Covid-related keywords: *Corona, Covid, Infektion, Lockdown, Impfen, Impfung, Impfstoff.* The selection of news based on the keywords ensured that all articles are related to events surrounding the coronavirus pandemic. The collected textual data were cleaned and preprocessed by transforming dates of publication from handwritten formats to the uniform datetime format and the removal of HTML tags. A schematic representation of the procedure used to compile FANG-COVID is shown in Figure 1.

In total, the FANG-COVID dataset comprises 41,242 news articles: 28,056 articles from three publishers are labeled as 'real' and 13,186 articles

[3] https://correctiv.org/

[4] https://www.newsguardtech.com/

[5] https://www.newsguardtech.com/ratings/rating-process-criteria/

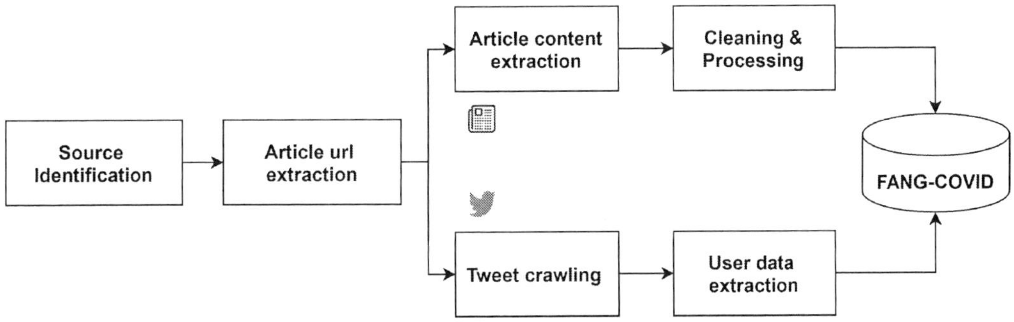

Figure 1: Procedure applied to compile the FANG-COVID dataset

are labeled as 'fake' based on the reliability of their source (see Tables 2 and 3 for details on the composition of the dataset). On average, news articles in FANG-COVID contain 803 word tokens and 43.8 sentences, with similar distributions for fake and real news articles. With regards to political orientation, the majority of the fake news publishers exhibited tendencies towards right wing populism, as common topics by these publishers involve allegations against immigrants (a topic that has been especially prevalent in Germany since the refugee crisis in 2015). The articles from unreliable sources are also characterized by a higher proportion of articles favouring the right-wing populist party "Alternative für Deutschland" (AfD) (see Figure 4 in the Appendix).

To facilitate research on the diffusion of fake news in social networks, FANG-COVID also contains rich information relating to the articles' spreading on social media. These data were collected using the snscrape[6] library, a Python scraper for social networking services. We gathered all tweets referring to any of the articles in the dataset, as well as reactions to these in the form of likes or retweets and additional information, such as which device the tweet was posted from as well as user-related data, such as the follower count, the number of posts or the date a user joined Twitter. Each news article is associated with a JSON array containing all tweets sharing its url, ordered by the time they were posted. Each tweet is represented as a JSON object containing specific information about each tweet, such as the number of likes and retweets as well as extensive data about the user sharing each tweet such as their follower count, their number of posts since joining Twitter as well as visual information in the form of their profile picture and banner. Overall, FANG-COVID contains social media information related to the news articles from a total of 363,393 tweets. On average, a real news article from our dataset was shared 8.4 times while a fake news article was shared 9.7 times. Out of all users sharing articles from our dataset, 52,289 distinct user profiles reposted real news articles while 7,861 users shared news articles labeled as fake.

4 *FANG-COVID:* Benchmark Experiments

In this section, we first describe the textual and social context representations used in the fake news detection model and the experimental setup, before presenting the empirical results of classification models trained on interpretable features and contextualized word embeddings. Specifically, in order to establish benchmarks for fake news detection on the FANG-COVID dataset and to provide initial insights into the features and approaches that prove to be effective for the detection of German fake news regarding COVID-19, we evaluate detection models based on interpretable Term Frequency Inverse Document Frequency (TF-IDF) and linguistic complexity features and compare their performance to classifiers based on a fine-tuned BERT language model with and without social context information.

4.1 Textual Representations

Interpretable representation: Our proposed interpretable text representation $T_i = t_t \oplus t_c$ consists of two concatenated vectors t_t, t_c where t_t is a 600-dimensional TF-IDF vector measuring the frequencies of single words and bigrams in a given text and t_c is a 718-dimensional vector capturing the linguistic complexity of a given text. This vector is generated using CoCoGen, a computational tool that implements a sliding window technique to calculate within-text distributions of feature scores (see

[6]https://github.com/JustAnotherArchivist/snscrape

Table 2: Text size statistics of real articles, fake articles and the whole dataset. Tokenization was performed using the Stanford CoreNLP library.

Measure	Real	Fake	All
Average number of tokens per article	784	803	790
Average number of sentences per article	50.40	43.82	48.30
Average number of tokens per sentence	15.68	18.32	16.36
Total number of types in corpus	424,529	270,961	543,720

Table 3: Distribution of articles and associated tweets across publishers along with average article length (in words)

Publisher	Number of Articles	Average article length	Number of Tweets	Number of distinct users sharing articles
Reliable Publishers:				
Sueddeutsche Zeitung	6,749	673.3	29,009	11,709
Tagesspiegel	11,623	699.7	75,100	22,248
ZEIT	9,684	1,023.7	130,945	34,264
Unreliable Publishers:				
AnonymousNews	229	689.3	8,078	1,368
Compact-Online	1,077	708.9	10,211	1,276
Contra-Magazin	998	691.2	2,621	181
FreieWelt	1,403	367.3	5,023	877
Journalistenwatch	3,675	683.1	61,299	3,480
Kopp-Report	204	1,017.0	1,932	436
Politikstube	602	239.5	3,896	649
Pravda-TV	1,117	1,612.6	4,575	496
RT-DE	2,442	504.7	15,986	2,131
Rubikon News	1,439	2,132.3	14,718	2,637

recently published papers that use this tool, (Ströbel et al., 2018; Kerz et al., 2020b,a; Qiao et al., 2020)). In contrast to the standard approach implemented in other tools for automated text analysis that rely on aggregate scores representing the average value of a feature in a text, the sliding-window approach generates a series of measurements representing the 'local' distributions of scores. A sliding window can be conceived of as a window of size ws, which is defined by the number of sentences it contains. The window is moved across a text sentence-by-sentence, computing one value per window for a given feature. The series of measurements faithfully captures a typically non-uniform distribution of features within a text and is referred here to as a 'contour'. To compute the value of a given feature in a given window m ($w(m)$), a measurement function is called for each sentence in the window and returns a fraction (wn_m/wd_m). The series of measurements generated by CoCoGen captures the progression of language performance within a text for a given indicator and is referred here to as a 'complexity contour' (see Figure 2 for illustration). CoCoGen uses the Stanford CoreNLP suite (Manning et al., 2014) for performing tokenization, sentence splitting, part-of-speech tagging, lemmatization and syntactic parsing (Probabilistic Context Free Grammar Parser (Klein and Manning, 2003)). For German, CoCoGen currently supports 118 linguistic feature scores that fall into five categories: (1) features of syntactic complexity (N=5), (2) features of lexical density, sophistication and variation (N=17), (3) features of morphological complexity (N=27), (4) information-theoretic features (N=1) and (5) LIWC (Linguistic Inquiry and Word Count) (Tausczik and Pennebaker, 2010) features (N=68).

Thus, for a given news article, CoCoGen outputs a list $S = [s_1, s_2, ..., s_l]$ of 118-dimensional sentence representations where l is the length of the input text in sentences. These sentence representations serve as input for a 2-layer bidirectional LSTM-network (Graves and Schmidhuber, 2005) with a hidden state size of 150. t_c consists of the concatenated outputs from each last hidden state layer from both directions as well as a 118-dimensional vector containing the sum $s_1 + ... + s_l$

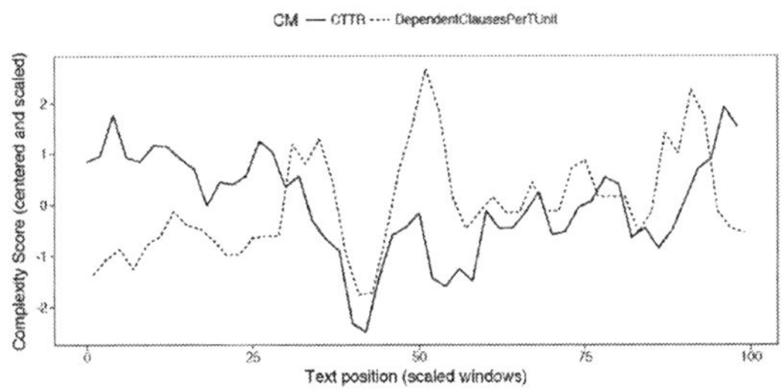

Figure 2: Schematic representation of 'complexity contours' for two out of 118 complexity measures investigated

of all feature values for each sentence.

Black-Box representation: As a textual black-box representation T_b, we use a pretrained German[7] BERT model (Devlin et al., 2019) and fine-tune six of its twelve encoding layers for our classification task. We use BERT's 768-dimensional output for its classification token [CLS] as our text representation. For texts of lengths greater than 512 tokens, we only keep the first 512 to serve as input to BERT as this method has been shown not to perform meaningfully worse than hierarchical methods (Sun et al., 2019).

4.2 Social Context Representation

As social context has been shown to be a valuable source of information for the detection of fake news (Shu et al., 2019c; Zhou and Zafarani, 2019), we employed a recurrent neural network-based representation for our social media data input for our classifiers, following an approach proposed in Ruchansky et al. (2017). For every article, a list of Twitter post representations $P = [p_1, p_2, ..., p_n]$ is constructed where p_i is an eight-dimensional vector representing user interactions with a tweet sharing the article as well as information about the user posting it. The list is ordered by the time the tweets were posted. The values contained in each vector are the tweet's number of likes, number of replies, number of retweets and its number of quotes as well as the poster's follower count, number of friends, total number of tweets and number of tweets they liked. The post representations serve as input to a two-layer bidirectional LSTM network with a hidden state size of 12. The final social context vector S is constructed by concatenating the four last hidden states from both layers in both directions as well as a five-dimensional vector containing values for the total number of tweets posting the corresponding news article as well as the total number of likes, replies, retweets and quotes to these posts. Thus, S is of dimension 53.

4.3 Experimental Setup

In this section we report on benchmark experiments conducted with different combinations of feature representations to assess how an explainable textual- and social context-based model compares to a black box model based on contextualised word embeddings in a binary classification task. Specifically, we evaluate the following four feature combinations: (1) Our interpretable textual representation T_i consisting of the TF-IDF vector and the linguistic complexity representation obtained from CoCoGen features, henceforth referred to as **TF-IDF + CoCoGen**, (2) the interpretable textual representation T_i and social context representation S, henceforth referred to as **TF-IDF + CoCoGen + Social Context**, (3) the black-box textual representation T_b obtained from BERT, henceforth referred to as **BERT** and (4) the black-box textual representation T_b and social representation S, henceforth referred to as **BERT + Social Context**.

For all feature combinations, we concatenate the individual feature vectors and use a three-layer perceptron to classify news articles as fake or real. We use binary cross entropy loss as our loss function:

$$\mathcal{L}(p, t) = -t \log(p) - (1 - t) \log(1 - p)$$

where t is the target value defined as 1 for fake news and 0 for articles labeled as real and p is the probability of a given news article being fake.

We tested our models using two data splits. First, we perform 5-fold cross validation over news articles from the whole dataset, including articles from all publishers in the train and test set. Second, we perform experiments on a randomly chosen publisher-separated split in which none of the publishers from the training set are included in the test set in order to determine whether the models learn to identify publishers-specific clues.

4.4 Ablation Study

In order to assess the relative importance of our neural networks' features for the detection of fake news, we performed a feature ablation study on the results from the 5-fold cross validation split using a modified version of an algorithm introduced by Díaz-Villanueva et al. (2010): For each

[7] https://deepset.ai/german-bert

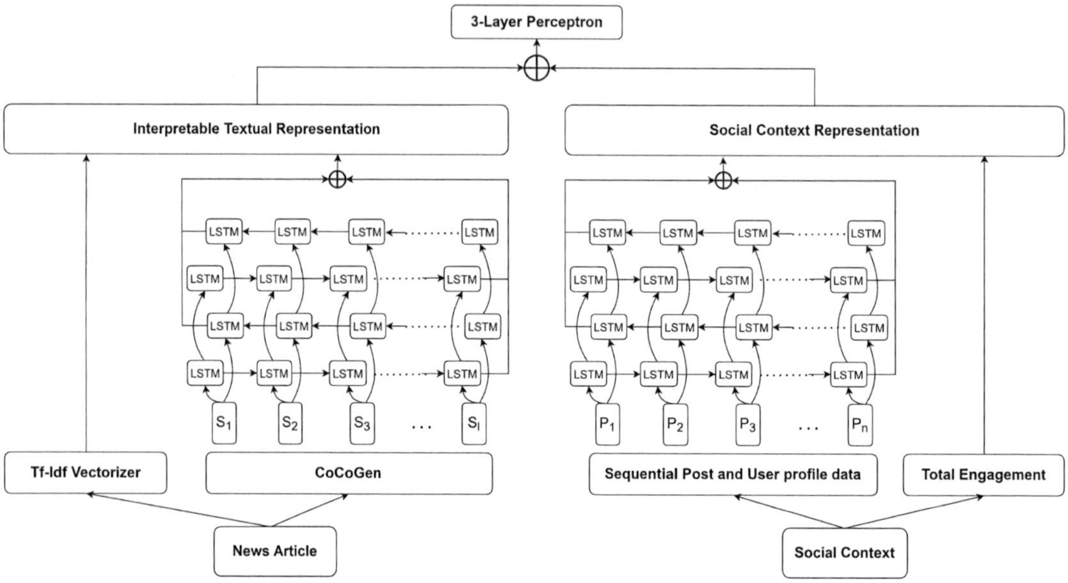

Figure 3: Architecture of proposed interpretable TF-IDF + CoCoGen+Social Context fake news detection model

step t, a neural network M_t is trained on a set of training data consisting of feature groups $F = \{f_1, f_2, ..., f_{D_t}\}$ where $f1, ..., f_{D_t}$ are the remaining feature groups at the current step, whose importance rank is to be determined. Let X_t denote the test dataset at time step t consisting of the feature set F_t and X_t^i denote the test dataset X_t with the values of features f_i being set to their average across the training dataset. Furthermore, let $acc(X)$ denote the classification accuracy of the given neural network M_t on test set X. For each time step t, the sensitivity score (Moody, 1994; Utans and Moody, 1991) $S_{i,t}$ for feature group f_i is computed as follows:

$$S_{i,t} = acc(X_t) - acc(X_t^i)$$

The most important feature group $f_{\hat{i}}$ at step t can be found by:

$$f_{\hat{i}} : \hat{i} =_{i:f_i \in F_t} (S_{i,t})$$

and the importance rank of feature group $f_{\hat{i}}$ is set as

$$Rank_{\hat{i}} = t$$

For the next step $t + 1$, feature group $f_{\hat{i}}$ is dropped from the training and test dataset that are used to train and evaluate the neural network:

$$F_{t+1} = F_t - \{f_{\hat{i}}\}$$

The process is repeated until step t' where $|F_{t'}| = 1$

5 Results

We outline our full classification results in Table 4. Our best performing models are the BERT and BERT + Social Context models which achieve superior results on both the 5-fold validation split as well as the publisher-seperated split. Notably, the proposed model relying solely on interpretable features achieves results that are comparable to those of the black box model relying on BERT embeddings. While the chosen social context representation could not add additional predictive power to the model solely relying on BERT embeddings, its addition to the interpretable text embeddings improved the model performance by a large margin on both data splits. The results of the models on the publisher-separated split suggest that both our interpretable models as well as the BERT-based models have learned publisher-specific features. These results indicate that future work should take measures that ensure that the models solve the task they are trained for, rather than learning stylistic features of specific sources (see Baly et al., 2020, for a related finding in the domain of prediction of political ideology).

For our interpretable model based on social context and textual data, the feature group of highest importance is the data provided about a user sharing an article, followed by CoCoGen features measuring the syntactic complexity of a given news article. Specifically, profiles sharing real news articles

Table 4: Results of fake news detection performance on FANG-COVID

Model	Accuracy	Precision	Recall	F1-Score
5-fold validation:				
TF-IDF + CoCoGen	0.888	0.839	0.798	0.817
TF-IDF + CoCoGen + Social Context	0.937	0.913	0.887	0.900
BERT	0.981	0.966	0.970	0.968
BERT + Social Context	0.981	0.957	0.976	0.966
Publisher-seperated split:				
TF-IDF + CoCoGen	0.758	0.590	0.524	0.555
TF-IDF + CoCoGen + Social Context	0.801	0.649	0.653	0.651
BERT	0.820	0.676	0.685	0.680
BERT + Social Context	0.824	0.672	0.695	0.683

Table 5: Results of feature ablation study for Tf-IDF+CoCoGen+Social Context, evaluated on 5-fold validation: The sensitivity of the most important feature at time step t is the difference between the accuracy before drop and after drop

Step	Most important feature	Accuracy before drop	Accuracy after drop
1	Twitter profile data	0.941	0.718
2	Syntactic complexity	0.901	0.600
3	Tweet engagement	0.880	0.711
4	Lexical features	0.875	0.810
5	TF-IDF	0.850	0.791
6	LIWC-features	0.827	0.798
7	Morphological features	0.791	0.752
8	Infotheoretic features	0.749	0.384

have significantly higher average follower counts, but a lower amount of friends than those sharing fake news, indicating that our model learned to recognize specifically reputable official sources and institutions that predominantly shared real news. Other than expected, our model furthermore capitalized on fake news being on average more syntactically and lexically complex than reliable news articles which contradicts previous research from the English language suggesting that fake news are designed to be specifically easy to read, thus avoiding longer sentences and sophisticated language (Horne and Adali, 2017). Surprisingly, TF-IDF vectors merely rank as the 5th strongest feature and LIWC features that have shown to be a powerful feature for English fake news detection (Qiao et al., 2020; Shu et al., 2019b) rank as the 6th most important feature group out of eight. The full ablation results can be found in Table 5.

6 Conclusion

The development of effective diagnostic and predictive models needed to combat the spread and consumption of disinformation requires high-quality benchmark datasets. In this paper, we introduced the FANG-COVID dataset, a new dataset for fake news detection in German, consisting of 40k+ real and fake news articles related to the COVID-19 pandemic along with data on their propagation on Twitter. To facilitate fake news related research, the dataset is publicly available to the research community on GitHub.

We further conducted benchmark experiments on the data that incorporated both uninterpretable and interpretable features to language-based fake news detection in conjunction with social media engagement and profile data. The results of these experiments indicate that models that combine interpretable language features with social network data can achieve comparable detection performance relative to those based on contextualized word embeddings. This finding is important in the light of the growing recognition of the need to move away from pure black-box models towards interpretable models for solving practical problems, in particular in the context of critical industries, including healthcare, criminal justice, and news (Rudin, 2019). This is due to the fact that human experts in a given application domain need both accurate but also understandable models (Loyola-Gonzalez, 2019).

Potentially, our work can be expanded upon with the addition of further linguistic features that can increase the predictive power of an interpretable model to match that of black box models. Furthermore, a wide range of data from the social context information provided in FANG-COVID can be integrated to build more sophisticated fake news detection models and to study the propagation of German fake news on social media. To address issues associated with the high correlation between the source of a news article and its class, approaches integrating adversarial objectives (Baly et al., 2020) could be evaluated.

References

Hadeer Ahmed, Issa Traore, and Sherif Saad. 2018. Detecting opinion spams and fake news using text classification. *Security and Privacy*, 1(1):e9.

Ramy Baly, Giovanni Da San Martino, James R. Glass, and Preslav Nakov. 2020. We can detect your bias: Predicting the political ideology of news articles. *CoRR*, abs/2010.05338.

Limeng Cui and Dongwon Lee. 2020. CoAID: COVID-19 Healthcare Misinformation Dataset. *arXiv e-prints*, page arXiv:2006.00885.

Limeng Cui, Suhang Wang, and Dongwon Lee. 2019. Same: Sentiment-aware multi-modal embedding for detecting fake news. In *Proceedings of the 2019 IEEE/ACM International Conference on Advances in Social Networks Analysis and Mining*, ASONAM '19, page 41–48, New York, NY, USA. Association for Computing Machinery.

Jacob Devlin, Ming-Wei Chang, Kenton Lee, and Kristina Toutanova. 2019. BERT: Pre-training of deep bidirectional transformers for language understanding. In *Proceedings of the 2019 Conference of the North American Chapter of the Association for Computational Linguistics: Human Language Technologies, Volume 1 (Long and Short Papers)*, pages 4171–4186, Minneapolis, Minnesota. Association for Computational Linguistics.

Wladimiro Díaz-Villanueva, Francesc J. Ferri, and Vicente Cerverón. 2010. Learning improved feature rankings through decremental input pruning for support vector based drug activity prediction. In *Trends in Applied Intelligent Systems*, pages 653–661, Berlin, Heidelberg. Springer Berlin Heidelberg.

Akansha Gautam, Venktesh V, and Sarah Masud. 2021. Fake news detection system using xlnet model with topic distributions: Constraint@aaai2021 shared task. *CoRR*, abs/2101.11425.

Anna Glazkova, Maksim Glazkov, and Timofey Trifonov. 2020. g2tmn at constraint@aaai2021: Exploiting CT-BERT and ensembling learning for COVID-19 fake news detection. *CoRR*, abs/2012.11967.

Alex Graves and Jürgen Schmidhuber. 2005. Framewise phoneme classification with bidirectional lstm and other neural network architectures. *Neural networks*, 18(5-6):602–610.

Benjamin D. Horne and Sibel Adali. 2017. This just in: Fake news packs a lot in title, uses simpler, repetitive content in text body, more similar to satire than real news. *CoRR*, abs/1703.09398.

Elma Kerz, Fabio Pruneri, Daniel Wiechmann, Yu Qiao, and Marcus Ströbel. 2020a. Understanding the dynamics of second language writing through keystroke logging and complexity contours. In *Proceedings of The 12th Language Resources and Evaluation Conference*, pages 182–188.

Elma Kerz, Yu Qiao, Daniel Wiechmann, and Marcus Ströbel. 2020b. Becoming linguistically mature: Modeling english and german children's writing development across school grades. In *Proceedings of the Fifteenth Workshop on Innovative Use of NLP for Building Educational Applications*, pages 65–74.

Johannes Kiesel, Maria Mestre, Rishabh Shukla, Emmanuel Vincent, Payam Adineh, David Corney, Benno Stein, and Martin Potthast. 2019. Semeval-2019 task 4: Hyperpartisan news detection. In *Proceedings of the 13th International Workshop on Semantic Evaluation*, pages 829–839.

Dan Klein and Christopher D Manning. 2003. Accurate unlexicalized parsing. In *Proceedings of the 41st annual meeting of the association for computational linguistics*, pages 423–430.

Sebastian Kula, Michał Choraś, Rafał Kozik, Paweł Ksieniewicz, and Michał Woźniak. 2020. Sentiment analysis for fake news detection by means of neural networks. In *Computational Science – ICCS 2020*, pages 653–666, Cham. Springer International Publishing.

Octavio Loyola-Gonzalez. 2019. Black-box vs. white-box: Understanding their advantages and weaknesses from a practical point of view. *IEEE Access*, 7:154096–154113.

Christopher D. Manning, Mihai Surdeanu, John Bauer, Jenny Finkel, Prismatic Inc, Steven J. Bethard, and David Mcclosky. 2014. The stanford corenlp natural language processing toolkit. In *In ACL, System Demonstrations*.

John Moody. 1994. Prediction risk and architecture selection for neural networks. In *From Statistics to Neural Networks*, pages 147–165, Berlin, Heidelberg. Springer Berlin Heidelberg.

Martin Müller, Marcel Salathé, and Per Egil Kummervold. 2020. Covid-twitter-bert: A natural language processing model to analyse COVID-19 content on twitter. *CoRR*, abs/2005.07503.

Daniele Orso, Nicola Federici, Roberto Copetti, Luigi Vetrugno, and Tiziana Bove. 2020. Infodemic and the spread of fake news in the covid-19-era. *European Journal of Emergency Medicine*.

Ray Oshikawa, Jing Qian, and William Yang Wang. 2020. A survey on natural language processing for fake news detection. In *Proceedings of the 12th Language Resources and Evaluation Conference*, pages 6086–6093, Marseille, France. European Language Resources Association.

Parth Patwa, Mohit Bhardwaj, Vineeth Guptha, Gitanjali Kumari, Shivam Sharma, Srinivas PYKL, Amitava Das, Asif Ekbal, Md Shad Akhtar, and Tanmoy Chakraborty. 2021. Overview of constraint 2021 shared tasks: Detecting english covid-19 fake news and hindi hostile posts. In *Combating Online Hostile Posts in Regional Languages during Emergency Situation*, pages 42–53, Cham. Springer International Publishing.

Parth Patwa, Shivam Sharma, Srinivas PYKL, Vineeth Guptha, Gitanjali Kumari, Md. Shad Akhtar, Asif Ekbal, Amitava Das, and Tanmoy Chakraborty. 2020. Fighting an infodemic: COVID-19 fake news dataset. *CoRR*, abs/2011.03327.

Martin Potthast, Johannes Kiesel, Kevin Reinartz, Janek Bevendorff, and Benno Stein. 2017. A stylometric inquiry into hyperpartisan and fake news. *arXiv preprint arXiv:1702.05638*.

Yu Qiao, Daniel Wiechmann, and Elma Kerz. 2020. A language-based approach to fake news detection through interpretable features and BRNN. In *Proceedings of the 3rd International Workshop on Rumours and Deception in Social Media (RDSM)*, pages 14–31, Barcelona, Spain (Online). Association for Computational Linguistics.

Natali Ruchansky, Sungyong Seo, and Yan Liu. 2017. Csi: A hybrid deep model for fake news detection. In *Proceedings of the 2017 ACM on Conference on Information and Knowledge Management*, CIKM '17, page 797–806, New York, NY, USA. Association for Computing Machinery.

Cynthia Rudin. 2019. Stop explaining black box machine learning models for high stakes decisions and use interpretable models instead. *Nature Machine Intelligence*, 1(5):206–215.

Gautam Kishore Shahi and D. Nandini. 2020. Fakecovid - a multilingual cross-domain fact check news dataset for covid-19. *ArXiv*, abs/2006.11343.

Kai Shu, Amrita Bhattacharjee, Faisal Alatawi, Tahora H. Nazer, Kaize Ding, Mansooreh Karami, and Huan Liu. 2020a. Combating disinformation in a social media age. *WIREs Data Mining and Knowledge Discovery*, 10(6):e1385.

Kai Shu, Limeng Cui, Suhang Wang, Dongwon Lee, and Huan Liu. 2019a. defend: Explainable fake news detection. In *Proceedings of the 25th ACM SIGKDD International Conference on Knowledge Discovery & Data Mining*, pages 395–405.

Kai Shu, Limeng Cui, Suhang Wang, Dongwon Lee, and Huan Liu. 2019b. Defend: Explainable fake news detection. In *Proceedings of the 25th ACM SIGKDD International Conference on Knowledge Discovery Data Mining*, KDD '19, page 395–405, New York, NY, USA. Association for Computing Machinery.

Kai Shu, Deepak Mahudeswaran, Suhang Wang, Dongwon Lee, and Huan Liu. 2020b. Fakenewsnet: A data repository with news content, social context, and spatiotemporal information for studying fake news on social media. *Big Data*, 8(3):171–188. PMID: 32491943.

Kai Shu, Amy Sliva, Suhang Wang, Jiliang Tang, and Huan Liu. 2017. Fake news detection on social media: A data mining perspective. *SIGKDD Explor. Newsl.*, 19(1):22–36.

Kai Shu, Suhang Wang, and Huan Liu. 2019c. Beyond news contents: The role of social context for fake news detection. In *Proceedings of the Twelfth ACM International Conference on Web Search and Data Mining*, WSDM '19, page 312–320, New York, NY, USA. Association for Computing Machinery.

Daniel H Solomon, Richard Bucala, Mariana J Kaplan, and Peter A Nigrovic. 2020. The "infodemic" of covid-19.

Marcus Ströbel, Elma Kerz, Daniel Wiechmann, and Yu Qiao. 2018. Text genre classification based on linguistic complexity contours using a recurrent neural network. In *MRC@ IJCAI*, pages 56–63.

Chi Sun, Xipeng Qiu, Yige Xu, and Xuanjing Huang. 2019. How to fine-tune BERT for text classification? *CoRR*, abs/1905.05583.

Yla R. Tausczik and James W. Pennebaker. 2010. The psychological meaning of words: Liwc and computerized text analysis methods. *Journal of Language and Social Psychology*, 29(1):24–54.

James Thorne, Andreas Vlachos, Christos Christodoulopoulos, and Arpit Mittal. 2018. FEVER: a large-scale dataset for fact extraction and VERification. In *Proceedings of the 2018 Conference of the North American Chapter of the Association for Computational Linguistics: Human Language Technologies, Volume 1 (Long Papers)*, pages 809–819, New Orleans, Louisiana. Association for Computational Linguistics.

Joshua A Tucker, Andrew Guess, Pablo Barberá, Cristian Vaccari, Alexandra Siegel, Sergey Sanovich, Denis Stukal, and Brendan Nyhan. 2018. Social media, political polarization, and political disinformation: A review of the scientific literature. *Political polarization, and political disinformation: a review of the scientific literature (March 19, 2018).*

J. Utans and J. Moody. 1991. Selecting neural network architectures via the prediction risk: application to corporate bond rating prediction. In *Proceedings First International Conference on Artificial Intelligence Applications on Wall Street*, pages 35–41.

Inna Vogel, Jeong-Eun Choi, and Meghana Meghana. 2020. Topic related corpus for fake news detection.

Inna Vogel and Peter Jiang. 2019a. Fake news detection with the new german dataset "germanfakenc". In *Digital Libraries for Open Knowledge - 23rd International Conference on Theory and Practice of Digital Libraries, TPDL 2019, Oslo, Norway, September 9-12, 2019, Proceedings*, pages 288–295.

Inna Vogel and Peter Jiang. 2019b. Fake news detection with the new german dataset "GermanFakeNC". In *International Conference on Theory and Practice of Digital Libraries*, pages 288–295. Springer.

William Yang Wang. 2017. "liar, liar pants on fire": A new benchmark dataset for fake news detection. In *Proceedings of the 55th Annual Meeting of the Association for Computational Linguistics (Volume 2: Short Papers)*, pages 422–426, Vancouver, Canada. Association for Computational Linguistics.

Yaqing Wang, Fenglong Ma, Zhiwei Jin, Ye Yuan, Guangxu Xun, Kishlay Jha, Lu Su, and Jing Gao. 2018. Eann: Event adversarial neural networks for multi-modal fake news detection. In *Proceedings of the 24th ACM SIGKDD International Conference on Knowledge Discovery Data Mining*, KDD '18, page 849–857, New York, NY, USA. Association for Computing Machinery.

Christian M Wellbrock. 2011. Die journalistische qualität deutscher tageszeitungen–ein ranking. *Medienwirtschaft*, 8(2):22–31.

Zhilin Yang, Zihang Dai, Yiming Yang, Jaime G. Carbonell, Ruslan Salakhutdinov, and Quoc V. Le. 2019. Xlnet: Generalized autoregressive pretraining for language understanding. *CoRR*, abs/1906.08237.

Xinyi Zhou, Apurva Mulay, Emilio Ferrara, and Reza Zafarani. 2020a. Recovery: A multimodal repository for COVID-19 news credibility research. *CoRR*, abs/2006.05557.

Xinyi Zhou, Jindi Wu, and Reza Zafarani. 2020b. SAFE: similarity-aware multi-modal fake news detection. *CoRR*, abs/2003.04981.

Xinyi Zhou and R. Zafarani. 2018. Fake news: A survey of research, detection methods, and opportunities. *ArXiv*, abs/1812.00315.

Xinyi Zhou and Reza Zafarani. 2019. Network-based fake news detection: A pattern-driven approach. *SIGKDD Explor. Newsl.*, 21(2):48–60.

A Appendix

A.1 Preprocessing:

The following preprocessing steps were taken before using our texts as input to our models (in order to avoid models relying on trivial features):

- removal of phrase 'Bleiben Sie aufmerksam!', very prevalent in PravdaTV's articles
- removal of advertisement paragraph for book "Illuminatenblut: Die okkulten Rituale der Elite" by PravdaTV" ('... Wenn Sie mehr über die heimlichen Machenschaften der Elite erfahren wollen,...')
- removal of paragraphs that contain (capitalized) 'COMPACT' and 'Am besten gleich hier bestellen'. Compact-Online spreads a lot of advertisement for their magazines in their articles, mentioning COMPACT-Sonderausgabe, COMPACT-Magazin, etc.; since their phrases were almost always similar, but not exactly the same, it was hard to find a systematic approach to remove these advertisements. Thus, we removed the paragraphs from these articles as a whole in order to make sure there's no bias in our dataset
- removal of text brackets with text () at the end of each article. Many publishers appended (dpa) or similar to their articles
- removal of 'von [Name]' at end of first paragraph. Some publishers used this to reference the author in their articles
- removal of pattern 'rt/dpa', 'ns/sna/tm' at the end of news text

Table 6: Data on the average user engagement for each article

Engagement Feature	Real	Fake
Feature per tweet:		
Number of likes	8.90	3.48
Number of retweets	2.72	1.85
Number of replies	1.40	0.50
Number of quotes	0.43	0.19
Feature per article:		
Number of tweets	8.4	9.7
Number of likes	74.6	33.9
Number of retweets	22.8	18.0
Number of replies	11.7	4.9
Number of quotes	3.6	1.9

Table 7: Data on the average user profile for each tweet sharing an article

Profile Feature	Real	Fake
Number of followers	129,714	2,618
Number of friends	1,304	1,791
Overall number of tweets	67,732	55,093
Overall number of liked tweets	23,565	23,197

Table 8: Data on the syntactic complexity of news articles

Syntactic Feature	Real	Fake
Mean Word Length (in characters)	5.78	5.90
Clauses per Sentence	1.74	1.90
Coordinate Phrases per Clause	0.44	0.57
Mean length of Clause (in tokens)	9.25	9.99
Mean length of Sentence (in tokens)	16.0	19.2

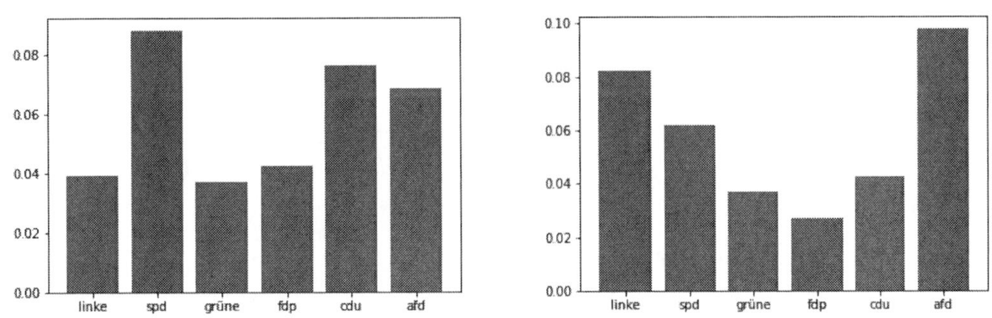

(a) Reliable publishers' mentions

(b) Unreliable publishers' mentions

Figure 4: Average number of mentions of political parties in the German parliament per news article by publisher

Combining sentence and table evidence to predict veracity of factual claims using TaPaS and RoBERTa

Martin Funkquist
martin.funkquist@gmail.com

Abstract

This paper describes a method for retrieving evidence and predicting the veracity of factual claims, on the FEVEROUS dataset. The evidence consists of both sentences and table cells. The proposed method is part of the FEVER shared task. It uses similarity scores between TF-IDF vectors to retrieve the textual evidence and similarity scores between dense vectors created by fine-tuned TaPaS models for tabular evidence retrieval. The evidence is passed through a dense neural network, that is trained on the FEVEROUS dataset, to produce a veracity label. The FEVEROUS score for the proposed model is 0.126 on the test dataset.

1 Introduction

Until recently, fact checking has been done solely by journalists and other human labor. With the large spread of information on the internet, the human labor component of fact checking has become a bottleneck. Vlachos and Riedel (Vlachos and Riedel, 2014) introduced the problem of automatic fact checking. Since then a lot of progress has been made, most notably with the release of the FEVER (Thorne et al., 2018) dataset, and succeeding systems using that dataset.

The FEVEROUS shared task (Aly et al., 2021) consists of retrieving evidence and predicting the veracity of a given claim, based on the retrieved evidence. This task can be divided into two separate tasks. The first is to retrieve the most relevant evidence from the given Wikipedia dataset. Here the evidence can be any form, such as sentences, table cells or list items. The second task is to predict the veracity for the claim, given the retrieved evidence.

In this paper a method for solving this task is proposed. The method can be divided into the following parts:

- Document retrieval
- Sentence extraction
- Table extraction
- Table cell extraction
- Claim veracity prediction

Each of the parts will be explained in detail later in this paper. The document retrieval and sentence extraction models are based on TF-IDF representation and cosine distances to get the most relevant documents and sentences. The table extraction part uses the model proposed by (Herzig et al., 2021), which uses dense representations from pre-trained TaPaS (Herzig et al., 2020) models to retrieve the most relevant tables. Similarly, the table cell extraction part uses a TaPaS model to retrieve the most relevant table cells from the previously retrieved tables. Lastly the claim veracity prediction model uses TaPaS and RoBERTa (Liu et al., 2019) representations of the retrieved evidence as input to a dense neural network that outputs the predicted veracity label of the given claim.

2 Related Work

Most previous research has been done on verification of claims based on textual evidence. However, a large amount of information on the internet is not in textual form, such as tables and databases. Chen et al introduced a dataset, TabFact (Chen et al., 2019), containing textual claims paired with tables and labelled either ENTAILED or REFUTED. Two methods for determining the veracity of the claim are also proposed, Table-BERT and Latent Program Algorithm (LPA). This paper describes a *closed setting*, where the table to use is given. In a real application an *open* setting would be encountered, where the evidence needs to be retrieved first, before veracity prediction can take place. The open setting scenario was studied by Schlichtkrull et al (Schlichtkrull et al., 2020) which introduced a model for retrieving tables before using these to predict a veracity label for a claim.

Proceedings of the Fourth Workshop on Fact Extraction and VERification (FEVER) at EMNLP 2021, pages 92–100
November 10, 2021. ©2021 Association for Computational Linguistics

The previously mentioned research has been investigating fact verification with either text or tables as evidence, but not both. UniK-QA (Oguz et al., 2020) is a question answering system that incorporates lists, tables and knowledge graphs. This is done by *flattening* the structured data into plain text using simple heuristics.

Chen et al introduced a dataset called HybridQA (Chen et al., 2020), consisting of questions paired with both tables and text that contain the answer. Thus, to get a good score on this dataset the provided model needs to be able to represent both tabular and textual data.

Pre-trained language models have turned out to be useful on downstream NLP tasks. When BERT (Devlin et al., 2018) was introduced it showed that a model can be trained on one task then be used to perform on another with good performance. A lot of other pre-trained models have been created after the introduction of BERT, one of them being RoBERTa (Liu et al., 2019). RoBERTa has the same architecture as BERT but is trained in a different way and on more data, which yields a better performance.

Most of the language models are pre-trained on textual data, but the FEVEROUS dataset requires reasoning over tabular data for some of the samples. TaPaS (Herzig et al., 2020) is one language model that is pre-trained on tables, instead of plain text. The input to the model includes tokens that represent the structure of the tables, such as row and column number.

3 Model

In this section the different parts of the model is described in detail. A graphical overview of the model is shown in Figure 1.

3.1 Document retrieval

For document retrieval, matching of TF-IDF vectors is used to efficiently compare a claim with all the documents in the dataset. Before creating the TF-IDF matrix, the words are stemmed to reduce the size of the matrix. To reduce the matrix even further the top 10% most frequent words are removed and all words that appeared less than 2 times were also removed. This results in a matrix of shape (N_{docs}, N_{tokens}), where $N_{docs} = 5421406$ and $N_{tokens} = 2634922$.

Preprocessing data To create the corpus only the sentence data for each document are used. As

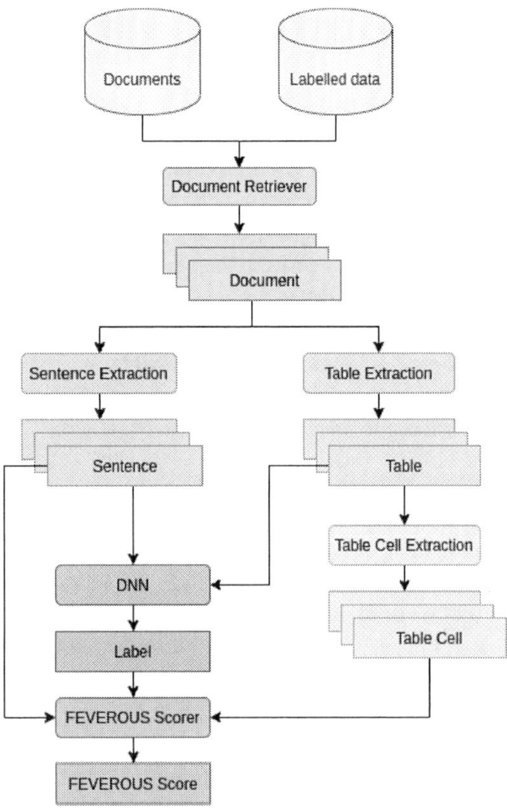

Figure 1: The design of the full model

there is more data than this, such as the tables and lists, the complete documents are not used in the retrieval step. However, the retrieval accuracy was considered sufficient, using only this reduced dataset.

Incorporating document title To improve the retrieval accuracy, a separate TF-IDF matrix is created using only the titles of the documents as the corpus. Since the title corpus is much smaller than the text corpus, it was possible to use n-grams in order to improve retrieval accuracy, with only a negligible increase in the size of the TF-IDF matrix. In this model bigrams are used for constructing the TF-IDF matrix.

3.2 Sentence extraction

For sentence extraction, a similar model as the one for document retrieval is used. Instead of dividing on distinct documents, each sentence in the top documents retrieved from the previous step is used. Then these sentences are matched with the claim using cosine similarity of the TF-IDF weighted vectors. Unigrams, bigrams and trigrams are used in order to create the TF-IDF matrix. The top *k* sentences are then selected as the evidence.

3.3 Table extraction

In the table extraction part, to get a more semantic representation of the tables, TaPaS (Herzig et al., 2020) is used. More specifically, the implementation of the dense table retriever described in (Herzig et al., 2021) is used[1]. Here the query and table representations are created from two separate TaPaS models. The output hidden representation of the [CLS] token is transformed through individual matrix projections into vectors, one for the query and one for the table, respectively. The matching score between a query and table is calculated by the dot product of the output vectors. Then the top *k* tables are returned. The dense table retriever is fine-tuned on the FEVEROUS dataset.

3.4 Table cell extraction

The model for extracting table cells is a fine-tuned TaPaS model. More specifically the model used is the TapasForQuestionAnswering from the Huggingface library[2], which is based on the model described in (Herzig et al., 2020). This model is first fine-tuned on the FEVEROUS dataset, then the fine-tuned model is used to extract the most relevant cells. Since the model only takes one table as input, each table is handled separately. A cell classification threshold is set to 0.1, to only retrieve the most relevant cells from each table. This means that there could be a varying amount of cells retrieved from each table. Because of this only the top m cells are kept, if the retriever would retrieve more than m cells. That leads to a maximum of $k \times m$ table cells for each claim, where k is the number of extracted tables.

3.5 Claim verification

In the last part of the model, a dense neural network is trained on the FEVEROUS dataset. This DNN consists of three dense layers, the first two with ReLU activations and the last with a Softmax activation for predicting the veracity of the given claim. The claim and top table are embedded using a pretrained TaPaS model and the sentence evidence is concatenated then embedded using a pretrained RoBERTa model. The TaPaS output are flattened before being concatenated with the RoBERTa output. The concatenated vector is then used as the input for the DNN. Note that the input to the TaPaS model is the *whole* highest scored table from the table extraction phase described in 3.3, and not the individual table cells extracted in section 3.4

One drawback with this model is that it only uses one table. The retrieved evidence may consists of more than one table, and it is not certain that this one table contains all the required information to give a valid prediction. Improvements to this model is discussed in Section 5.4.

The DNN is shown in Figure 2.

4 Results

4.1 Document Retrieval

The incorporation of titles using TF-IDF improved the accuracy of the document retrieval from 56.16% to 81.44%. However, note that when both title and text TF-IDF were used, the model returned a maximum of 10 documents (documents that is retrieved by both the text and title TF-IDF is only

[1] `https://github.com/google-research/tapas/blob/master/DENSE_TABLE_RETRIEVER.md`

[2] `https://huggingface.co/transformers/model_doc/tapas.html#tapasforquestionanswering`

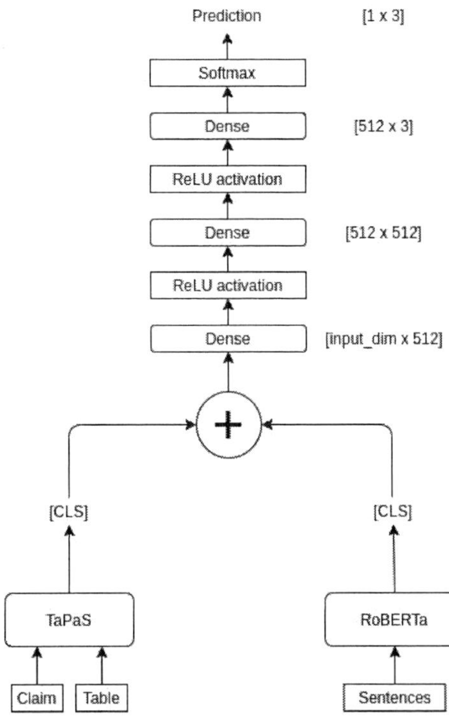

Figure 2: The design of the DNN for predicting the veracity of a claim

counted once), but in the case of only the text TF-IDF, a set of 5 documents were retrieved.

Comparing these results to the baseline document retrieval component of the FEVER system (Thorne et al., 2018) which is 77.24% for the top 10 retrieved documents, this seems like a sufficient score for document retrieval part of the system.

4.2 Sentence extraction

When retrieving the top k sentences, the result of the sentence extraction is as follows, for $k = 5$:

- Precision: 24.17
- Recall: 64.59
- F1: 35.18

Precision and recall is only calculated on the claims that have associated sentence evidence. If the examples that only contain table evidence were included, the precision would be lower.

4.3 Table extraction

The accuracy of the table extraction is measured with precision@k, and is shown in Table 1. As the results for the top 5 tables are good, this value is used in the end to end system.

Train		Dev	
k	**precision**	**k**	**precision**
1	0.59	1	0.75
5	0.81	5	0.91
10	0.87	10	0.95
15	0.90	15	0.96
50	0.96	50	0.99
100	0.97	100	0.995

Table 1: Results for the table retrieval using TaPaS on the train and dev set

4.4 Table cell extraction

The result for the table cell extraction is shown in Table 2. The accuracy of the cell extraction is limited by the table retrieval accuracy. Therefore, having higher accuracy than the retrieval part of the model is not possible.

The precision is low, which may be explained by the model extracting 5 cells from each of the 5 extracted tables, resulting in a total of 25 cells for each claim, and the evidence for most claims usually consists of just a few table cells.

	Tables only	**All**
Precision	04.95	10.09
Recall	29.89	61.95
F1	08.50	17.35

Table 2: Scores on the dev dataset for the table cell extraction, when considering only examples with table evidence and all examples

4.5 Claim verification

The accuracy of the claim verification part is calculated as the total amount of correct predictions divided by the total number of examples. The oracle results (e.g. the model is given the correct evidence) on the dev set are 0.68.

As shown in Table 3, the model only predicted SUPPORTS and REFUTES labels. Some reasons for this is discussed later in this paper.

The confusion matrix in Figure 3 shows that the model has some sense of which claims are supported and which ones are refuted.

4.6 FEVEROUS score

The final result is the FEVEROUS score, which measures the overall performance of the model. This is the only score available for the unlabelled test set. The score for this test set is presented in

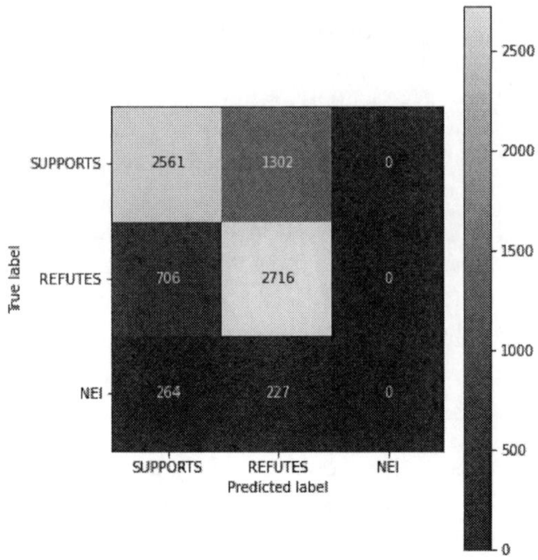

Figure 3: Confusion matrix of the predicted labels

Label	Predicted	Actual
SUPPORTS	3533	3869
REFUTES	4243	3417
NOT ENOUGH INFO	0	490

Table 3: The true labels compared to what the model predicted

Table 4, along with the score for the baseline model (Aly et al., 2021). As seen in the table, the model presented in this paper did not beat the baseline model.

	Baseline	Test
Feverous score	0.19	0.13
Label accuracy	0.53	0.43
Evidence precision	0.12	0.06
Evidence recall	0.29	0.28
Evidence F1	0.17	0.10

Table 4: Feverous score result on the unlabelled test set and baseline model.

The results presented previously has been on the train and dev datasets, and has been presented for each individual component of the model. The FEVEROUS score is the first score that measures the accuracy of the whole model, and might be the reason for the large drop in accuracy, since the errors propagate through the model.

5 Discussion

One improvement to the algorithm could be to incorporate the table caption into the table representation. Currently that information is discarded, but for some tables it could be crucial to know that to make a valid interpretation of the table. By studying the dataset, one could find that some required evidence are the table captions.

Another extension would be to add the page title or surrounding context into the representation of the table. Tables are rarely presented without some context around them, and for the algorithm to give a valid prediction, it might need to know the surrounding context, the same way as human beings would.

5.1 Table size restrictions

The tables that are too large to fit the TaPaS model are filtered out. The cap is set at $n_{rows} = 64$, $n_{cols} = 32$ and $n_{cells} = 512$. This means that evidence inside larger tables will never be retrieved with this model. If the size limitation problem would be solved, the accuracy of the model might increase.

However, with the given size limits only 424 tables that are needed for verification is filtered out. This results in 0.77% of the total amount of required tables, on the train and dev set. Therefore, increasing the maximum possible size of the tables will not likely lead to a significantly better score, unless the test set has a much larger portion of large tables.

5.2 Limit on the amount of retrieved cells

For the table retriever component, each table was limited to retrieve the top 5 cells. This means that if more than 5 cells in a single table were part of the evidence, these cells would never be retrieved. Here an improvement could be to analyze the probabilities for all table cells simultaneously, in order to select the most relevant cells from all tables, instead of only the most relevant cells from each table separately, as done in this model.

There are 12904 claims in the train and dev datasets that need more than 5 table cells as evidence from at least one table. This is 16.3% of the total amount of claims, which is a significant amount. Thus, removing the limit of 5 cells per table might contribute to an increased score.

5.3 Improvements on the veracity prediction model

As shown in the results for the veracity prediction model, the model did not predict any NOT ENOUGH INFO (NEI) labels. One reason for this could be that the dataset is not balanced and contains significantly more data samples for the other labels. This could be solved by sampling NEI data points as done in the FEVEROUS baseline (Aly et al., 2021). Without the sampling of NEI samples the baseline model does not predict any NEI labels correctly.

The test set consists of 19% NEI samples, while the train set has 3% and the dev set has 6%. Since the veracity prediction model did not predict any NEI labels for any of the datasets, this hurts the accuracy on the test set more than the accuracy on the other datasets.

Another reason why the model does not predict any NEI labels could be because the evidence retrieved for the NEI samples may not be as relevant as the evidence for the other labels. Therefore, the model did not find a good correlation between the NEI evidences.

The confusion matrix in Figure 3 shows that the model predicts the SUPPORTS and REFUTES labels for the NEI samples about an equal amount of times. There is no clear sign that it has a bias towards predicting one or the other. This might mean that the model has no idea of how to treat NEI samples.

5.4 Extending the veracity prediction network input

As previously mentioned, one drawback with the veracity prediction network is that it only takes one table as input. This way it discards the other tables that have been retrieved, because all tables except the top one, are not used for predicting the veracity. Thus, a possible improvement to the method would be to take all the retrieved tables into consideration.

The train and dev datasets have a total of 6624 samples which have multiple tables as evidence. With a total of 79181 samples this means that 8.37% of the samples needs multiple tables to determine the correct label of the claim. This is a significant portion of the samples and therefore incorporating multiple tables into the label prediction model could potentially yield an increased score.

The current model has a large input representation, of the size $l_R \times d_R + l_T \times d_T$, where $l_R = 256$ is the RoBERTa sequence length, $d_R = 768$ is the RoBERTa hidden dimension, $l_T = 512$ is the TaPaS sequence length and $d_T = 128$ is the TaPaS hidden dimension. This adds up to a total input dimension of 262144, which is fairly large. The main reason that only one table was used in the claim verification model is because of this large input dimension. Using all of the k extracted tables by concatenating the vector representations would yield a larger input dimension. For $k = 5$ the input dimensions of the DNN would increase to 524288 as the TaPaS sequence length would be $l_T = 2560$.

In the proposed input representation each word in the sentences and each cell in the table have their own representation. One reduction in the dimensionality could be to represent each sentence as a vector, instead of each individual word. A similar strategy could be used for the tables. A set of cells could have a common vector representation instead of each individual cell having its own representation, as in the current state of the model.

5.5 Future work

One obvious task to investigate would be to include several tables in the prediction part, as described in the previous section. This could be done by creating a model to represent multiple tables, or extending the input layer of the proposed prediction model.

Another interesting topic would be to investigate the possibility of training a BERT based Transformer model that has the ability to take both tables and sentences as inputs, and output the veracity as the hidden representation of the [CLS] token, and at the same time provide the most relevant table cells. This could even be extended to input a set of say 5 documents containing both text and tables, and the model would predict the aforementioned elements. But it seems infeasible due to the large input representations that would be needed to represent the full documents.

6 Conclusion

This article describes a method for solving the FEVEROUS shared task introduced by (Aly et al., 2021). The system consists of two main parts, the retrieval part and the verification part. In the retrieval part, documents are first retrieved, then sentences and table cells are extracted from these documents. For the verification part, the previously retrieved evidence, in form of sentences and table cells, are used to make a prediction about the veracity of a given claim.

While the results show that this method may not be feasible in a real world application, there are parts that show promising results. The problem of automatic fact checking is difficult and includes several NLP topics, such as information extraction and natural language inference. Certainly there will be further advances in this topic, which may result in a system that is usable in real world applications.

Acknowledgements

Thanks to Rami Aly, Christos Christodoulopoulos, Oana Cocarascu, Zhijiang Guo, Arpit Mittal, Michael Schlichtkrull, James Thorne and Andreas Vlachos for organizing the FEVER 2021 workshop.

References

Rami Aly, Zhijiang Guo, Michael Sejr Schlichtkrull, James Thorne, Andreas Vlachos, Christos Christodoulopoulos, Oana Cocarascu, and Arpit Mittal. 2021. FEVEROUS: fact extraction and verification over unstructured and structured information. *CoRR*, abs/2106.05707.

Wenhu Chen, Hongmin Wang, Jianshu Chen, Yunkai Zhang, Hong Wang, Shiyang Li, Xiyou Zhou, and William Yang Wang. 2019. Tabfact: A large-scale dataset for table-based fact verification. *CoRR*, abs/1909.02164.

Wenhu Chen, Hanwen Zha, Zhiyu Chen, Wenhan Xiong, Hong Wang, and William Yang Wang. 2020. HybridQA: A dataset of multi-hop question answering over tabular and textual data. In *Findings of the Association for Computational Linguistics: EMNLP 2020*, pages 1026–1036, Online. Association for Computational Linguistics.

Jacob Devlin, Ming-Wei Chang, Kenton Lee, and Kristina Toutanova. 2018. BERT: pre-training of deep bidirectional transformers for language understanding. *CoRR*, abs/1810.04805.

Jonathan Herzig, Thomas Müller, Syrine Krichene, and Julian Martin Eisenschlos. 2021. Open domain question answering over tables via dense retrieval. *CoRR*, abs/2103.12011.

Jonathan Herzig, Pawel Krzysztof Nowak, Thomas Müller, Francesco Piccinno, and Julian Eisenschlos. 2020. TaPas: Weakly supervised table parsing via pre-training. In *Proceedings of the 58th Annual Meeting of the Association for Computational Linguistics*, pages 4320–4333, Online. Association for Computational Linguistics.

Yinhan Liu, Myle Ott, Naman Goyal, Jingfei Du, Mandar Joshi, Danqi Chen, Omer Levy, Mike Lewis, Luke Zettlemoyer, and Veselin Stoyanov. 2019. Roberta: A robustly optimized BERT pretraining approach. *CoRR*, abs/1907.11692.

Barlas Oguz, Xilun Chen, Vladimir Karpukhin, Stan Peshterliev, Dmytro Okhonko, Michael Sejr Schlichtkrull, Sonal Gupta, Yashar Mehdad, and Scott Yih. 2020. Unified open-domain question answering with structured and unstructured knowledge. *CoRR*, abs/2012.14610.

Michael Sejr Schlichtkrull, Vladimir Karpukhin, Barlas Oguz, Mike Lewis, Wen-tau Yih, and Sebastian Riedel. 2020. Joint verification and reranking for open fact checking over tables. *CoRR*, abs/2012.15115.

James Thorne, Andreas Vlachos, Christos Christodoulopoulos, and Arpit Mittal. 2018. FEVER: a large-scale dataset for fact extraction and verification. *CoRR*, abs/1803.05355.

Andreas Vlachos and Sebastian Riedel. 2014. Fact checking: Task definition and dataset construction. In *Proceedings of the ACL 2014 Workshop on Language Technologies and Computational Social Science*, pages 18–22, Baltimore, MD, USA. Association for Computational Linguistics.

A Dataset statistics

It can be valuable to take a look at the statistics of the dataset in order to examine where the model could do wrong. Table 5 shows some statistics for the FEVEROUS dataset. As can be seen in the label statistic, there are many more samples with labels SUPPORTS and REFUTES than NOT ENOUGH INFO. This may be the reason for the model not predicting any NOT ENOUGH INFO labels. It may not have learned what separates these labels from the others, due to the lack of examples, or it could simply assume that the distribution of labels will be the same always and be satisfied with only optimizing on predicting the other labels. Thus, one improvement in the training phase could be to sample NOT ENOUGH INFO examples for the Wikipedia data, as done in the FEVEROUS baseline system.

Worth noting in Table 5 is that a total of 4921 (about 6%) of the claims have evidence that is neither a sentence nor a table cell. The model proposed in this paper will never return any of these evidences. An extension would then be to include this type of evidence in a future iteration of the model.

The distribution of the different types of evidence is shown in Figure 4. There are very few samples that have more than 5 sentences as evidence, which means that not many examples will be missed due to a known limitation in the model. The model currently only returns a maximum of 25 table cells, and there are a few examples that have more cells than this as the evidence. However, this is comparatively small compared to the total number of examples, which means that the majority of errors are not due to this limitation of the system, given that the distribution of data samples is similar for the test set.

	Total	**Train**	**Dev**
Samples	79181	71291	7890
w. single evidence	72945	65764	7181
w. multiple evidence	6236	5527	709
w. sentence evidence	56139	50484	5655
w. table evidence	47174	42611	4563
w. other evidence	4921	4423	498
Labels			
SUPPORTS	45743	41835	3908
REFUTES	30696	27215	3481
NOT ENOUGH INFO	2742	2241	501

Table 5: Feverous score result on the unlabelled test set.

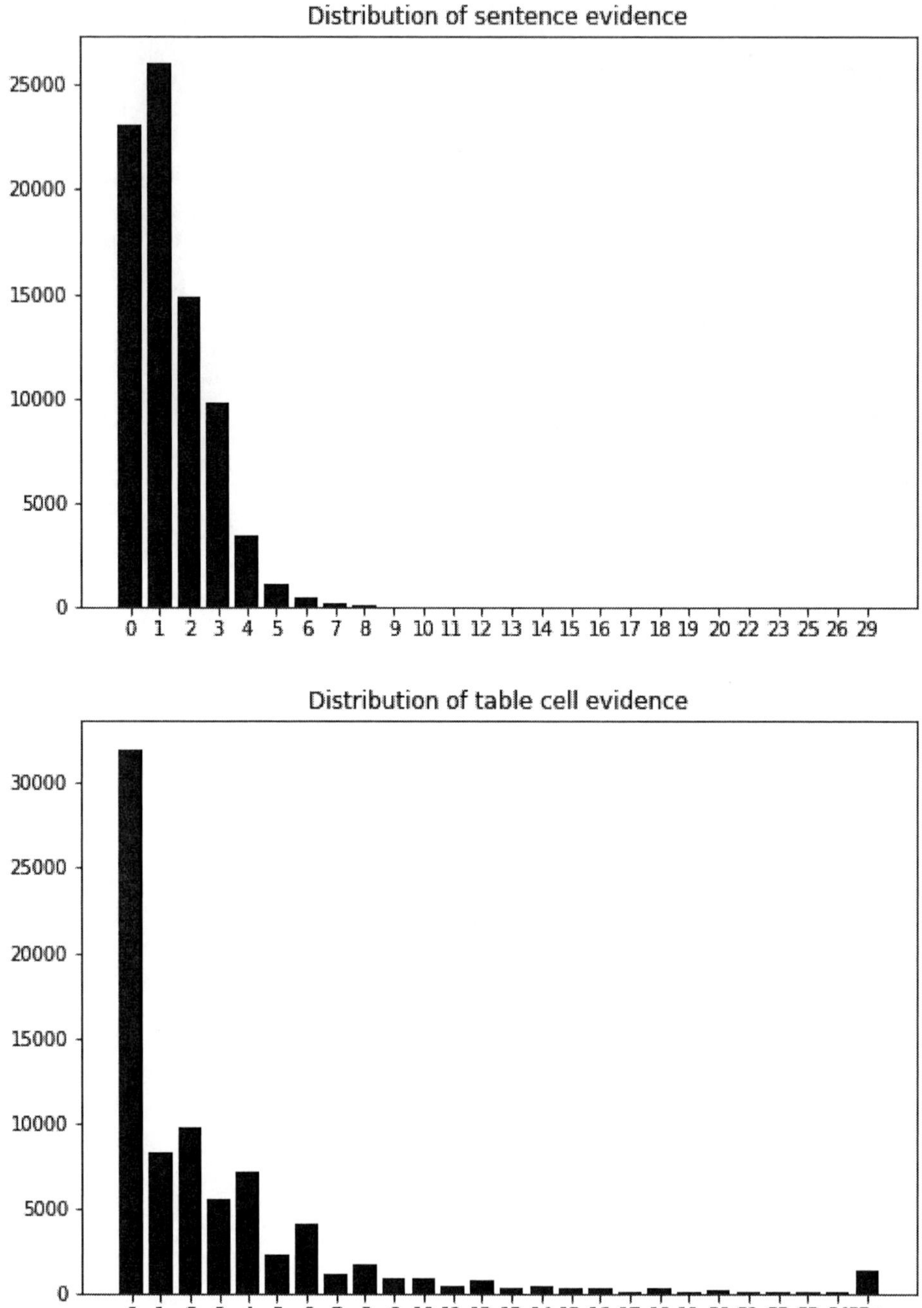

Figure 4: The distribution of claims with the given sentence evidence and table cell evidence respectively

Automatic Fact-Checking with Document-level Annotations using BERT and Multiple Instance Learning

Aalok Sathe*
Massachusetts Institute of Technology
asathe@mit.edu

Joonsuk Park
University of Richmond
NAVER AI Lab
park@joonsuk.org

Abstract

Automatic fact-checking is crucial for recognizing misinformation spreading on the internet. Most existing fact-checkers break down the process into several subtasks, one of which determines candidate evidence sentences that can potentially support or refute the claim to be verified; typically, evidence sentences with gold-standard labels are needed for this. In a more realistic setting, however, such sentence-level annotations are not available. In this paper, we tackle the natural language inference (NLI) subtask—given a document and a (sentence) claim, determine whether the document supports or refutes the claim—only using document-level annotations. Using fine-tuned BERT and multiple instance learning, we achieve 81.9% accuracy, significantly outperforming the existing results on the WikiFactCheck-English dataset.

1 Introduction

As the volume of information present on the internet steeply increases, automatic fact-checking has become a promising approach to identify and stop the spread of misinformation. Active research in this area has been supported in part by a handful of carefully curated datasets (Thorne et al., 2018a; Hanselowski et al., 2019; Wadden et al., 2020).

While these datasets have been playing a crucial role in the development of the latest fact-checkers, they do not faithfully represent the reality in certain aspects. First, these datasets come with short evidence snippets for the claims; most existing fact-checkers rely on such sentence-level evidence annotations to build the natural language inference (NLI) component of their systems—e.g. given an evidence sentence and a claim sentence, determine if the claim is supported (Thorne et al., 2018b). Second, most of the datasets consist of synthetic claims written by annotators based on snippets of evidence. Both aspects render it difficult to readily apply the findings in real applications.

Field	Content
id	115724
claim	The hindwings are uniform grey with a narrow marginal line.
context	Eupoca sanctalis is a moth in the Crambidae family. [...]
refuted	The hindwings are uniform blue with a broad marginal line.
url	http://digitalcommons.unl.edu/[...]

Table 1: Example entry from WikiFactCheck-English. The URL is for the evidence document cited in support of the claim in the Wikipedia article.

WikiFactCheck-English (Sathe et al., 2020) was constructed to address the aforementioned concerns. The dataset consists of 124k entries each consisting of a claim[1], context, and evidence document extracted from English Wikipedia articles. (See Table 1 for an example.) We believe that the real claims and lengthy evidence documents without sentence-level annotations will lead to fact-checkers that can better handle claims in the wild.

In this paper, we tackle the NLI subtask—given a document and a (sentence) claim, determine whether the document supports or refutes the claim—only using document-level annotations. We improve on existing systems trained and tested on the WikiFactCheck-English dataset during both steps of the 2-step pipeline: evidence retrieval and support verification. We find that fine-tuned BERT with multiple instance learning (MIL)—to use multiple candidate evidence sentences—results in about 13% increase in accuracy over the baseline. However, incorporating Sentence-BERT (SBERT) (Reimers and Gurevych, 2019) to identify candidate evidence sentences during evidence

* Work done while at the University of Richmond

[1] 34k of these come with manually written 'refuted' claims.

Proceedings of the Fourth Workshop on Fact Extraction and VERification (FEVER) at EMNLP 2021, pages 101–107
November 10, 2021.

retrieval does not lead to a noticeable improvement.

2 Related Works

Many recent works on automatic fact-checking have attempted to employ Transformers, BERT in particular. This was motivated by BERT having showed promising results for many NLP tasks (Devlin et al., 2019). To mention a few relevant examples, Soleimani et al. (2020) tackle the shared task from the third FEVER workshop (Christodoulopoulos et al., 2020) by constructing a 2-step pipeline. They use BERT in the evidence retrieval step to rank evidence by relevance. Then, BERT is employed once more in the support verification step to make the final prediction using the retrieved evidence. We also have a 2-step pipeline, but methods used in each step is distinct from their work.

Lee et al. (2020) take a new approach using BERT to the otherwise traditional pipeline of fact-checking in FEVER-like tasks. The authors treat BERT as a knowledge base and use its masked language modeling predictions to decide the factual correctness of the claim. While it is a novel approach, it does not provide a promising performance gain in practice. Also, we are working with a dataset where the claims are extracted from Wikipedia, but BERT uses Wikipedia as part of its training. For these reasons, we decided that this approach would not be suitable in our work.

Zhong et al. (2020) highlight the complexity of the fact-checking task, where more than one sentence collectively support or refute a claim. Thus, the authors create semantic graphs and reason over these structures using graph convolutional network and graph attention netowrk. There report improvement in performance in the FEVER task (Thorne et al., 2018a). In our work, we assume a simple semantic structure of evidence sentences. This is based on an observation that when people cite a document in support of their factual claim in Wikipedia, the claim tends to be one of the main points of the document. And points are typically stated in a single sentence or span over consecutive sentences.

The work we build off of in this paper is from Sathe et al. (2020). The authors released a new fact-checking dataset with only document-level annotations that we use in this work. Along with it, they presented baseline systems consisting of a two-step pipeline: evidence retrieval and support verification. In our work, we adopt the same pipeline but make improvements to each step using BERT-based approaches. Also, unlike their approach, we retrieve multiple sentences during the evidence retrieval step and compute the final aggregated prediction using multiple instance learning.

3 Method

We tackle the NLI subtask of automatic fact checking—given a relevant document (a list of sentences E_c) and a claim c, determine whether the E_c supports or refutes c. This is done in two-steps: (1) evidence retrieval and (2) support verification, as shown in Figure 1. The same pipeline was used in Sathe et al. (2020); we improve both steps using BERT-based approaches and multiple instance learning to make use of multiple candidate evidence sentences.

3.1 Evidence Retrieval

The evidence retrieval step involves retrieving candidate evidence sentence(s) from the evidence document E_c that either supports or refutes the claim c. We retrieve the top k sentences $(e_1, e_2, ..., e_k) \in E_c$ that are most similar to c. These in turn are likely to be relevant for verifying c.

We improve on the Levenshtein distance (LD) used in the baseline (Sathe et al., 2020), by incorporating SBERT (Reimers and Gurevych, 2019). SBERT uses siamese and triplet networks to derive sentence embeddings capturing semantic similarities. Because the claims and evidence documents in the WikiFactCheck-English dataset are drawn from distinct sources, they are often dissimilar in their content and style. Thus, we expect SBERT capturing semantic similarity to be more effective than LD capturing surface-level textual similarity. We use a pretrained SBERT architecture fine-tuned to STS-B (semantic textual similarity benchmark), part of the popular NLU benchmark set 'GLUE' (generalized language understanding and evaluation) (Wang et al., 2018).

Given the large number of sentences in E_c, we first filter out sentences least-likely to be the evidence sentence: Of the sentence in E_c that have at least 1 word overlap with the claim, we use SBERT with a classification layer outputting a scalar similarity score to determine k most similar sentences for $k = 1, 3, 5$.

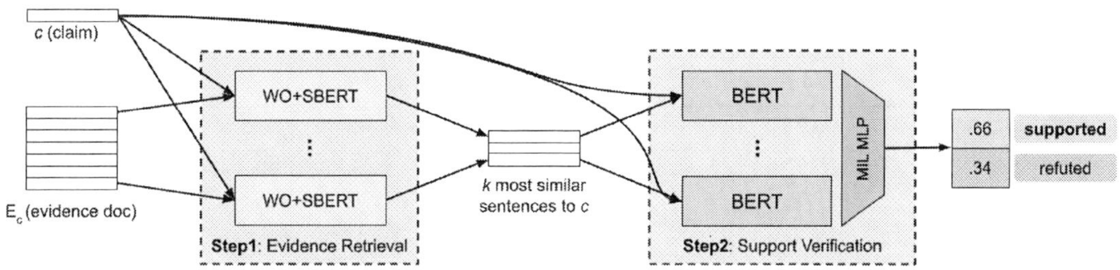

Figure 1: The 2-step pipeline to determine if evidence document E_c supports or refutes claim c. The final output is a distribution over probabilities of E_c supporting and refuting c. The components depicted are of our best performing system: the evidence retrieval step consists of word overlap (WO) and Sentence-BERT (SBERT); the support verification step consists of BERT and multiple instance learning (MIL).

3.2 Support Verification

The support verification step takes a claim c and a list of candidate evidence sentence(s) $e_1, e_2, ..., e_k \in E_c$ from the previous step and outputs a distribution over two labels denoting the relative likelihood of whether the claim is 'supported' or 'refuted' by E_c. Our approach to this step involves two subparts: natural language inference (NLI) and attention-based aggregation. Again, E_c may contain one or more sentences that support or refute c, but there is no sentence-level gold-standard label for NLI for each sentence in E_c.

Thus, we use multiple instance learning (MIL) (Angelidis and Lapata, 2018; Ilse et al., 2018) to learn sentence-level labels in a semi-supervised manner by aggregating over multiple labels and computing loss at the document level.

In the following, $\mathbf{BERT}\langle[\texttt{CLS}]...\rangle$ denotes the contextualized representation of the $[\texttt{CLS}]$ token obtained after passing in $[\texttt{CLS}], \mathrm{E}_1, \mathrm{E}_2, \ldots [\texttt{SEP}], \mathrm{C}_1, \mathrm{C}_2, \ldots$ as the input to BERT. Here, the [CLS] token is a special token whose representation is meant to capture relevant features of the input for classification (Devlin et al., 2019).

We first initialize a binary ("supported" and "refuted") NLI classifier using $\mathbf{BERT}\langle[\texttt{CLS}]...\rangle$:

$$\mathbf{y}' = ReLU\,(W \cdot \mathbf{BERT}\langle[\texttt{CLS}]...\rangle + b_W) \quad (1)$$

where $\mathbf{y}'$ contains the predictions for the claim and evidence sentence pairs.

Notice that for a claim c and top-k candidate evidence sentences $e_1, e_2, \ldots, e_k$, we have k input pairs $\langle e_i, c\rangle$. For each pair, we have an NLI prediction $\mathbf{y}'_i$. However, we only have the ground truth label corresponding to $\langle E_c, c\rangle$. Therefore, we will use another MLP to transform the same representation used for NLI to compute softmaxed attention weights $\mathbf{a}$ over the sentences.

$$\mathbf{a}' = Sigmoid\,(V \cdot \mathbf{BERT}\langle[\texttt{CLS}]...\rangle + b_V) \quad (2)$$

$$\mathbf{a} = Softmax(\mathbf{a}') \quad (3)$$

Here, each element $\mathbf{a}_i$ of $\mathbf{a}$ is the attention weight for aggregating the predictions for $\langle c, e_i\rangle$. Then our aggregated document-level predicted label is:

$$\mathbf{y} = \mathbf{a}^T \mathbf{y}' \quad (4)$$

where $\mathbf{y}$ is a vector giving the probability distribution over the two labels, "supported" and "refuted". Loss is computed using Cross Entropy loss with the appropriate ground truth label. In the case when $k = 1$, the attention weight for the single prediction is by default 1, and this automatically reduces to not using MIL.

4 Experiments

4.1 Setup

The experiments were conducted on the WikiFactCheck-English dataset. We trained the models using a randomly sampled set of 10k supported claims, each with a corresponding refuted claim, for a total of 20k examples selected from the training set. Then, the performances were measured on the heldout test set of about 10k supported claims, each with a corresponding refuted claim, for a total of about 20k examples to match the setup from Sathe et al. (2020).

We performed a hyperparameter search for learning rates between $1e{-}5$ to $5e{-}4$ in increments of powers of 10; for gradient accumulation steps between 4 and 16 in increments of 4; pretrained BERT models among `bert-base-uncased` (the 'vanilla' BERT) and `bert-base-mnli` (vanilla BERT finetuned on the MNLI dataset from Williams et al. (2018)).

System	System Components			Performance			
	Evidence Retrieval	k	Support Verification	Prec.	Rec.	F1	Acc.
Sathe et al. (2020)	(WO +) LD	1	Logistic Regression	.664	.729	.695	.680
LD + BERT	(WO +) LD	1	BERT	.856	.748	.798	.811
	(WO +) LD	3	BERT (with MIL)	.845	**.767**	.804	.813
	(WO +) LD	5	BERT (with MIL)	.847	**.767**	.805	.815
SBERT + BERT	(WO +) SBERT	1	BERT	.853	.746	.796	.809
	(WO +) SBERT	3	BERT (with MIL)	.855	.762	.806	.816
	(WO +) SBERT	5	BERT (with MIL)	**.857**	**.767**	**.810**	**.819**

Table 2: We take the best performing system (with respect to accuracy) by Sathe et al. (2020) as the baseline. In that system, Levenshtein distance (LD) is used to find k=1 most similar sentence to the claim in the evidence document, among the sentences that have at least one word overlap (WO) with the claim. Then, logistic regression is used to make a prediction. LD + BERT improves on the baseline in the support verification step using BERT and larger k's—# of candidate evidence sentences—with multiple instance learning (MIL). SBERT+BERT improves on LD+BERT by using SBERT to find k most similar sentences to the claim among those with one or more WO.

4.2 Results and Analysis

As summarized in Table 2, the best performing system, SBERT+BERT with $k = 5$, achieves 81.9% accuracy and 81.0% F1. This is a significant improvement over the best performing system from Sathe et al. (2020). Most of the improvement is attributable to the use of fine-tuned BERT during support verification; simply replacing logistic regression with BERT in the inference stage leads to 13% increase in accuracy. This is expected given the strong performance of BERT on various NLP tasks.

Small additional gains seem to result from using multiple candidate evidence sentences. For $k = 1, 3, 5$, there is a mostly consistent upward trend in performance across the board, though the magnitude is small. The increase in performance is greater between $k = 1$ and 3, compared that between to 3 and 5, meaning the positive impact may diminish as k increases. In theory, using multiple candidate evidence sentences can be helpful in at least two ways. First, it can reduce the error propagating from evidence retrieval to support verification. That is, it is less likely that the true evidence sentence is not included in the top-5 most similar sentences than in the top-1. Second, multiple sentences may collectively serve as evidence for a given claim. In this case, each evidence sentence would partially verify the claim, thus having a single evidence sentence would not be enough.

Incorporating SBERT in evidence retrieval improves the performance only when multiple evidence sentences are used. And when it does help, the difference is marginal. This suggests that identifying evidence sentences based on LD, which quantifies the textual similarity, is comparable to relying on SBERT, which is intended to measure semantic similarity. We suspect that this could be due to the characteristics of this particular dataset; the evidence documents are previously published documents cited in support of factual claims made on Wikipedia articles. Often, these claims are very similar to a sentence in the document, as there is little incentive to rephrase the claim. This is different from other datasets in which annotators are instructed to write novel claims based on evidence sentences or snippets.

5 Conclusion and Future Work

We presented a 2-step pipeline to determine if a document supports or refutes a claim only using document-level annotations. Fine-tuned BERT with MIL to use multiple candidate evidence sentences resulted in about 13% increase in accuracy over the baseline. However, incorporating SBERT in evidence retrieval did not lead to additional gains that are noticeable.

In the future, we want to leverage the context, as sentences in this dataset, and in the wild, are often not self-contained. We expect the context to be useful for disambiguating keywords in both evidence retrieval and support verification. Note that both the claim and evidence sentences have contexts, and the context of an evidence sentence is a potential evidence sentence itself. Both opens up many possibilities to be explored.

Acknowledgments

We would like to thank the University of Richmond and the Thomas F. and Kate Miller Jeffress Memorial Trust, Bank of America, Trustee for their generous support for this project. We also thank the anonymous reviewers for their comments.

References

Stefanos Angelidis and Mirella Lapata. 2018. Multiple instance learning networks for fine-grained sentiment analysis. *Transactions of the Association for Computational Linguistics*, 6:17–31.

Pepa Atanasova, Preslav Nakov, Lluís Màrquez, Alberto Barrón-Cedeño, Georgi Karadzhov, Tsvetomila Mihaylova, Mitra Mohtarami, and James Glass. 2019. Automatic fact-checking using context and discourse information. *Journal of Data and Information Quality (JDIQ)*, 11(3):1–27.

Lukas Biewald. 2020. Experiment tracking with weights and biases. Software available from wandb.com.

Yonatan Bilu, Daniel Hershcovich, and Noam Slonim. 2015. Automatic claim negation: why, how and when. In *Proceedings of the 2nd Workshop on Argumentation Mining*, pages 84–93.

Peter Bloem. 2019. Transformers from scratch.

Samuel R. Bowman, Gabor Angeli, Christopher Potts, and Christopher D. Manning. 2015. A large annotated corpus for learning natural language inference. In *Proceedings of the 2015 Conference on Empirical Methods in Natural Language Processing (EMNLP)*. Association for Computational Linguistics.

John Burger and Lisa Ferro. 2005. Generating an entailment corpus from news headlines. pages 49–54. Association for Computational Linguistics.

Christos Christodoulopoulos, James Thorne, Andreas Vlachos, Oana Cocarascu, and Arpit Mittal, editors. 2020. *Proceedings of the Third Workshop on Fact Extraction and VERification (FEVER)*. Association for Computational Linguistics, Online.

Giovanni Luca Ciampaglia, Prashant Shiralkar, Luis M Rocha, Johan Bollen, Filippo Menczer, and Alessandro Flammini. 2015. Computational fact checking from knowledge networks. *PloS one*, 10(6):e0128193.

Ido Dagan, Bill Dolan, Bernardo Magnini, and Dan Roth. 2010. Recognizing textual entailment: Rational, evaluation and approaches–erratum. *Natural Language Engineering*, 16(1):105–105.

Jacob Devlin, Ming-Wei Chang, Kenton Lee, and Kristina Toutanova. 2019. Bert: Pre-training of deep bidirectional transformers for language understanding. In *NAACL-HLT (1)*.

Andrea Esuli and Fabrizio Sebastiani. 2006. Sentiwordnet: A publicly available lexical resource for opinion mining. In *LREC*, volume 6, pages 417–422. Citeseer.

William Ferreira and Andreas Vlachos. 2016. Emergent: a novel data-set for stance classification. pages 1163–1168.

Matt Gardner, Joel Grus, Mark Neumann, Oyvind Tafjord, Pradeep Dasigi, Nelson F Liu, Matthew Peters, Michael Schmitz, and Luke Zettlemoyer. 2018. Allennlp: A deep semantic natural language processing platform. In *Proceedings of Workshop for NLP Open Source Software (NLP-OSS)*, pages 1–6.

Swapnil Ghuge and Arindam Bhattacharya. 2014. Survey in textual entailment.

Suchin Gururangan, Swabha Swayamdipta, Omer Levy, Roy Schwartz, Samuel Bowman, and Noah A Smith. 2018. Annotation artifacts in natural language inference data. In *Proceedings of the 2018 Conference of the North American Chapter of the Association for Computational Linguistics: Human Language Technologies, Volume 2 (Short Papers)*, pages 107–112.

Andreas Hanselowski, Christian Stab, Claudia Schulz, Zile Li, and Iryna Gurevych. 2019. A richly annotated corpus for different tasks in automated fact-checking. In *Proceedings of the 23rd Conference on Computational Natural Language Learning (CoNLL)*, pages 493–503, Hong Kong, China. Association for Computational Linguistics.

Andrew Hickl, John Williams, Jeremy Bensley, Kirk Roberts, Bryan Rink, and Ying Shi. 2006. Recognizing textual entailment with lcc's groundhog system. volume 18.

Christopher Hidey, Tuhin Chakrabarty, Tariq Alhindi, Siddharth Varia, Kriste Krstovski, Mona Diab, and Smaranda Muresan. 2020. Deseption: Dual sequence prediction and adversarial examples for improved fact-checking. In *Proceedings of the 58th Annual Meeting of the Association for Computational Linguistics*, pages 8593–8606.

Matthew Honnibal and Ines Montani. 2017. spaCy 2: Natural language understanding with Bloom embeddings, convolutional neural networks and incremental parsing. To appear.

M Ilse, JM Tomczak, and M Welling. 2018. Attention-based deep multiple instance learning. *Proceedings of Machine Learning Research*, 80:2127–2136.

Tushar Khot, Ashish Sabharwal, and Peter Clark. 2018. Scitail: A textual entailment dataset from science question answering. In *Thirty-Second AAAI Conference on Artificial Intelligence*.

Nayeon Lee, Belinda Z Li, Sinong Wang, Wen-tau Yih, Hao Ma, and Madian Khabsa. 2020. Language models as fact checkers? In *Proceedings of the*

Third Workshop on Fact Extraction and VERification (FEVER), pages 36–41.

Edward Loper and Steven Bird. 2002. NLTK: The natural language toolkit. In *Proceedings of the ACL-02 Workshop on Effective tools and methodologies for teaching natural language processing and computational linguistics*, pages 63–70.

Daniel Marcu and Abdessamad Echihabi. 2002. An unsupervised approach to recognizing discourse relations. In *ACL*, pages 368–375.

George A Miller. 1995. Wordnet: a lexical database for english. *Communications of the ACM*, 38(11):39–41.

Ankur Parikh, Oscar Täckström, Dipanjan Das, and Jakob Uszkoreit. 2016. A decomposable attention model for natural language inference. In *Proceedings of the 2016 Conference on Empirical Methods in Natural Language Processing*, pages 2249–2255.

Joonsuk Park and Claire Cardie. 2012. Improving implicit discourse relation recognition through feature set optimization. In *Proceedings of the 13th Annual Meeting of the Special Interest Group on Discourse and Dialogue*, SIGDIAL '12, pages 108–112, Stroudsburg, PA, USA. Association for Computational Linguistics.

Verónica Pérez-Rosas, Bennett Kleinberg, Alexandra Lefevre, and Rada Mihalcea. 2018. Automatic detection of fake news. In *Proceedings of the 27th International Conference on Computational Linguistics*, pages 3391–3401.

Bryan A Plummer, Liwei Wang, Chris M Cervantes, Juan C Caicedo, Julia Hockenmaier, and Svetlana Lazebnik. 2015. Flickr30k entities: Collecting region-to-phrase correspondences for richer image-to-sentence models. In *Proceedings of the IEEE international conference on computer vision*, pages 2641–2649.

Yada Pruksachatkun, Jason Phang, Haokun Liu, Phu Mon Htut, Xiaoyi Zhang, Richard Yuanzhe Pang, Clara Vania, Katharina Kann, and Samuel Bowman. 2020. Intermediate-task transfer learning with pretrained language models: When and why does it work? In *Proceedings of the 58th Annual Meeting of the Association for Computational Linguistics*, pages 5231–5247.

Nils Reimers and Iryna Gurevych. 2019. Sentence-bert: Sentence embeddings using siamese bert-networks. In *Proceedings of the 2019 Conference on Empirical Methods in Natural Language Processing and the 9th International Joint Conference on Natural Language Processing (EMNLP-IJCNLP)*, pages 3982–3992.

Anna Rogers, Olga Kovaleva, and Anna Rumshisky. 2021. A Primer in BERTology: What We Know About How BERT Works. *Transactions of the Association for Computational Linguistics*, 8:842–866.

Aalok Sathe, Salar Ather, Tuan Manh Le, Nathan Perry, and Joonsuk Park. 2020. Automated fact-checking of claims from wikipedia. In *Proceedings of The 12th Language Resources and Evaluation Conference*, pages 6874–6882.

Karishma Sharma, Feng Qian, He Jiang, Natali Ruchansky, Ming Zhang, and Yan Liu. 2019. Combating fake news: A survey on identification and mitigation techniques. *ACM Transactions on Intelligent Systems and Technology (TIST)*, 10(3):21.

Amir Soleimani, Christof Monz, and Marcel Worring. 2020. Bert for evidence retrieval and claim verification. In *European Conference on Information Retrieval*, pages 359–366. Springer.

James Thorne, Andreas Vlachos, Christos Christodoulopoulos, and Arpit Mittal. 2018a. Fever: a large-scale dataset for fact extraction and verification. In *Proceedings of the 2018 Conference of the North American Chapter of the Association for Computational Linguistics: Human Language Technologies, Volume 1 (Long Papers)*, pages 809–819.

James Thorne, Andreas Vlachos, Oana Cocarascu, Christos Christodoulopoulos, and Arpit Mittal. 2018b. The fact extraction and verification (fever) shared task. In *Proceedings of the First Workshop on Fact Extraction and VERification (FEVER)*, pages 1–9.

Ashish Vaswani, Noam Shazeer, Niki Parmar, Jakob Uszkoreit, Llion Jones, Aidan N Gomez, Łukasz Kaiser, and Illia Polosukhin. 2017. Attention is all you need. In *Advances in neural information processing systems*, pages 5998–6008.

Andreas Vlachos and Sebastian Riedel. 2014. Fact checking: Task definition and dataset construction. pages 18–22.

Soroush Vosoughi, Deb Roy, and Sinan Aral. 2018. The spread of true and false news online. *Science*, 359(6380):1146–1151.

David Wadden, Shanchuan Lin, Kyle Lo, Lucy Lu Wang, Madeleine van Zuylen, Arman Cohan, and Hannaneh Hajishirzi. 2020. Fact or fiction: Verifying scientific claims. In *Proceedings of the 2020 Conference on Empirical Methods in Natural Language Processing (EMNLP)*, pages 7534–7550, Online. Association for Computational Linguistics.

Alex Wang, Amanpreet Singh, Julian Michael, Felix Hill, Omer Levy, and Samuel Bowman. 2018. Glue: A multi-task benchmark and analysis platform for natural language understanding. In *Proceedings of the 2018 EMNLP Workshop BlackboxNLP: Analyzing and Interpreting Neural Networks for NLP*, pages 353–355.

William Yang Wang. 2017. "liar, liar pants on fire": A new benchmark dataset for fake news detection. In *Proceedings of the 55th Annual Meeting of the*

Association for Computational Linguistics (Volume 2: Short Papers), pages 422–426.

Adina Williams, Nikita Nangia, and Samuel Bowman. 2018. A broad-coverage challenge corpus for sentence understanding through inference. In *Proceedings of the 2018 Conference of the North American Chapter of the Association for Computational Linguistics: Human Language Technologies, Volume 1 (Long Papers)*, pages 1112–1122.

Thomas Wolf, Julien Chaumond, Lysandre Debut, Victor Sanh, Clement Delangue, Anthony Moi, Pierric Cistac, Morgan Funtowicz, Joe Davison, Sam Shleifer, et al. 2020. Transformers: State-of-the-art natural language processing. In *Proceedings of the 2020 Conference on Empirical Methods in Natural Language Processing: System Demonstrations*, pages 38–45.

Wenpeng Yin and Dan Roth. 2018. Twowingos: A two-wing optimization strategy for evidential claim verification. In *Proceedings of the 2018 Conference on Empirical Methods in Natural Language Processing*, pages 105–114.

Wanjun Zhong, Jingjing Xu, Duyu Tang, Zenan Xu, Nan Duan, Ming Zhou, Jiahai Wang, and Jian Yin. 2020. Reasoning over semantic-level graph for fact checking. In *Proceedings of the 58th Annual Meeting of the Association for Computational Linguistics*, pages 6170–6180.

Neural Re-rankers for Evidence Retrieval in the FEVEROUS Task

Mohammed Saeed, Giulio Alfarano, Khai Nguyen, Duc Pham, Raphaël Troncy and Paolo Papotti
EURECOM, France
{FirstName.LastName}@eurecom.fr

Abstract

Computational fact-checking has gained a lot of traction in the machine learning and natural language processing communities. A plethora of solutions have been developed, but methods which leverage both structured and unstructured information to detect misinformation are of particular relevance. In this paper, we tackle the FEVEROUS (Fact Extraction and VERification Over Unstructured and Structured information) challenge which consists of an open source baseline system together with a benchmark dataset containing 87,026 verified claims. We extend this baseline model by improving the evidence retrieval module yielding the best evidence F1 score among the competitors in the challenge leaderboard while obtaining an overall FEVEROUS score of 0.20 (5th best ranked system).

1 Introduction

The volume of potentially misleading and false claims has surged with the increasing usage of the web and social media. No barriers exist for publishing information which make anyone capable of diffusing false or biased claims while reaching large audiences with ease (Baptista and Gradim, 2020). One approach of dealing with this ordeal is computational fact-checking (Wu et al., 2014), where the automation of the verification pipeline or parts of it is flourishing due to advances in natural language processing (Nakov et al., 2021; Saeed and Papotti, 2021). Along these lines, several datasets and fact-evaluation algorithms have been proposed (Kotonya and Toni, 2020).

In this paper, we report on our effort in tackling the FEVEROUS challenge (Aly et al., 2021). The provided dataset consists in a set of textual claims verified against evidence retrieved from a corpus of English Wikipedia pages. The claims are labeled as *supported, refuted* or *NEI* (Not Enough Information). Evidence can be unstructured (such as sentences) or structured (such as general tables, infoboxes, lists, etc.). The task is to return the right label with the correct evidence. The baseline model is divided in two main parts: an evidence retrieval part and a verdict prediction part. The evaluation is performed through the so-called FEVEROUS score which is computed considering both the correct retrieval of the evidence and the correct label predictions. In this paper, we propose an enhanced version of this baseline model that focuses on the retrieval component through a re-ranking process of pages, resulting in a more precise model.

In the remainder of this paper, we first describe briefly the challenge task and the supplied data, and we detail our extension (Section 2). We then provide experimental results obtained on the development dataset and we discuss observations on analyzed errors (Section 3). We conclude with a discussion of other research directions that can be applied to improve results for the FEVEROUS task (Section 4).

2 Method

We begin by reviewing the given baseline, and then propose an extension to it that improved the precision and recall of the page-retrieval module in exchange for more computation time.

2.1 FEVEROUS Baseline

In FEVEROUS (Aly et al., 2021), the aim is to find out the veracity of a claim c. This is done by: (i) acquiring a set of evidence E which could contain sentences extracted from a Wikipedia page, or cell(s) from a Wikipedia table, and (ii) predicting a label $y \in \{\text{Supports, Refutes, NEI}\}$.

The proposed baseline is simple yet competitive (Aly et al., 2021). For (i), a combination of entity-matching and TF-IDF scoring are used to identify the most prominent Wikipedia pages (Chen et al., 2017). k pages are selected by matching entities extracted from the claim to Wikipedia pages.

Proceedings of the Fourth Workshop on Fact Extraction and VERification (FEVER) at EMNLP 2021, pages 108–112
November 10, 2021.

If needed, remaining pages are identified using TF-IDF matching between the claim and the introductory sentence of the page. Given the extracted Wikipedia pages, sentences are scored through a dot product with the claim in the TF-IDF space, where the top l sentences are retrieved. Similarly, the top q tables are extracted where the TF-IDF vector of the table title is used to represent a table. The tables are then linearized, pre-processed to respect the input-size limit of the classifier (Oguz et al., 2020), and then used, alongside the claim, to fine-tune a RoBERTa model (Liu et al., 2020) on a binary token classification task.

For (ii), given the retrieved evidence, the final verdict is predicted using a RoBERTa model with a sequence-classification layer which is fed with sequentially concatenated claim and evidences as input. The model has been trained on a set of labelled claims (71,291 samples) with their associated evidence.

2.2 Proposed Extension

It is clear that to enhance the system, evidence retrieval should be a top priority as identifying the correct evidence is crucial for the verdict predictor to function properly. We focus on enhancing the identification of Wikipedia pages by utilizing advances in the information retrieval (IR) community where neural ranking models have been proposed for better data retrieval (Mitra et al., 2016; Hui et al., 2018).

A simple IR pipeline comprises a two-stage reranking process where: (a) first, a large number of documents to a given query are retrieved from a corpus using a standard mechanism such as TF-IDF or BM25; (b) second, the documents are scored and reranked using a more computationally-demanding method. Given that neural ranking methods have shown success in the IR community (Guo et al., 2019), we used this method as part of our extension.

For (a), we use the current page-retriever based on entity-matching and TF-IDF to retrieve a higher number of pages. For (b), the re-ranker model provides a score s_i indicating how relevant a page p_i is to an input claim c. The re-ranker is based on a pre-trained BERT model (Devlin et al., 2019) that is fine-tuned on the passage re-ranking task of the MS MACRO dataset (Nguyen et al., 2016) to minimize the binary cross-entropy loss:

$$L = -\sum_{i \in I^+} log(s_i) - \sum_{i \in I^-} log(1 - s_i) \quad (1)$$

where I^+ and I^- are the set of indices of the relevant and non-relevant pages respectively in the top-1,000 MS MACRO documents retrieved with BM25 (Nogueira and Cho, 2019). We designate a page re-ranker model as a function $PR(m)$ which take a set of relevant pages for a claim, which are usually scored by a less-computationally demanding method such as TF-IDF to limit the set of candidates, scores them, and outputs the top m pages.

3 Experiments

Model. We rely on the cross-encoder model fine-tuned on the MS MARCO Passage Ranking task (Reimers and Gurevych, 2019) provided on the Hugging Face model hub. We feed the claim with every extracted page into the re-ranker model to obtain scores used to re-rank the respective pages.
Settings. We set $k = 150$ and $m = 5$ where 150 pages are first extracted through entity-matching+TF-IDF, scored with the re-ranker model, and then the top-5 pages for each claim are extracted. The remainder of the pipeline remains intact ($l = 5$, $q = 3$). We designate this pipeline by $BLpage(150) \rightarrow PR(5) \rightarrow tfidf(5, 3)$. Our code can be found at `https://gitlab.eurecom.fr/saeedml/eurecom-fever`.
Results. We see improvement with the page re-ranker as the coverage of documents has increased compared to the baseline. Hence, for $k = 5$, the retriever without the re-ranker achieves a document coverage of 69% on the dev set, while the addition of the re-ranker enhances the coverage to around 79%, which, in turn, improves the FEVEROUS and F1 scores, compared to the initial baseline (Table 1, in bold). While the page re-ranker improves the document coverage, we do not observe pronounced improvements on the system as a whole. Even with a better page retriever, an increase in FEVEROUS and F1 scores requires improvements also in the sentence and cell evidence retrievers.

Although more time-demanding, the re-ranker gives more subtle results than an entity-matching approach (Aly et al., 2021). For example, given the following excerpt of a claim: "**Family Guy is an American animated sitcom that features five main voice actors [...] and has appeared in 22 (out of 349) episodes [...] that has appeared**

	FS	LA	EP	ER	E-F1
$BL(5,5,3)$	0.19	0.54	0.12	0.29	0.17
$BL(5,5,3)_{full}$	0.186	0.533	0.119	0.289	0.168
$BLpage(50) \rightarrow PR(5) \rightarrow tfidf(5,3)$	0.129	0.468	0.120	0.201	0.151
$BLpage(150) \rightarrow PR(5) \rightarrow tfidf(5,3)$	**0.218**	**0.548**	**0.145**	**0.339**	**0.203**
$BLpage(150) \rightarrow PR(5) \rightarrow BM25(5,3)$	0.205	0.550	0.127	0.321	0.182
$BLpage(150) \rightarrow PR(5) \rightarrow SR(5) \rightarrow tfidf_{table}(3)$	0.184	0.501	0.130	0.283	0.179

Table 1: Results on the dev set showing the FEVEROUS Score (FS), the Label Accuracy (LA), the Evidence Precision (EP), the Evidence Recall (ER), and the Evidence F1-score (E-F1) of the different system variants.

in 90 episodes.", one can directly see that the retrieved pages should be related to the series "**Family Guy**". The baseline fails to predict the correct page `Family Guy`, and instead matches with entities such as `Guy` and `American`, and Wikipedia pages for numbers such as `90` and `22`. Additionally, some pages retrieved with TF-IDF do not relate to the claim at hand: `John Manwood (MP)` and `John Manwood`. The page re-ranker, on the other hand, manages to get the correct page in the top-5 predictions, where all other predictions are related: `List of Family Guy guest stars`, `List of Family Guy episodes`, `Blue Harvest` (an episode from the TV series), `List of Family Guy cast members`, and `Family Guy`. Finally, we observe that the entity-matching process is brittle and fails to match the sub-string "Angela Santomero" to the page `Angela C. Santomero` as it only performs exact string matching.

There are some cases where entity-matching+TF-IDF outperformed the re-ranker: some of those are cases where the Wikipedia page content is small and does not bring much benefit on a semantic level and this is where TF-IDF works better. We observe that we tend to miss the correct page when there are several pages who share similar semantics. For example, given the claim: "**Seven notable animated television series, including Super Why!, a children's educational show created by Angela C. Santomero and Samantha Freeman Alpert, Phineas and Ferb and WordGirl, were released in September 2007.**", the page re-ranker retrieves TV shows that are produced `Angela C. Santomero`). However, the correct page `Phineas and Ferb` does not appear in the top-5 predictions, and other pages take the lead, whereas the baseline can identify the correct page by entity matching, although its predictions are not as coherent as those of the page re-ranker.

k	FEVEROUS Score	Time(mins)
200	0.216	140
300	0.224	210
500	0.219	345

Table 2: Results on the dev set showing the FEVEROUS Score and the recorded time for the re-ranking processing for varying values of k.

Other Attempts. We have experimented with varying the number of extracted pages k. We measure also the time taken for re-ranking. Table 2 shows the results. We observe that increasing the number of pages to extract does not always increase the FEVEROUS score, as more candidate pages act as distractors to the other modules in the pipeline.

We have attempted to perform other extensions to the system that we describe below (Table 1).

Firstly, we specified the re-ranking system to extract less pages (50), but it worsened the scores. This configuration is defined as $BLpage(50) \rightarrow PR(5) \rightarrow tfidf(5,3)$.

Furthermore, we applied the same re-ranking approach at the sentence level. After obtaining 150 pages from the page re-ranker, we continue to retrieve all sentences from every page and re-rank them using the same passage re-ranking model (Nguyen et al., 2016), ($BLpage(150) \rightarrow PR(5) \rightarrow SR(5) \rightarrow tfidf_{table}(3)$). However, despite great outputs of page re-ranker, we could not obtain better results from sentences re-ranker than TF-IDF.

Regarding how relevant sentences and tables are chosen as evidence, apart from TF-IDF + Cosine Similarity, we also experimented with the Okapi BM25 scoring function (Robertson et al., 1995). This is applied after the pages are re-ranked, ($BLpage(150) \rightarrow PR(5) \rightarrow BM25(5,3)$). Surprisingly, although BM25 is generally preferred for document retrieval, in our case, it did not lead to better results compared to TF-IDF. One possible cause might lie in text preprocessing, as we did not fully explore different combinations of preprocessing functions.

Lastly, we attempted to improve the verdict predictor by (i) fine-tuning the verdict classifier on the full training dataset ($BL(5,5,3)_{full}$) and by (ii) utilizing other pre-trained models that are either larger or were pre-finetuned on a NLI dataset. However, we did not observe significant improvements from them since their performance on the dev set was either on par or slightly worse than the baseline model signaling that the focus enhancing of the second part of the system requires more significant changes.

4 Conclusion and Future Directions

In this work, we have proposed the inclusion of a neural re-ranker model as a refinement step after standard methods such as TF-IDF. While being more intensive on the computational side, we do see improvements on the document-retrieval side where results are more sound. There are of course more directions that are worth exploring to improve the results further.

Sentence retrieval could be improved by incorporating a pre-trained neural network that performs semantic matching between the claims and the sentences. One instance of such models is where the text sequences are encoded, then passed through an alignment layer that computes aligned representations of the encoded input sequences, followed by a matching layer that performs the semantic matching (Nie et al., 2018). Such models have been applied on the FEVER dataset (Thorne et al., 2018) and have been shown to outperform the TF-IDF approach (Nie et al., 2018).

Cell retrieval could be enhanced by utilizing pre-trained models over tables that outperform pre-trained models over text (Herzig et al., 2021). Several systems that exploit table structure have been proposed for the task of fact-checking a claim over a table. However, not all of them can be used in every setting as each system holds different attributes and dimensions that need to be comprehended to better integrate them in certain tasks (Saeed and Papotti, 2021). For example, some systems such as SCRUTINIZER (Karagiannis et al., 2020) are dependent on the table-schema and would not benefit in the FEVEROUS scenario where tables have varying schema. Yet, other systems such as TAPAS (Herzig et al., 2020) are schema-independent and can be fine-tuned on the available FEVEROUS dataset to provide a score for a given table, thus acting as a table ranker module. Some of these systems can be even directly trained on the data, to get domain-specific models. Once the tables have been identified, a classifier can be trained on top of models that output cell representations of a table, such as TaBERT (Yin et al., 2020) and TURL (Deng et al., 2020), to extract the key cells for verdict prediction. Also, fine-tuning the re-ranker models on the given data is a viable approach. Finally, more sophisticated entity matching algorithms could have been explored to avoid the "exact match" issues that we observed with the baseline's entity matching (C. et al., 2018).

References

Rami Aly, Zhijiang Guo, Michael Sejr Schlichtkrull, James Thorne, Andreas Vlachos, Christos Christodoulopoulos, Oana Cocarascu, and Arpit Mittal. 2021. FEVEROUS: fact extraction and verification over unstructured and structured information. *CoRR*, abs/2106.05707.

João Pedro Baptista and Anabela Gradim. 2020. Understanding fake news consumption: A review. *Social Sciences*, 9(10).

Paul Suganthan G. C., Adel Ardalan, AnHai Doan, and Aditya Akella. 2018. Smurf: Self-service string matching using random forests. *Proc. VLDB Endow.*, 12(3):278–291.

Danqi Chen, Adam Fisch, Jason Weston, and Antoine Bordes. 2017. Reading Wikipedia to answer open-domain questions. In *Association for Computational Linguistics (ACL)*.

Xiang Deng, Huan Sun, Alyssa Lees, You Wu, and Cong Yu. 2020. Turl: Table understanding through representation learning. *Proc. VLDB Endow.*, 14:307–319.

Jacob Devlin, Ming-Wei Chang, Kenton Lee, and Kristina Toutanova. 2019. BERT: Pre-training of deep bidirectional transformers for language understanding. In *ACL*, pages 4171–4186.

Jiafeng Guo, Yixing Fan, Liang Pang, Liu Yang, Qingyao Ai, Hamed Zamani, Chen Wu, W. Bruce Croft, and Xueqi Cheng. 2019. A deep look into neural ranking models for information retrieval. *CoRR*, abs/1903.06902.

Jonathan Herzig, Thomas Müller, Syrine Krichene, and Julian Eisenschlos. 2021. Open domain question answering over tables via dense retrieval. In *Proceedings of the 2021 Conference of the North American Chapter of the Association for Computational Linguistics: Human Language Technologies*, pages 512–519, Online. Association for Computational Linguistics.

Jonathan Herzig, Pawel Krzysztof Nowak, Thomas Müller, Francesco Piccinno, and Julian Eisenschlos. 2020. TaPas: Weakly supervised table parsing via pre-training. In *Proceedings of the 58th Annual Meeting of the Association for Computational Linguistics*, pages 4320–4333, Online. Association for Computational Linguistics.

Kai Hui, Andrew Yates, Klaus Berberich, and Gerard de Melo. 2018. Co-pacrr: A context-aware neural ir model for ad-hoc retrieval. In *Proceedings of Web Search and Data Mining 2018*.

Georgios Karagiannis, Mohammed Saeed, Paolo Papotti, and Immanuel Trummer. 2020. Scrutinizer: A mixed-initiative approach to large-scale, data-driven claim verification. *Proc. VLDB Endow.*, 13(11):2508–2521.

Neema Kotonya and Francesca Toni. 2020. Explainable automated fact-checking: A survey. In *Proceedings of the 28th International Conference on Computational Linguistics*, pages 5430–5443, Barcelona, Spain (Online). International Committee on Computational Linguistics.

Yinhan Liu, Myle Ott, Naman Goyal, Jingfei Du, Mandar Joshi, Danqi Chen, Omer Levy, Mike Lewis, Luke Zettlemoyer, and Veselin Stoyanov. 2020. RoBERTa: A robustly optimized BERT pretraining approach.

Bhaskar Mitra, Fernando Diaz, and Nick Craswell. 2016. Learning to match using local and distributed representations of text for web search. *CoRR*, abs/1610.08136.

Preslav Nakov, David P. A. Corney, Maram Hasanain, Firoj Alam, Tamer Elsayed, Alberto Barrón-Cedeño, Paolo Papotti, Shaden Shaar, and Giovanni Da San Martino. 2021. Automated fact-checking for assisting human fact-checkers. In *IJCAI*, pages 4826–4832. ijcai.org.

Tri Nguyen, Mir Rosenberg, Xia Song, Jianfeng Gao, Saurabh Tiwary, Rangan Majumder, and Li Deng. 2016. MS MARCO: A human generated machine reading comprehension dataset. *CoRR*, abs/1611.09268.

Yixin Nie, Haonan Chen, and Mohit Bansal. 2018. Combining fact extraction and verification with neural semantic matching networks. *CoRR*, abs/1811.07039.

Rodrigo Nogueira and Kyunghyun Cho. 2019. Passage re-ranking with BERT. *CoRR*, abs/1901.04085.

Barlas Oguz, Xilun Chen, Vladimir Karpukhin, Stan Peshterliev, Dmytro Okhonko, Michael Sejr Schlichtkrull, Sonal Gupta, Yashar Mehdad, and Scott Yih. 2020. Unified open-domain question answering with structured and unstructured knowledge. *CoRR*, abs/2012.14610.

Nils Reimers and Iryna Gurevych. 2019. Sentence-bert: Sentence embeddings using siamese bert-networks. In *Proceedings of the 2019 Conference on Empirical Methods in Natural Language Processing*. Association for Computational Linguistics.

Stephen Robertson, S. Walker, S. Jones, M. M. Hancock-Beaulieu, and M. Gatford. 1995. Okapi at trec-3. In *Overview of the Third Text REtrieval Conference (TREC-3)*, pages 109–126. Gaithersburg, MD: NIST.

Mohammed Saeed and Paolo Papotti. 2021. Fact-checking statistical claims with tables. *IEEE Data Eng. Bull.*, 44(3).

James Thorne, Andreas Vlachos, Christos Christodoulopoulos, and Arpit Mittal. 2018. FEVER: a large-scale dataset for fact extraction and VERification. In *Proceedings of the 2018 Conference of the North American Chapter of the Association for Computational Linguistics: Human Language Technologies, Volume 1 (Long Papers)*, pages 809–819, New Orleans, Louisiana. Association for Computational Linguistics.

You Wu, Pankaj K. Agarwal, Chengkai Li, Jun Yang, and Cong Yu. 2014. Toward computational fact-checking. *Proc. VLDB Endow.*, 7(7):589–600.

Pengcheng Yin, Graham Neubig, Wen tau Yih, and Sebastian Riedel. 2020. TaBERT: Pretraining for joint understanding of textual and tabular data. In *Annual Conference of the Association for Computational Linguistics (ACL)*.

A Fact Checking and Verification System for FEVEROUS Using a Zero-Shot Learning Approach

Orkun Temiz, Özgün Ozan Kılıç, Arif Ozan Kızıldağ, Tuğba Taşkaya Temizel
Graduate School of Informatics
Middle East Technical University
{orkun.temiz, ozank, arifozan, ttemizel}@metu.edu.tr

Abstract

In this paper, we propose a novel fact checking and verification system to check claims against Wikipedia content. Our system retrieves relevant Wikipedia pages using Anserini, uses BERT-large-cased question answering model to select correct evidence, and verifies claims using XLNET natural language inference model by comparing it with the evidence. Table cell evidence is obtained through looking for entity-matching cell values and TAPAS table question answering model. The pipeline utilizes zero-shot capabilities of existing models and all the models used in the pipeline requires no additional training. Our system got a FEVEROUS score of 0.06 and a label accuracy of 0.39 in FEVEROUS challenge.

1 Introduction

Misinformation on online mediums has caused several problems in recent years. For instance, during the initial spread of the Covid-19 pandemic, inappropriate treatments or incorrect statistics have been widely disseminated through posts. Manually checking the content of such posts against the fact checking sites is not feasible as it is labor intensive. As a remedy, many automated fact-checking solutions have started to emerge in the last decade.

To challenge researchers and advance the domain in this research area, the Fact Extraction and Verification (FEVER) (Thorne et al., 2018) challenge was introduced in 2018. This challenge contained 185,445 claims, and the most successful group (Nie et al., 2019) obtained a 0.63 fever score in the test set. In 2021, a new challenge, Fact Extraction, and VERification Over Unstructured and Structured information (FEVEROUS) (Aly et al., 2021) was organized with a new dataset comprising 87,026 claims where the average length of the claims increased significantly. A Wikipedia dump with more than 5.4 million articles was provided for claim verification, which included sentences and other page elements such as lists and table cells as potential evidence while the previous challenge's dataset contained only sentences. Moreover, the total number of page elements included in the dump increased significantly compared to the previous challenge. Although FEVEROUS challenge contains less number of claims, it has a higher complexity than FEVER challenge. In this challenge, participants were not only required to label each claim as *"SUPPORTS," "REFUTES,"* or *"NOT ENOUGH INFO"* but also provide the correct evidence for it.

The baseline model in FEVEROUS challenge obtained around 18% FEVEROUS score. This model contains two steps, which are retrieval and verdict prediction. The model firstly retrieves relevant pages and then sentences and cells separately from each page. During cell retrieval, tables are linearized to obtain the most relevant cells. Then cell retrieval is handled as a binary sequence labeling task. Verdict prediction is made using the Robustly Optimized BERT Pretraining Approach (RoBERTa) model (Liu et al., 2019). In addition, the FEVEROUS score assumes that the prediction is correct when the label is correct and a set of evidence is present in the predicted evidence.

In this challenge, we developed a pipeline that utilizes zero-shot learning capabilities of existing models where we have considered claims as a question and our retrieved documents as a solution text instead of extracting cells and sentences after the document retrieval. We applied different question answering (QA) models to solve the claim for sentences and cells. We obtained our labels from sentences by using Natural Language Inference (NLI) model. After that, we added the cells after the sentence solutions. Our model obtained 0.06 FEVEROUS score, 0.39 label accuracy, and 0.06 evidence F1 score.

Proceedings of the Fourth Workshop on Fact Extraction and VERification (FEVER) at EMNLP 2021, pages 113–120
November 10, 2021. ©2021 Association for Computational Linguistics

Table 1: The details of the top approaches with respect to document retrieval, sentence retrieval, and claim verification tasks in the first FEVER challenge compared to the FEVER and the FEVEROUS baseline models

	Document Retrieval	Sentence/Cell Retrieval	Claim Verification
FEVER-baseline (Thorne et al., 2018)	TF-IDF	TF-IDF	Decomposable attention
FEVEROUS-baseline (Aly et al., 2021)	TF-IDF	TF-IDF	RoBERTa
UNC-NLP (Nie et al., 2019)	ESIM	ESIM	ESIM
UCL Machine Reading Group (Yoneda et al., 2018)	Logistic regression	Logistic regression	ESIM + aggregation
Team Athene (Hanselowski et al., 2018)	MediaWiki API	ESIM	ESIM

1.1 Related Works

In the first FEVER challenge, the top three groups used Enhanced Sequential Inference Model (ESIM) (Chen et al., 2017) with modifications. The UNC-NLP team (Nie et al., 2019) used Neural Semantic Matching Network (NSMN) for both retrieval and verification tasks while modifying ESIM with additional shortcut connections and changing the output layer to max-pool. Team Athene (Hanselowski et al., 2018) made use of Wikipedia's MediaWiki API to search named entities and ESIM in sentence retrieval and claim verification by extending it to generate a ranking score. This extension adds a hidden layer with a single neuron output and gives the claim together with an input sentence. Finally, UCL Machine Reading Group (Yoneda et al., 2018) employed logistic regression in document and sentence retrieval by utilizing keywords, and features of sentences, respectively. In addition, they aggregated the labels created by ESIM with different models including logistic regression and Multi-Layer Perceptron (MLP) with two layers for claim verification. Their results showed that aggregation with MLP yielded a better result than other aggregation methods.

The FEVEROUS (Aly et al., 2021) baseline model applies TF-IDF for document and sentence retrieval, like the first FEVER challenge (Thorne et al., 2018). On the other hand, the FEVEROUS baseline uses RoBERTa instead of the decomposable attention model for claim verification. Table 1 shows the methodological details of the approaches performed well at the FEVER shared task and the FEVEROUS baseline model. Moreover, Akkalyoncu Yilmaz et al. (2019) retrieved documents while utilizing Bidirectional Encoder Representations from Transformers (BERT) (Devlin et al., 2019) model for re-ranking results returned by Anserini. Soleimani et al. (2020) applied BERT for sentence retrieval and claim verification while fine-tuning it for each task separately. On the other hand, they made use of Wikipedia's MediaWiki API, similar to Team Athene (Hanselowski et al., 2018) for document retrieval.

2 Method

In the following subsections, we will explain how our system works. An overview of the system in the form of pseudocode is given in Algorithm 1.

2.1 Preprocessing & Keyword Extraction

The claims themselves were directly used to form the base query for retrieving the relevant pages. Since some claims had alternative space characters, these were replaced with a single standard space character. The queries were enhanced with the relevant keywords, which were formed by the named entities extracted from the text using spaCy (n.d.). To improve spaCy's performance, other candidate entities with capitalized first letters were also added. Moreover, to handle the cases where spaCy could not detect the whole word chunk (i.e. Adam Smith), the contingency parser was employed to detect noun chunks. If the named entity found by spaCy was located inside a noun chuck, we added that noun chunk to the keyword list. Date entities

Algorithm 1 The pseudocode of our proposed pipeline

```
Input:
claims: A list including the claims that will be verified.
raw_docs: A database including the Wikipedia documents provided by FEVER.
indexed_docs: A formatted sentence corpus of the provided Wikipedia documents, indexed using Anserini.
Initialize:
results ← [] // Create a list with eventual dimensions of [claims.length,3] to store the claim, predicted label, and predicted evidence
for each c in claims do
    Extract entities from claim c using spaCy, uppercase detection, and chunking, store it in entities
    Obtain a query by appending entities to claim c, and set it into query
    Obtain the most relevant documents based on query from indexed_docs and set it into docs[doc_title, doc_content, relevance]
    Apply string matching to document titles from docs with entities, maximize relevance scores of the matched documents (see Section 3.1 for its explanation)
    sentence_evidence ← { } // Create empty sets that will be filled with evidence
    table_evidence ← { }
    for each d in docs do
        if sentence_evidence.length < 5 then
            Divide document d into subdocuments subdocs (See Section 2.3)
            for each sd in subdocs do
                Retrieve the evidence sentence and its immediate predecessor as ev using c, sd, and BERT QA model
                Add ev.sentence_ids, doc_title of d, and ev's confidence score (according to the universal sentence encoder) to sentence_evidence
            end for
        end if
        if table_evidence.length < 25 then
            Extract the document tables from raw_docs, normalize their formats (see Section 2.3), and set them into tables
            Retrieve cell values from tables that match entities, and add all the cell IDs from their corresponding rows to table_evidence
            Apply TAPAS QA model to c and tables, and add the retrieved cells' IDs to table_evidence
        end if
    end for
    Rank evidence in sentence_evidence based on confidence scores
    // Ensure evidence do not exceed the limit (5 and 25 for sentence and table evidence, respectively) by slicing them, combine them and push to the results list
    predicted_evidence ← sentence_evidence[0:5] + table_evidence[0:25]
    Verify claim c using c, sentence_evidence[0:5], and XLNET model, set it into predicted_label
    results.push([c, predicted_label, predicted_evidence])
end for
Output:
results: A list with claims, their predicted label, and predicted evidence.
```

were ignored. These obtained entities were concatenated twice to the query to give them more weight, since our document retrieval module uses OKAPI BM25 (Robertson et al., 1994), where including a phrase more than once causes the module to give it more weight in the document retrieval process.

2.2 Document Retrieval

To retrieve Wikipedia texts efficiently, we use Anserini indexing, which uses OKAPI BM25 (Robertson et al., 1994) for indexing the Wikipedia pages. Anserini (Yang et al., 2017) is a toolkit developed on Apache Lucene, open-source search software. To use Anserini indexing, we transformed the Wikipedia dump into an indexable format while discarding lists, tables, and section titles. Then, we indexed it using Anserini toolkit with the help of Pyserini (Lin et al., 2021), a Python interface for Anserini. We fed the query and the keywords in a concatenated way to the Anserini. By retrieving 70 pages per claim, and also obtaining the documents that link to the retrieved relevant documents, the algorithm could successfully retrieve all of the documents that have the necessary evidence for 7255 claims out of the 7891 (91.94%) from the development set. However, we later saw that better document retrieval does not always translate well to evidence retrieval and verification. These settings were causing the retrieved evidence to be noisy and taking too much time. Therefore, looking for the incoming links was later scrapped, and only 10 documents were retrieved for every claim to speed up the process.

2.3 Evidence Selection

In this section, we selected the sentences related to or considered as potential evidence with respect to the query from the retrieved Wikipedia pages. To select the relevant parts, we employed BERT-large-cased (Devlin et al., 2019) question answering model instead of a sentence similarity model even though the claims were not including a question. Although sentence similarity models were highly used in FEVER (Thorne et al., 2018) tasks, with the help of QA models, search may grasp the nuance and semantic meaning of the query better than sentence similarity models. In line with our approach, Google also employs a BERT question answering model for its searches (Nayak, 2019).

Since BERT is able to handle a maximum of 512 tokens at once and Wikipedia pages contain long texts, we split the retrieved text into chunks of 10 sentences. This way, we were also able to retrieve more than one answer from one document, since we would get an answer from each split. Although splitting the page helped with the token limit, it did not ensure that truncation would not occur. For this purpose, after the initial split, we split the chunks further with 10% overlapping words into chunks of at most 512 words in order not to lose the semantic meaning of the chunks. Then, the QA model was applied to all the chunks and the answer with the highest score was labeled as the final answer. As evidence identifiers such as "sentence_1" created noise and negatively affected the QA model, these identifiers were cleaned. After that, we retrieved the sentence including the answer and its preceding one to ensure to obtain the full answer. Correct evidence identifiers were then obtained through the returned pieces of evidence as the answer. Then, we sorted them with the universal sentence encoder according to its similarity (confidence) score with the query (Cer et al., 2018). We found that retrieving pages related to people with very similar names to the "PERSON" entity in the query was throwing the results off. To tackle this issue while sorting the answers, we doubled the similarity score obtained after a softmax normalization if the document title matched the "PERSON" named entity recognized by the spaCy. Page title and person entity are considered to be matched when one includes the other. For the task scoring constraints, we kept only the top 5 pieces of evidence. As a result of the textual QA module, we ended up with a query, its answers and the confidence scores between the query and the textual answers. Also, note that since we got a sentence which included the answer, and the sentence before it, a full answer text may contain more than one evidence. In Wikipedia pages, evidence or answers may have been located in the provided table cells. To address this gap, we employed two methods; The first method involved using the non-person entities from the claim and matching them with the cell values from the tables of the relevant page. A cell value was considered to be a match when its original or link-removed version had a Levenshtein ratio of 0.8 or higher with the non-person entity.

The second method involved using TAPAS (TAble PArSing) (Herzig et al., 2020), a weakly supervised transformer-based question answering model developed by Google Research. Given a table with column header names and cell values, the model can predict the answer according to the given query, similar to the textual question answering model, except our answer is cell values instead of text chunks. To make this method work, tables of relevant pages were obtained in a normalized form such that cells with row/column spans larger than one are divided into 1x1 cells sharing the same value, compatible with the model. Since TAPAS requires tables to have column headers, the table rows were removed from the beginning one by one until the first row included the header cells. Dividing the cells into 1x1 cells and duplicating their values led some tables to be very crowded and caused memory issues. To address this problem, firstly, if a row has more than 700 characters combined, the row is removed. Secondly, if the final table has more than 1000 tokens when it is tokenized, it is skipped as a whole. We chose to do so due to the time constraints and our anecdotal findings of marginally large tables having tangential information.

These two methods were applied to the pages in order from the highest to the lowest confidence scores, and only the first 25 cells (belonging to the most relevant evidence's pages) were kept. Since cells usually do not form complete sentences, we did not use them in the textual entailment step to decide whether a claim is supported or not. Internal links to other Wikipedia pages are formatted in the dataset as "[[Page_ID|Visible text]]" where "Page_ID" denotes the identifier through which the page can be accessed (like "https://en.wikipedia.org/wiki/Page_ID") while "Visible text" denotes the text (mostly the linked page's title) shown to the user. Since these links create noise and prevent matches, they are simplified to obtain plain text cells with both cell evidence retrieval methods.

2.4 Textual Entailment

For the entailment model, we used XLNET (Yang et al., 2019) trained on the composition of SNLI (Bowman et al., 2015), MultiNLI (Williams et al., 2018), FEVER (Thorne et al., 2018), ANLI (Williams et al., 2020) and NLI (Nie et al., 2019) datasets. By using the pre-trained model, we evaluated the entailment between the textual answers and the query. As a result of the textual entailment model, we retrieved the Support, Contradict or Neutral (*NOT ENOUGH INFO*) scores between one query and one answer instance.

2.5 Heuristic Verdict Assignment

After utilizing the textual entailment module, we concluded the final verdict, which will be one of Support, Contradict or Neutral (*NOT ENOUGH INFO*) via the following heuristic:

- If there was no answer with a similarity score of 0.6 between the query and the answer threshold, it was assigned as Neutral.
- If the "neutral" score between the query and the answer was higher than 0.8, it was counted as a Neutral vote. For the other cases, we look for the contradiction and entailment scores between the query and the answer. If the entailment score was higher, we added one vote for Support label. If the contradiction score was higher, we added one vote for the Contradict label.
- At the end, a majority vote was taken between the "Support" and "Contradict" label votes and then we determined the final verdict.

If the outcome is Neutral, we can conclude that there is no information, which support or contradict the claim in the Wikipedia pages. Even if the verdict was *NOT ENOUGH INFO*, we still fetched the evidence as well.

3 Results and Discussion

Based on the official leaderboard (Fact Extraction and VERification, 2021), our pipeline's scores along with the baseline, minimum, and maximum FEVEROUS scores are shown in Table 2. Excluding the baseline, our FEVEROUS score is the ninth out of 12 groups.

The label accuracy of our method (0.39) is relatively close to the baseline (0.48). For reference, the accuracy obtained with random guesses on the development set is 0.33 while randomly guessing the label using the class distribution yields an accuracy of 0.45.

Our pipeline's success in identifying the expected evidence and consequently our FEVEROUS score are significantly lower than the baseline. Having a recall of 0.10 and precision of 0.05 suggests we have more false positives than false negatives. The fact that we also retrieved the previous sentence of the sentence retrieved from the question answering model may have an effect on this, but a significantly lower evidence precision compared to

Table 2: Our model's results compared to the baseline, minimum, and maximum FEVEROUS scores among the participant groups

	FEVEROUS Score	Accuracy	Evidence F1	Evidence Precision	Evidence Recall
Maximum	0.2701	0.5607	0.1308	0.0773	0.4258
FEVEROUS Baseline	0.1770	0.4760	0.1610	0.1121	0.2855
Ours	**0.0636**	**0.3897**	**0.0634**	**0.0462**	**0.1011**
Minimum	0.0223	0.3999	0.0282	0.0245	0.0330

the evidence recall is seemingly the norm among the participant groups.

We had not run the final version of the pipeline on the whole development set before our test submission. We later ran it on the development set and obtained very similar results (a FEVEROUS score of 0.0642 and label accuracy of 0.3867), which suggests dataset splits are well-balanced. The confusion matrix for the development set is shown in Table 3.

Table 3: Confusion matrix for the development set predictions with the base model, *"N.E.I."* indicating *NOT ENOUGH INFO* label

		Predicted		
		SUPPORTS	REFUTES	N.E.I.
Actual	SUPPORTS	1009	1366	1533
	REFUTES	530	1834	1117
	N.E.I.	112	181	208

3.1 Limitations, Improvements, and Future Work

Numerous improvements can be made on the pipeline. Based on the confusion matrix for the development set, our pipeline is seemingly too much inclined towards finding that there is not enough information as 2858 claims from the development set are labeled as *NOT ENOUGH INFO* compared to the expected number of 501 while only 208 of them were true positives. This suggests the claim verification model requires fine-tuning. Even a more heuristic solution can slightly improve the results. Since the mean and median number of expected non-cell evidence were approximately two, we observed that randomly assigning the label as either *SUPPORTS* or *REFUTES* for claims that have more than two retrieved non-cell evidence increases the label accuracy to 0.51 and the FEVEROUS score to 0.07. We found that it is also possible, to some extent, to verify the claims based on whether the retrieved documents mention entities extracted from the claim. We naively assumed that if a claim's entities are completely matched in the documents, the claim is correct. If most of the entities were not found, then there was not sufficient information. Using the ratio of entities matched in the documents and some threshold values, we obtained a lowered FEVEROUS score (0.0457) but a higher label accuracy (0.4593). More importantly, we saw that applying this naive approach only when the predicted label is wrong (4839 claims out of 7890) significantly improves both FEVEROUS score (0.0812) and label accuracy (0.6718). While this is not applicable when we do not have the expected label, this suggests that a complementary naive approach can significantly improve the results if we can identify which cases are more likely to be misclassified.

Due to time constraints, several parameters (like the number of retrieved documents) were kept at minimal and not optimized. While we limited document retrieval to 10 results per claim, we had observed that some expected Wikipedia pages for the claims in the development set were being retrieved at much lower ranks (such as 50 and up). As explained, deep learning models used within the pipeline are pre-trained models that are not fine-tuned for this task. Fine-tuning these parameters and models may yield better results. However, using a subset of the development set, we saw that retrieving 70 results for each claim only improved the label accuracy by 0.02 and FEVEROUS score did not change while the pipeline became 5-6 times slower.

We found that people's names in the claims and their Wikipedia pages do not always perfectly match. For example, Sir Arthur Conan Doyle was mentioned in a claim as *"Conan Doyle"* while his Wikipedia page was called *"Arthur Conan Doyle."* Our pipeline requires the entity to be included in the page title or the page title to be included in an entity to double its confidence score, so these simple differences could be handled. However, while it is rarer, we saw that certain entities have more significant differences between their mentioned names and their Wikipedia page titles. For example, Eleanor Francis *"Glo"* Helin was mentioned as *"E. F. Helin"* in a claim while her Wikipedia page was titled *"Eleanor F. Helin."* For these cases, removing the disambiguation parentheses, using a Levenshtein ratio threshold, and initial matching when there is initialism involved may improve the results. Since these name differences can be seen anywhere, a more flexible and tolerating approach may be helpful while dealing with entities. With a subset of the development set, using Levenshtein ratio as an alternative to partial matching (without dealing with initialism) increased FEVEROUS score by about 0.01, which is not significant.

Fundamentally changing some parts of the pipeline may have positive effects as well. Our question answering model can retrieve multiple evidence sentences, but the retrieved sentences must be in consecutive order since the model actually retrieves a piece of the document that is deemed relevant which can span multiple sentences. This limitation is partially alleviated since we split all the documents into chunks of sentences before using the question answering model. Separately feeding each piece of evidence or splitting the documents using a sliding window approach with a small window may improve the results, but it would also increase the inference time. Similarly, splitting the tables further can prevent truncation and may improve evidence recall. While tables may mislead the model, the existence of matching entities in them may, in general, give some clues about the claim's veracity. Based on the complicatedness of the claims, it might be possible to improve the results by adjusting the entailment score when there is table cell evidence.

Inference takes a considerable amount of time as the pipeline becomes more complex with multiple models. Due to verification and evidence retrieval taking roughly eight or nine seconds per claim, we ran the pipeline with two computers in parallel. Reducing the inference time can help with speeding up the iterative improvements and experimentation.

4 Conclusion

In this work, we proposed a fact extraction and verification pipeline that mainly uses Anserini to retrieve documents, a BERT-based question answering model to retrieve textual evidence, TAPAS to retrieve table cell evidence, and an XLNET-based entailment model to judge the claim without fine-tuning them. We believe parameter optimization and challenge-specific fine-tuning can significantly improve the results.

References

Zeynep Akkalyoncu Yilmaz, Shengjin Wang, Wei Yang, Haotian Zhang, and Jimmy Lin. 2019. Applying BERT to document retrieval with birch. In *Proceedings of the 2019 Conference on Empirical Methods in Natural Language Processing and the 9th International Joint Conference on Natural Language Processing (EMNLP-IJCNLP): System Demonstrations*, pages 19–24, Hong Kong, China. Association for Computational Linguistics.

Rami Aly, Zhijiang Guo, Michael Sejr Schlichtkrull, James Thorne, Andreas Vlachos, Christos Christodoulopoulos, Oana Cocarascu, and Arpit Mittal. 2021. FEVEROUS: Fact Extraction and VERification over unstructured and structured information.

Apache Lucene. Apache Lucene - welcome to Apache Lucene.

Samuel R. Bowman, Gabor Angeli, Christopher Potts, and Christopher D. Manning. 2015. A large annotated corpus for learning natural language inference. In *Proceedings of the 2015 Conference on Empirical Methods in Natural Language Processing*, pages 632–642, Lisbon, Portugal. Association for Computational Linguistics.

Daniel Cer, Yinfei Yang, Sheng-yi Kong, Nan Hua, Nicole Limtiaco, Rhomni St John, Noah Constant, Mario Guajardo-Céspedes, Steve Yuan, Chris Tar, et al. 2018. Universal sentence encoder. *arXiv preprint arXiv:1803.11175*.

Qian Chen, Xiaodan Zhu, Zhen-Hua Ling, Si Wei, Hui Jiang, and Diana Inkpen. 2017. Enhanced LSTM for natural language inference. In *Proceedings of the 55th Annual Meeting of the Association for Computational Linguistics (Volume 1: Long Papers)*, pages 1657–1668, Vancouver, Canada. Association for Computational Linguistics.

Jacob Devlin, Ming-Wei Chang, Kenton Lee, and Kristina Toutanova. 2019. BERT: Pre-training of deep bidirectional transformers for language understanding. In *Proceedings of the 2019 Conference of the North American Chapter of the Association for Computational Linguistics: Human Language*

Technologies, Volume 1 (Long and Short Papers), pages 4171–4186, Minneapolis, Minnesota. Association for Computational Linguistics.

Fact Extraction and VERification. 2021. 2021 shared task. [Online] Available at: https://fever.ai/task.html [Accessed August 8, 2021].

Andreas Hanselowski, Hao Zhang, Zile Li, Daniil Sorokin, Benjamin Schiller, Claudia Schulz, and Iryna Gurevych. 2018. UKP-Athene: Multi-sentence textual entailment for claim verification. In *Proceedings of the First Workshop on Fact Extraction and VERification (FEVER)*, pages 103–108, Brussels, Belgium. Association for Computational Linguistics.

Jonathan Herzig, Pawel Krzysztof Nowak, Thomas Müller, Francesco Piccinno, and Julian Eisenschlos. 2020. TaPas: Weakly supervised table parsing via pre-training. In *Proceedings of the 58th Annual Meeting of the Association for Computational Linguistics*, pages 4320–4333, Online. Association for Computational Linguistics.

Jimmy Lin, Xueguang Ma, Sheng-Chieh Lin, Jheng-Hong Yang, Ronak Pradeep, and Rodrigo Nogueira. 2021. Pyserini: A Python toolkit for reproducible information retrieval research with sparse and dense representations. In *Proceedings of the 44th International ACM SIGIR Conference on Research and Development in Information Retrieval*, SIGIR '21, page 2356–2362, New York, NY, USA. Association for Computing Machinery.

Yinhan Liu, Myle Ott, Naman Goyal, Jingfei Du, Mandar Joshi, Danqi Chen, Omer Levy, Mike Lewis, Luke Zettlemoyer, and Veselin Stoyanov. 2019. RoBERTa: A robustly optimized BERT pretraining approach. *arXiv preprint arXiv:1907.11692*.

Pandu Nayak. 2019. Understanding searches better than ever before. [Online] Available at: https://blog.google/products/search/search-language-understanding-bert/ [Accessed August 8, 2021].

Yixin Nie, Haonan Chen, and Mohit Bansal. 2019. Combining fact extraction and verification with neural semantic matching networks. In *Proceedings of the AAAI Conference on Artificial Intelligence*, volume 33, pages 6859–6866.

Stephen E Robertson, Steve Walker, Susan Jones, Micheline M Hancock-Beaulieu, Mike Gatford, et al. 1994. Okapi at TREC-3. In *Proceedings of the Third Text REtrieval Conference (TREC 1994)*.

Amir Soleimani, Christof Monz, and Marcel Worring. 2020. BERT for evidence retrieval and claim verification. In *Advances in Information Retrieval*, pages 359–366, Cham. Springer International Publishing.

spaCy. n.d. spaCy · Industrial-strength Natural Language Processing in Python. [Online] Available at: https://spacy.io/ [Accessed August 8, 2021].

James Thorne, Andreas Vlachos, Christos Christodoulopoulos, and Arpit Mittal. 2018. FEVER: A large-scale dataset for fact extraction and VERification. In *Proceedings of the 2018 Conference of the North American Chapter of the Association for Computational Linguistics: Human Language Technologies, Volume 1 (Long Papers)*, pages 809–819, New Orleans, Louisiana. Association for Computational Linguistics.

Adina Williams, Nikita Nangia, and Samuel Bowman. 2018. A broad-coverage challenge corpus for sentence understanding through inference. In *Proceedings of the 2018 Conference of the North American Chapter of the Association for Computational Linguistics: Human Language Technologies, Volume 1 (Long Papers)*, pages 1112–1122, New Orleans, Louisiana. Association for Computational Linguistics.

Adina Williams, Tristan Thrush, and Douwe Kiela. 2020. ANLIzing the adversarial natural language inference dataset. *arXiv preprint arXiv:2010.12729*.

Peilin Yang, Hui Fang, and Jimmy Lin. 2017. Anserini: Enabling the use of Lucene for information retrieval research. In *Proceedings of the 40th International ACM SIGIR Conference on Research and Development in Information Retrieval*, pages 1253–1256.

Zhilin Yang, Zihang Dai, Yiming Yang, Jaime Carbonell, Russ R Salakhutdinov, and Quoc V Le. 2019. XLNet: Generalized autoregressive pretraining for language understanding. *Advances in neural information processing systems*, 32.

Takuma Yoneda, Jeff Mitchell, Johannes Welbl, Pontus Stenetorp, and Sebastian Riedel. 2018. UCL machine reading group: Four factor framework for fact finding (HexaF). In *Proceedings of the First Workshop on Fact Extraction and VERification (FEVER)*, pages 97–102, Brussels, Belgium. Association for Computational Linguistics.